A VOICE FOR FREEDOM

Volume 1

David Ivon Jones in Wales and South Africa
Articles & Speeches 1901-1924

Edited and Foreword by *Meic Birtwistle* & *Robert Griffiths*

A VOICE FOR FREEDOM

Volume 1

David Ivon Jones in Wales and South Africa
Articles & Speeches 1901-1924

Edited and Foreword by *Meic Birtwistle* & *Robert Griffiths*

Print edition: 978-1-899155-99-6
Digital edition: 978-1-899155-98-9

Published by Praxis Press 2024
Email: praxispress@me.com
Website: www.redletterspp.com

Praxis Press
c/o 26 Alder Road
Glasgow, G43 2UU
Scotland, Great Britain

CONTENTS

FOREWORD

THIS BOOK would not have been possible without the inspiration and assistance of a number of people and their institutions.

The inspiration originated with a wonderful television documentary film – 'The African from Aberystwyth' (1986) – researched, written and presented by the late and hugely missed Professor Gwyn Alf Williams, and produced by his chief collaborator in so many other memorable history programmes, Colin Thomas. Much of the research in South Africa had been conducted with extraordinary thoroughness by the Baruch Hirson, who later co-wrote The Delegate for Africa: David Ivon Jones 1883-1924 (1985). Sadly, like co-author Gwyn, he is no longer with us but we hope this present volume does justice to their labours.

Even before these works were completed, the South African Communist Party reproduced some of Jones' writings in South African Communists Speak (1981). Earlier still, in 1974, the party's journal The African Communist had carried a biographical article about him by A Lerumo (alias Michael Harmel).

Other historians and academics also deserve credit for their part in helping to recover the record of the extraordinary man from a hillside farm on the outskirts of Aberystwyth in west Wales. Notable among them are

Professors Lucien van der Walt (Rhodes University) and Wessel Visser (formerly of Stellenbosch University), together with Dr Marieta Buys and her staff at the Stellenbosch University Library. Between them, they provided an invaluable and indispensable collection of documents and sources for this volume and the next.

In Britain, Dr Rhodri Llwyd Morgan and his staff have provided every facility to study the correspondence of David Ivon Jones at the National Library of Wales, Aberystwyth. Likewise, Dr Meirion Jump and staff at the Marx Memorial Library in London have given generous assistance to our research.

Finally, we would like to thank Laurette Picand, Roger Jones and Byron Ashton for supplying some helpful papers and publication. Not least, we must express our gratitude to Tonwen Davies and Irene Green for their support, advice and forbearance during the preparation of this book.

* * *

Jones was a product of his times. This is reflected in his use of language in terms of gender and race. While we have tried to maintain the integrity of the original text as far as possible, we have edited some of the racial terms current in South Africa in his early years. For example, Jones correctly condemned the use of the 'N-word' as a derogatory term for the black majority, yet in his early years in Africa he also casually used another term, known today as the 'K-word', which in today's South Africa is seen as similarly derogatory, as is another term for the Khoikhoi people.

While we have deliberately avoided using these terms in full in the text, using 'N*', 'K*' and H* instead, the reader will clearly see that as Jones' political understanding of the role and experiences of the black majority in South Africa deepened, so too his language shifted from these terms to phrases such as 'native worker' and then on to categories such as the 'black proletariat'. While this clearly reflects the positive influence of the Communist International's anti-imperialist and anti-colonialist perspectives, it is also a testament to Jones' own political development, as his travels led him to gradually shake off well meaning but patronising attitudes towards the non-white populations of the British Empire – to the point where he recognised the struggles against white supremacy as part of a wider struggle for socialism and communism.

Nevertheless, nothing else he said or wrote has been edited, except where a word has clearly been omitted or rendered incorrectly when previously printed. However, some inconsistencies of punctuation have been rectified or brought into line with more modern usage, notably in the use of italics when referring to publication titles.

David Ivon Jones often wrote with elegance and erudition. His style of English is of its time and some of his similes, metaphors and idioms sound somewhat awkward, hackneyed and even archaic today. Others may strike today's reader as novel and fresh.

Unfortunately, specific editions of the journals that carrying his most extensive account in English of the 'Rand Revolt' of 1922 are missing from various collections. A retranslation of the article from German has therefore been used in this volume. His report in the original English will be included next year in Volume 2, *A Voice for Freedom: David Ivon Jones in Revolutionary Russia.*

Full responsibility for the selection, editing and translation of the articles and speeches in both volumes rests with the editors.

Meic Birtwistle
Robert Griffiths
Cardiff, June 2024

ABOUT THE EDITORS

MEIC BIRTWISTLE is an historian and journalist who lives in David Ivon Jones' home county of Ceredigion. His mother's family were staunch Unitarians from 'Y Smotyn Du / The Black Spot', heartland of that radical sect . His home now is the village on Y Mynydd Bach where the Jones family originally resided.

He wrote his MA on the Agricultural Workers of Cardiganshire and has published articles in the Welsh Labour History Journal *Llafur*. His book Rhyfelgan tells of Welsh language songs from the Great War.

A current affairs and documentary maker who worked in television at HTV and BBC Wales, he writes regularly for the daily socialist newspaper the *Morning Star.* A proud member of the National Union of Journalists he served on its national executive for a number of years.

ROBERT GRIFFITHS is a former tutor for the TUC and Workers Education Association and Senior Lecture in Labour History and Political Economy at University College of Wales, Newport. He has been General Secretary of the Communist Party since 1998 and is chair of the Cymru-Cuba society.

His previous books include *Streic! Streic! Streic!* (1986), *Driven by ideals – a history of ASLEF* (2005), *Killing No Murder – South Wales and the Great Railway Srike of 1911* (2009), *Granite and honey: the story of Phil Piratin, Communist MP* (2012) with Kevin Marsh, *Marx's Das Kapital and capitalism today* (2018) and *Reddest of the Reds: SO Davies, MP and miners' leader* (2019). He has also written pamphlets on current political and economic issues, China and Welsh communist poet TE Nicholas.

He is currently working on a volume of artcles on Welsh working-class history and lives in Caerllion, Newport

BIOGRAPHY
David Ivon Jones 1883-1924

'THE DELEGATE FOR AFRICA', as David Ivon Jones was later to be known in revolutionary circles, was born near Aberystwyth in Cardiganshire, west Wales, in 1883 (the year that Karl Marx died).

His roots were indeed radical ones. His family originally hailed from Y Mynydd Bach ('The Small Mountain'), a poor and mountainous farming area in the county. This community had been the centre of a lengthy guerrilla struggle, 'Rhyfel y Sais Bach' ('The War of the Little Englishman'), of squatters and small farmers against the enclosure of common land by an English landowner. And his great grandfather had led the progress of Methodism locally. Subsequently, David's grandfather John Ivon Jones became a leading campaigner for Liberalism and radical causes in Aberystwyth. An antiquarian and literary figure, he passed on this radicalism and bardic name, Ivon, to his grandson. However, David Ivon's parents died when he was young, leaving him to be raised by various relatives.

In Lampeter and then Aberystwyth, the young David was soon working as a grocer in the family business. But he came under the influence of the former Unitarian minister George Eyre Evans and soon deserted his family's austere Calvinistic Methodism for the radical Unitarian sect. With strong roots in Cardiganshire, it had recently opened a new chapel in Aberystwyth. David was publicly berated by Calvinistic Methodists in his shop and on the street for having joined the people of 'Y Smotyn Du' ('The Black Spot'), as the dangerous Unitarian presence in Cardiganshire was derisively known. As Gwyn A Williams, the Welsh Marxist historian and co-biographer of David Ivon Jones, explained: 'In Aberystwyth at the time, the word "Unitarian" carried the same stigma as the word "Communist" in later years'.

Jones became the secretary and treasurer of Aberystwyth Unitarian Chapel, which developed into a particular hotbed of religious and political unorthodoxy. The chapel records show the congregation inviting striking miners to their services, collecting for the Penrhyn quarrymen locked out for three years and hosting Miss Von Pretzold of Prussia – the first woman to be ordained in Britain.

According to Islwyn ap Nicholas in *Heretics at Large – The Story of a Unitarian Chapel* (1977): 'Ivon appeared to be a Christian Humanist, unless this is a contradiction in terms. Indeed, he was more of a humanist than anything else and he always stressed the social and economic teachings of Jesus'.

Among David's shop accounts book with its lists of payments for coal, rent, steak and vinola there are quotations from Plato and Kant as well as poetry and translations into Welsh, for example of Ebenezer Elliott's radical hymn, 'The People's Anthem' (1848) in December 1905:

WHEN wilt thou save the people?
O God of mercy! when?
Not kings and lords, but nations!
Not thrones and crowns, but men!

Pa bryd iacheir y bobl?
O dywed Ior, pa bryd?
Y bobl Arglwydd tirion,
Nid gorseddfeingiau'r byd.

Tuberculosis – the particular curse of his home county – was to cut short David Ivon's residence in Cardiganshire. The chapel minutes note that in 1907 he 'left to seek health in New Zealand', following many in his family who had emigrated to the colonies. However, after a short time working as a rabbit farmer he was lured to the Orange Free State in South Africa to work in shops owned by two of his brothers.

He arrived in South Africa in November 1910, after which his early admiration of the Boers for their 'bravery' in two wars against British imperialism quickly dissipated. He saw in them a gun-toting version of the same narrowness, bigotry and hypocrisy of the Calvinism he had witnessed back home. He also became increasingly aware of the position of the black natives – even more so the women – as 'slaves in everything but name'. In 1912, he had welcomed the formation of the South African Native National Congress (later renamed the ANC) as part of the drive to 'national self-consciousness', but nonetheless joined the pro-segregation South African Labour Party (SALP). Still more of a liberal than a socialist, he moved closer to some of the social-democrats before the 1913 ore-miners strike on the Witwatersrand changed his outlook profoundly. The 'Randowners', their government and British troops crushed the white workers with brutal force as the province was plunged into a civil war which also included anti-Indian violence and looting. Jones had left his clerical job in a power station to join the struggle, helping the miners' union as a book-keeper. The following January, martial law was declared in the main towns and cities to crush an attempted general strike. Repression of the unions, the SALP and various socialist groups further radicalised him as his organisational skills came to the fore in election campaigns. He was elected general secretary of the SALP in August 1914 as the party expanded rapidly in appeal and size. Devouring ILP (Independent Labour Party) and other left-wing and Marxist publications from George Evans and other Welsh friends and organisations across Britain, he abandoned all vestiges of religious belief and embraced socialism.

Tensions within the SALP finally resulted in a major rupture over the First World War as Jones and a section of the party leadership stuck to the anti-war principles now being dumped by most parties of the Second (Socialist) International. He attacked pro-war Christians and journalists who perpetrated the 'colossal swindle in terms of religion and honour' which was leading British and German workers to butcher one another. He resigned as SALP general secretary and in September 1915 became the editor of a new paper, The International and secretary of the breakaway International Socialist League (ISL). He urged Karl Liebknecht to lead a new international body of anti-war socialist parties. His editorials explained the significance of the February and October revolutions in Russia in 1917.

While still grappling with the race question and whether or for how long the more organised whites would play the leading role within an alliance of all workers, Jones played a major part in the formation of the country's first all-black trade union, namely, the short-lived Industrial Workers of Africa. Very much under his influence, the ISL published propaganda in the African languages, proposed working-class unity, challenged white racism and demanded equal status in industry and society for black workers. In *The International*, he struck a ground-breaking note in support of black Africans:

> An Internationalism which does not concede the fullest rights which the Native working class is capable of claiming will be a sham. One of the justifications for our withdrawal from the Labour Party is that it gives us untrammelled freedom to deal, regardless of political fortunes, with the great and fascinating problem of the Native.

In 1919, he co-wrote with LH Greene a leaflet under the title: 'The Bolsheviks are Coming!' Addressed 'to the workers of South Africa, Black as well as White' in English, Sotho and Zulu, it declared: 'While the black worker is oppressed, the white worker cannot be free'. This was a fundamental break from the concept of the white working class – mostly racist in its aims and aspirations – as the vanguard of political change in South Africa. For producing this dangerous leaflet, the two authors were fined and sentenced to four months of imprisonment, though this was later quashed on appeal.

In November 1920, David Ivon left South Africa for Europe. For the sake of his health, he spent time in Nice where he wrote a report in March 1921 for the executive committee of the Communist International (ECCI) on 'Communism in South Africa'. An outstanding survey of the complex economic, social, cultural and political conditions in the country, analysing its class and racial divisions, the report apparently had a major impact on Lenin and the Comintern [Communist International]. Jones also visited Wales briefly, but without the time to see many of his old friends. He had received an invitation to attend the Third Congress of the Communist International in 1921 in Moscow as a delegate from South Africa, together with Sam Barlin. In the session of July 12, Jones proposed that the congress 'resolves to further the movement among the working masses of Africa... and desires the Executive to take a direct initiative in promoting the awakening of the African Negroes as a necessary step to the world revolution'. It was agreed to refer the proposal to the Comintern executive committee (ECCI). In his speech, Jones quoted Marx on how veiled wage slavery in Europe was founded upon the open slavery of colonies in the New World. The Comintern had adopted a comprehensive policy on the colonial question, but along with the parties it had been weak in applying it. He described the position in South Africa as a replica of the world situation in miniature: a mass of native workers side by side with a white 'labour aristocracy' of skilled workers. It was proving very difficult to recruit militant workers to the Communist Party from the country's very small labour aristocracy. But whereas the South African delegates at this Comintern congress were white, the 'native working mass as a whole is going to be a brilliant example for communism'. He continued:

> They are ripe for communism. They are absolutely propertyless. They are stripped of every vestige of property and caste prejudice. The African natives are a labouring race, still fresh from ancestral communal traditions. I will not say that the native workers are well organised, or have a general conception of communism or even of trade unionism, as yet. But they have made several attempts at liberation by way of industrial solidarity. They only need awakening. They know they are slaves, but lack the knowledge how to free

> themselves... The solution of the problem, the whole world problem is being worked out in South Africa on the field of the working-class movement.

The congress agreed that he should represent South Africa as a consultative voice on the Comintern executive committee. Remaining in Moscow for health reasons, he missed the founding congress of the Communist Party of South Africa (CPSA) at the end of July. Instead, he devoted his time learning Russian and became one of the first translators of Lenin's works into English (technically David Ivon's second language after Welsh).

In this period, too, he accumulated immense knowledge and understanding of life in Soviet Russia and Ukraine, gleaned from his own direct experience there, travelling, meeting people and studying local publications. His descriptions and assessments of early Soviet policies and their impact will be revelatory to some readers today, particularly those reared in an era where so much of the post-1917 history of Russia and the Soviet Union is presented in a wholly one-sided and negative way.

Jones composed numerous articles for Russian, British and CPSA publications. For instance, in the Communist Party of Great Britain's journal *The Communist Review* (February 1922), he wrote approvingly of Soviet support for the more radical and democratic elements among the poor peasants in their revolt against the bourgeois leadership and wealth of the Russian Orthodox Church. This was the way to win the Christian peasantry to the revolution. Forcing atheism upon them would fail, because 'only the industrial proletariat and its fighting advance guard, the Communist Party, is able to carry science into all realms, and can thus dispense with supernatural idols'. In March 1924, David Ivon's article urged revolutionaries to read and ponder the earliest works of Lenin, demonstrating his own expansive knowledge not only of Lenin's writings but also those of Plekhanov, Martov and other leading figures in the Russian movement. His skilled analysis explained Lenin's early conception of the alliance needed between the industrial working class and the peasantry.

But by now, David Ivon's years of unstinting political toil had taken a heavy toll on his health and the Russian climate no doubt added to the burden. Although the Comintern despatched this highly regarded revolutionary to Yalta for recuperation from another tuberculosis attack, he died there on May 31, 1924, according to legendary trade union and Comintern envoy Tom Mann who was in Russia at the time. David Ivon had, in effect, martyred himself in the cause of world socialism.

In his 'Political Testament', written on his deathbed, Jones urged his comrades to 'carry out the great revolutionary mission imposed on colonies in general and South Africa in particular with revolutionary devotion and dignity, concentrating on shaking the foundations of world capitalism and British imperialism'. As he wrote to the CPSA general secretary WH 'Bill'

Andrews: 'We stand for Bolshevism, and in all minds Bolshevism stands for the Native worker'.

He was buried in the Novodevichy Cemetery in Moscow, to be joined alongside later by South African Communist Party leaders Moses Kotane and JB Marks. A 20-strong deputation from the South African government and embassy visited the graves in 2015, shortly before the remains of Kotane and Marks were returned to South Africa at their families' request. They also paid their respects at the headstone of David Ivon Jones.

The 'Delegate for Africa' is now commemorated by a plaque on the Unitarian chapel in his native Aberystwyth. But it is in South Africa that his legacy is particularly treasured today by the SACP and the African National Congress.

This collection of his articles and speeches testifies to his deep humanitarian and communist principles. They embody and express his love for his Welsh homeland, for his adopted South Africa and its native peoples and for revolutionary Russia and its working class and peasantry. He was a patriot and an internationalist, who unsparingly committed himself to the liberation of people everywhere.

THE INTERNATIONAL,
Official Organ of
THE COMMUNIST PARTY
(S.A. Section of the Communist International).
(Secretary-Editor,, W. H. Andrews.)
Annual Subscription, 10/-; half-yearly, 5/-
Party Offices:
Bundle Orders of One Dozen and over: 2/- per dozen.
Nos. 4 & 6, TRADES HALL, RISSIK STREET, JOHANNESBURG.

Vol. IX. JUNE 5th, 1924. No. 420.

D. Ivon Jones.

On Monday morning a cable was received from Moscow announcing the death of our late secretary and editor, David Ivon Jones.

The news was not unexpected, as our comrade has long been seriously ill, and for the last two years, with a brief interval in Moscow, has been in the tuberculosis institute in Yalta, on the shores of the Black Sea.

His career in the Labour and Socialist movement was a brief but brilliant one.

Born in Aberystwith, Wales, in 1883, Comrade Jones had few pleasant recollections of his childhood and youth, and his early hardships sowed the seeds of the disease which carried him off in what should have been the prime of his manhood.

For health reasons he emigrated to New Zealand, of which country he always spoke with affection.

His health improved as a result of his open-air life in that fine climate, but having a desire to travel he left for South Africa about fourteen years ago, and first came in touch with the Labour movement in Germiston, where he was employed as a clerk in the V.F.P. office during the Georgetown by-election. There he met the writer, and notwithstanding strong temperamental differences, a strong personal friendship sprang up.

When the 1913 strike spread to Vereeniging, our comrade came out on strike from the V.F.P. station there, being the only office worker to range himself alongside the men. This decided his future activities, for of course he was victimised by his late employers. He was then engaged in the office of the Mine Workers' Union for a few months to assist the secretary, Tom Matthews, in reorganising the office, and throwing himself with ardour into a study of and active participation in the Labour movement, he was soon after appointed general secretary to the South African Labour Party. This position he filled with conspicuous ability until the division on the War reached its climax at the special conference of the Party held in Johannesburg in August, 1915, when he with a majority of the Executive and many members were expelled for refusing to sign the infamous pledge to assist the Botha-Smuts Government in its War policy.

The anti-war section immediately formed the International Socialist League, with Comrade Jones as secretary and editor of its paper, "The International." His clear vision and rapid grasp of new situations, his facile pen and ardent and poetic temperament had full play in the new revolutionary movement. Speaking, writing, studying and engaging in the unceasing debates and discussions which were a feature of those stirring times when old ideas had to be discarded and new points of view acquired, relentless in his revolutionary enthusiasm, yet genial and lovable to all his comrades and even to his political opponents, Comrade Jones was the incarnation of all that was best in the new movement.

The pace, however, was too hot for his enfeebled frame, and he was forced to retire, but being under the necessity, like all proletarians, of earning his living, he accepted a position in Comrade Pettersen's office in Durban, and later spent some months in the Mozambique coastal belt. Returning to Johannesburg, he resumed the editorship of "The International" for a few months, but had to desist, and at the invitation of a friend proceeded in 1920 to Nice in the vain quest of health. Keenly interested in the Russian Revolution, he made his way through Italy, Germany and Sweden to Moscow, where he represented the International Socialist League at the 3rd Congress of the Communist International.

Comrade Jones had a gift for languages; besides his native Welsh and English, he read and spoke Dutch, German and Russian, and would read Spanish, Italian and Portuguese papers when they came to hand.

He continued to contribute valuable articles on tactics to "The International" and to the English and Russian Communist Press and periodicals. His brochure, "Communism in South Africa," is well known, and he was the author of a number of pamphlets, one of which, "The Bolsheviks are Coming," was the cause of his arrest, imprisonment and trial for sedition in Maritzburg, in company with Comrade Laurie Greene. He was convicted, but on appeal to the Supreme Court the conviction was quashed.

Comrade Jones was recognised by the Russian comrades as a sound propagandist of proletarian revolutionary tactics, and were it not for the tragedy of his health would undoubtedly have become a considerable international figure.

His courage, both moral and physical, were undoubted. In the 1913 siege of the Trades Hall, again when the mob broke up the May Day demonstration in 1917, and on many other occasions, this was put to the severest test, and he never flinched. In his small body he carried a lion's heart, is a frequent comment by those who knew him. But that which gives him a prominent place in the roll of proletarian fighters is his whole-hearted devotion to the cause of the workers. From the time that he saw his path clearly he never wavered and never looked back. Whatever doubts and backslidings others may have expressed or shown, Comrade Ivon remained firm in his faith in the certainty of the ultimate triumph of the revolutionary working-class.

Many will mourn his loss in Russia and Britain as well as in South Africa, but the best tribute we can pay to his memory, and the one he would wish, is to carry on the work which, splendidly equipped as he was for it, he so reluctantly and tragically had to lay down

Obituary for David Ivon Jones in the Communist Party of South Africa's journal *The International* (1924)

1

A WELSH MISCELLANY

Welsh Gazette and *West Wales Advertiser* (1901-1905)

CYMRU FU ['Wales Past']

Caer Alltgoch

December 12 1901

This British Caer or Fort is situated on the summit of Alltgoch hill, about two miles north-east of Lampeter. Judging from its size and position, it seems to have been a very important station with the Britons at one time. Looking due north, towards Teify Valley the position of Loventium, the Roman station can be seen five or six miles away; one can picture the British Warriors watching the movements of the Roman Legions far up the valley, from this Alltgoch hill. Across the valley to the east Caer Forus is situated above Cellan, and by performing a right about turn motion Caer Pantcou can be seen directly opposite, across and above the Dulas. The question naturally arises what Caers are in sight of Caer Forus and Pantcou, for doubtless, a long chain of caers existed (of which these were only links), each one in signalling communication with the other. The chain of Caers would be a very interesting subject for investigation to anyone who could trace it across the country. Caer Alltgoch is always designated the "Roman Camp" by the inhabitants, probably for the reason that the Romans adapted the British Caers they captured to their own use and garrisoned them with

Roman soldiers, hence the reason this Caer is called "Roman," though it was originally a British Caer. What looks like an old British road can still be seen between Alltgoch and Loventium, or rather the British caer which occupied that site previous to the settlement of the Romans there; a further proof of the importance of Caer Alltgoch in this neighbourhood.

December 19 1901

Like all British camps, this is oval in form. Its dimensions are, roughly speaking, about 770 yards long from north to south by 90 yards wide. It has one entrance on the west side, about ten yards wide. The ffos, or moat. can only be faintly traced, but it is more distinct near the entrance and to the north-east, where a shallow ffos remains, about 20 yards wide. We were informed that it has been deeper within living memory, but that it has been filled up in some parts with rubbish. The height of the vallum is about 5 feet on the east side and from 9 to 12 feet to the north, and on the west, where there is a sharp declivity towards the Alltgoch. At the north end a few portions of the ramparts still remain; evidently more labour was expended on this part of the fortifications, as the land here, being a gradual slope, did not afford such a natural defence as the steep sides of the Alltgoch on the west. At the south end, there is a small clump of rushes on damp soil, which suggests the locality of the wells, which existed in every camp; our guide informed us that it only yields water in rainy weather. It is worthy of notice that a well exists a few yards below the walls of the Caer, which he declared is infallible during the longest droughts; it is quite possible that the water was drawn to this one, for convenience, from the original well within the walls of the Caer.

December 26 1901

In the wood called Alltgoch, below the Caer are ruins of a Druidical circle; hardly anything can be seen now except a few massive boulders, though we can still roughly trace a circle of two rows among the trees. It is evident that it was not destroyed by the Romans, as it is mentioned in Meyrick's History of Cardiganshire, as intact: it is more than probable that some nineteenth century "Vandalls" (to use a hackneyed term), were its destroyers, for nearly every stone has a hole bored in it, in which they put the charge of gunpowder by which the great stones were blasted; though our guide's explanation was otherwise, viz., that they se...ed the Druids for candlesticks. A few yards below Alltgoch farm at the foot of the hill, there is an old yew tree, which has a strange out-of-place look near the larch and other forest trees of the adjacent wood; it is believed that an early British church, or at least a burial ground existed there of which this yew is a solitary survival: here we have a striking picture of the advance of Christianity in the Caer, the Druidical Circle, and the Yew.

Canwyll Gorff [Corpse Candle], Llangwyryfon

January 9 1902

Although the darkness of superstition, which once spread itself over the whole of Wales, is fast becoming dispelled by the bright rays of education and enlightenment, yet there remain among the hills of Cardiganshire, many old characters who retain a belief in the superstitious omens of a bygone age. I have heard several tales which go to prove this, and the following is one which was told to me one night by an old lady, who had witnessed more than three score years and ten glide into a memory of the past. She was a member of the C.M. Chapel of Llangwyryfon, and in her time used to attend all the services with great regularity, One dark night in winter, while returning home by herself from the society, past a narrow lane leading to an adjacent farm she chanced to look over the hedge in the direction of the house, and lo! she saw a feeble, yet a clear light coming along the lane at a slow regular pace. Knowing instinctively as she did, that this must be a "Canwyll Gorff" (corpse candle) she hastened on with all the speed at her command in order to pass the entrance first, because then she would not in any case be forced to come in contact with it. As she walked on she became timid and could not dream of looking along the lane; for the "Canwyll Gorff" must be by this time very near the main road. At last however when she was safe and had left the lane well behind her, she summoned up courage to look back, and to her delight and relief saw the fatal "Canwyll Gorff" grow dim in the distance. She watched its route carefully and patiently now, to its destination the churchyard, and finally saw it disappear behind the crest of the hill which she had but recently traversed. After the light was gone she felt a queer sensation of fear and wonder creeping over her, and a feeling of loneliness among departed spirits coming on. She still gazed for some time over the brow of the hill which had hid from her view the mysterious light and then retraced her weary steps homeward. What troubled her most when she realised the situation was the fact that the husband of the farm-house, from which the "Canwyll Gorff" had come had been for some considerable time dangerously ill. Eventually she came to the sad conclusion that it would be no great wonder in view of her remarkable vision to see him soon leaving the land of the living. For a time however the old man got better; but alas there was no cure for him, because his "Canwyll Gorff" had undoubtedly left him, and in a year or so, he too left behind him this land of sorrows and mysteries for other realms beyond the human ken. That is the tale of the "Canwyll Gorff" as I heard it many years ago.

DEWI WYRE ['GRANDSON DAVID']

Welsh Superstitions

January 30 1902

A short time ago I witnessed what seemed to be the survival of an old

Welsh superstition, when a tradesman, desiring to present a customer with a knife, made a clause that he (the customer) should in return pay a nominal charge of a penny, or any other coin of the realm; explaining that, unless it were done, it would result in ill-luck for them both. On enquiring, I found that it was not done in mere caprice, but from an unshaken belief in the old superstition. I understand that this custom applies only to a knife, or any other like instrument. I have failed to come across any mention of this custom by authorities on Welsh folk-lore, excepting Wirt Sikes, who states in his *British Goblins*,"that a knife in Welsh Ghost-lore bears the same charm for exorcizing *gwyllion* or ghosts, as the rowan branch for the *Tylwyth Teg*, ['Fairies']" and further, that to give or receive a knife from a friend is a sign that enmity shall exist between the parties, or that "it cuts friendship." Can any reader relate some personal experiences regarding this strange old custom, with or without variations to the above? A few suggestions as to its origin would also be very interesting, for its antiquity cannot be denied; in fact, Wirt Sikes suggests a connection between it and Arthur's *Excalibur*; this raises the question – is it a purely Welsh custom.
DAFYDD O BONT STEPHAN ['DAVID FROM LAMPETER']

Dialectical "Baby-Talk"

April 2 1903

In a recent number of *Celtia*, the organ of the Pan-Celts, a review appeared of a French work by Maurice Grammont, contributed to the *Melanges Linguistiques*; being a study of baby-talk as an aid to researchers into the evolution of languages. The reviewer quotes some of the peculiarities of an Italian infant's speech, one of which he termed a "metathesis," the meaning of which will be the better demonstrated in his own words. – *Coupe* (for *bouquet*) also involves a metathesis, which is further exemplified in *coupou* (for *beaucoup*) and *cape* (for *paquet*). The reviewer, in concluding, urges his readers to take observations on the language of Welsh infants, to facilitate researches into the evolution of the Welsh language and its history. Not being a family man myself, nor having many opportunities of coming into contact with infants, I do not purpose adding to the list of infantile speech abnormalisms quoted by the reviewer; but a few examples of the metathesis he mentions may be observed in the dialect of South Cardiganshire or *godre'r sir* as it is called, which would not be out of place if inserted in *Cymru Fu*. It will be found that this "metathesis" has an especial tendency in words ending with "l" that have also the termination "ydd," thus, *hulydd* (a strainer) is pronounced *huddyl*, and *cywilydd* [shame] is transformed into *cwiddil*. One hears *gomrod* not *gormod* [too much], and it is interesting to note how "n" following a soft consonant is disliked by the Cardi's palate, he inserts a vowel between, and says *eginiol* for *egniol* [energetic], we see something similar in *onfi* for *ofni* [to fear]. Why so? It is hard to explain.

Again note the substitution of *"dd"* for *"f"* in *tyfu* (to grow) which they pronounce *tyddu;* but when we hunt for an explanation we are baffled by coming across a reversion of this abnormalism, for when a South Cardi sees anything expensive [*drud*], instead of saying *yn ddrud* he mutters *yn brud,* although 1 believe this is a Carmarthenshire influence for it is not heard except near the borders of both counties.

April 9 1903

To help solve the problem which was first *tyddu* or *tyfu,* and *drud* or *brud,* we should do well to compare the English "about" with the Welsh *oddeutu,* colloquially pronounced *obeutu,* to which again compare the Latin *apud.* In suggesting the latter comparison I admit that I foolishly venture beyond my depth. As we have begun on the peculiarities of South Cardiganshire dialect, a few more examples would not be amiss here, although they do not bear on the theory propounded in *Celtia.* A few of them seem very strange, not to say solitary, amongst the rough speech of Teify's banks. Consider the word "still," which probably owes its origin to the Flemings of the "Little England beyond Wales" in Dyfed; for whence have such words as these their origin, certainly not in the modern inroads of the English language, for they have been in use from time immemorial; while "still" is a word lost to spoken English of to-day in the sense given it by the South Cardiland folk. I do not mean the "still" that the dictionary defines "to this time" nor the still which is meant for "not-withstanding," but the "still" that we read in Watts' well-known hymn – "Satan finds some mischief still" etc. which, I believe, is lost to the English language as spoken at the present time; that is in the sense in which it is used in Lower Cardiganshire.

April 16 1903

Taking into consideration the meagreness of the communications between this part of Wales and England when the word "still" in the sense mentioned was in use in the latter country, it appears at once impossible to have been borrowed from England, therefore we must look for an explanation to the industrious Flemings who were colonized in Dyfed to harass the wild and warlike spirits of the Welsh Princes. A peculiarity appertaining to this word "still" is that, often, when intended to convey the meaning in a superlative degree, its Welsh equivalent, *gwastad,* is linked on, and both pronounced with emphasis – "still *wastad.*" Another example of this is found in the word *biti* (small), evidently derived from the English "bit." At what period and by what source was this "bit" borrowed we have no conclusion to arrive at other than that it was a companion of "still" in its transition; now, the pure Welsh for *biti* is *bach;* and when a Teify Vale farmer desires to impress the littleness of an object in a superlative sense he couples the English corruption with the Welsh perfection and produces – *"biti bach."*

THE LEISURE HOUR

Self-Respect and Usefulness

April 2 1903

Of all things, the best and most needful to impress children with is, a sense of their self- respect and their usefulness as members of humanity. Once impress a child with a respect for his good name and character and he will never stoop easily to do wrong. A respect for one's self is at the root of every manly virtue and every good quality. The next best thing is a sense of their usefulness. Let a child know that he is useful in a small way and he will try his utmost to be useful in a great many ways. A sense of his usefulness will draw out all the hidden resources in his character, and bring them more in touch with all things around him. There is nothing so good to root out idleness and selfishness as this sense of self-respecting morality and usefulness. It makes him ready to dare and to suffer, to face the world without flinching for truth and love and any good principle. It increases his brotherly love and neigbbourly kindness. It fits him out for a citizen life, and makes him a good member for home and for society. To bring out these dualities in our children we have got to do something ourselves. We must first of all learn to cultivate the same feelings of self-respect and usefulness among ourselves. Though it may sound strange, we must first of all learn to respect the feelings of our own children. How sadly and often how shamefully we disregard their tender feelings. How often unthinkingly and arrogantly we outrage their innate sense of self-respect and their tender emotions. Yes, we must learn to respect them ourselves first. Fathers and mothers must give up their false idea of superiority and learn to respect everything good and true in their children. It is the best and the only way to bring out and develop those qualities in them. Every education begins at home and with the parents. It is the parents' glory and the parents' greatest responsibility that they are principally instrumental in the making of their children's character and their children's lives.

In Early Spring

April 9 1903

The waking woods are filled with glee;
Each bush and tree,
Tho' leafless yet, has now its chorister
That merrily flits and flashes here and there,
And shakes the laughing music from his throat
Uprising as a fountain flies
The singer of the skies;

And, drop-like falling, every liquid note
In rapture ripples, ripples thro' the air.
Sequestered sings
The mellow blackbird from afar,
Who blithely prodigal of priceless things,
His jewels all around him flings --
Melodious numbers, radiant as a star.

Tho' leafless yet the trees,
A thousand fronds, uncurling one by one
To meet the wooing, kind, caressing sun,
A thousand tender shoots
Put forth around the roots,
And brave the healthful freshness of the breeze --
An air austere
That says the time of summer is not here:
A fuller joy shall be;
To-day is prophecy --
Not yet the glory of the perfect year.

The Daffodil

April 16 1903

A thing of beauty is a joy for ever … and such are daffodils:

"With the green world they live in." – Keats.

"Fair daffodils we weep to see. You haste away so soon." – [Robert] Herrick.

Few words cover a thing better than the Welsh word for daffodil, *Croeso Gwanwyn* (welcome spring). The daffodil is not so much admired for its brilliant yellow flowers, graceful as they are, as for the season in which it appears. It comes in the sweet spring-time of the year, when the earth awakes from her slumber. It is a true Spring flower, and is closely associated with sunshine and song. It is probably for this reason, more than for any other, that it has won the affections, and is such a favourite of the poets. Shakespeare says that:

When daffodils begin to peer...
Why, then comes the sweet of the year.

Another poet tells us that the period of joy and gladness is come:

When apple trees in blossom are,
And cherries of a silken white,
And kingcups deck the meadows fair,
And daffodils in brooks delight.

Still, the common English daffodil has a peculiar charm of its own; and nothing equals the bright freshness of the Lent lily, as it is sometimes called. Its favourite haunts are old gardens, orchards, and parks, where its golden blossoms appear to advantage, and are rendered the more attractive by the ground of green sward which surrounds them. Here they may be allowed to grow wild, without let or hindrance, and they require no care whatever, unless it be protection against pilferers. As their leaves die down soon after flowering, they are well out of the way before hay time, and are in no danger of scythe or mower. Wordsworth describes a charming scene in the following verses which we quote at length:

I wandered lonely as a cloud
That floats on high o'er vales and hills,
When all at once I saw a crowd
A host of golden daffodils,
Beside the lake beneath the trees
Fluttering and dancing in the breeze.

Continuous as the stars that shine
And twinkle on the milky way,
They stretched in never-ending line
Along the margin of a bay;
Ten thousand saw I at a glance
Tossing their head in sprightly dance.

The waves beside them danced, but they
Out-did the sparkling waves in glee;
A poet could not but be gay
In such a jocund company!
I gazed – and gazed – but little thought
What wealth the show to me had brought.

For oft, when on my couch I lie
In vacant or in pensive mood,
They flash upon that inward eye
Which is the bliss of solitude;
And then my heart with pleasure fills,
And dances with the daffodils.

In some parts of Wales the daffodil is known *Cenhinen Pedr* (Peter's leek); but it is commonly known by some corruption of its English name as Daffy-dwn-dilly and the like. A similar form is found in the old rhyme –

Daff-a-down-dill

Has now come to town,
In a yellow petticoat
And a green gown.

This was used, in days gone by, by country children when the daffodils made their annual appearance in early spring.

Its botanical name, Narcissus, recalls the classic myth of the beautiful youth who fell in love with his own image reflected in a well, and pined away until he was changed into the flower that bears his name.

Herrick's verses to this old-fashioned flower are well known. He sang in a different strain to Wordsworth. Sadness breathes in every line of his. To him the flower was an unmistakable symbol of the shortness of life, and death.

When a daffodil I see
Hanging down her head towards me,
Guess I may what I must be:
First, I shall decline my head
Secondly, I shall be dead;
Lastly, safely buried.

LLOFFION

Y Cynhauafwr

Gorffennaf 9 1903

Y mae gan y cynhauaf gwair, yr hwn sydd yn tynnu gymaint o sylw pryderus yr amaethwr y dyddiau hyn, ei lenyddiaeth cyfreithiol ei hun yn Lloegr, medd gohebydd yn y "*Daily Post*." Yn yr hen amser gynt yr oedd gorfodiaeth ar y deiliaid i dori a chywain gwair eu meistriaid. Yr oedd deiliad yn Badbury, fel engraifft, yn rhwym o ladd gwair ei arglwydd am un diwrnod, am yr hyn y derbyniau bryd o fara a chaws ddwy waith yn nghwrs y dydd; yna yr oedd yn rhaid iddo gywain yr un gwair, a caffai grymman neu bwn o wair am ei drafferth. Derbyniau y cynhauafwyr hefyd rhyngddynt ddeuddeg ceiniog, neu ddafad, yr hon oeddent i ddewis o gorlan eu harglwydd wrth yr olwg yn unig. Mewn lleoedd eraill cawsai y cynhauafwr yr hyn elwid ganddynt yn "haveroe", hyny yw, gymaint o laswellt ag a allasai godi ar ei bigfforch heb dori ei choes; tal arall i gynhauafwr am waith diwrnod ydoedd gymaint o wair ag allasai gofleidio yn ei freichiau. Mewn un maenordy pan byddai gwair ei arglwydd wedi ei dori gan y deiliad, yr oedd yn deilwng o "knitch" o wair, sef gymaint ag allsai godi a'i fys cyfuwch a'i benlin. Byddai'n ddyddorol cael ychydig len-gwerin Gymreig yn nglyn a'r cynhauaf gwair. – IVONFAB.

William Ellery Channning

Gorffennaf 16 1903

Ychydig amser yn ol dathlwyd canmlwyddiant genedigaeth Emerson – prif feddyliwr fagodd America yn y ganrif o'r blaen; ychydig wythnosau yn ddiweddarach dathlwyd canmlwyddiant ordeiniad William Ellery Channing i'r weinidogaeth Undodaidd. Pwy ydoedd Emerson? "Cyfaill a chyn-northwydd y rhai a ddymunant fyw yn yr ysbryd," ydoedd desgrifiad Mathew Arnold o waith a neges Ralph Waldo Emerson; "Gorweddai ei fawredd yn ei bersonoldeb aruchel, ac wrth ddarllen ei weithiau esgyna ein hysbrydoedd i awyrgylch newydd," medd un arall.

Beth ydoedd neges Channing, ei gyd-oeswr, ynte? Gellir dweyd mai dyngarwr ydoedd yn yr ystyr uwchaf ac eangaf o'r gair; ac urddas y natur ddynol ydoedd hoff destyn ei ymddiddan a'i ysgrifeniadau. Dyma'r hyn ddywed y papur Americanaidd, *Christian Register*, am ei chydwladwr nodedig, – "Tu allan i gylchoedd Undodaidd teimlir a hoffir ei ddylanwad gan lawer yn Ewrop a'r Amerig nas adwaenant ef fel arweinydd chwyldroad crefyddol, ond fel noddwr rhyddid cyffredinol – hawliau dyn ac egwyddorion ar ba rai y sylfaenwyd y werin-lywodraeth Americanaidd. Y mae ei ysgrifeniadau wedi dod i lawer o wladgarwyr fel ysgrythyrau sanctaidd, wedi eu hannerch i bawb a ymdrechant yn erbyn gormes; ac i'r rhai a weithiant er dyrchafiad yr hil ddynol; o herwydd chwiliodd Channing am y gwirionedd; i fesur cafodd afael ynddo, ac ymddiriedodd iddo'n llwyr. Deil ei ddywediadau a chynnydda ei glod. Sylweddolwyd ei annerchiadau ar gaethwasaeth yn y diwedd pan rhyddawyd y caethwas; a darllenir ei bregeth ar ryfel byd yr amser na bydd rhyfel mwyach."

Ni chaed erioed well engraifft o dalent a thlodi wedi cydgyfarfod yn yr un person nac yn Robert Burns, y bardd Ysgottig bydenwog. Bywyd helbulus a gadd ef; ac eto, yr wythnos ddiweddaf gwerthwyd un copi o'r argraffiad cyntaf o'i ganeuon am fil o bunau.

"Heb lafur nid oes cyrraedd gorphwys; ac nis gellir cael buddugoliaeth heb ymladd." – THOMAS A. KEMPIS

Tafodiaeth Deheu Ceredigion

Gorffennaf 23 1903

Yn nghanol y llu cynnyrchion barddonol Cymreig – rhagorol, diddrwg-didda a gwael – sydd yn cael eu cyhoeddi yn barhaus o'r wasg Gymreig, nis gallwn lai na sylwi ar "Gan Shacci'r Gwas" gan Sarnicol yn yr *Ymofynydd* cyfisol. Heblaw ei rhagoroldeb, yr hyn ddena sylw y darllenydd ydyw ei bod yn ysgrifenedig yn nhafodiaeth Deheu Ceredigion yr hyn rydd rhyw newydd-deb a naturioldeb atdyniadol iddi. Ni chynnygwn adrodd yr ystori, oherwydd amherir hi yn y trosglwyddiad. Gwasanaethed a ganlyn i ddangos gallu darluniadol ei hawdwr, rhan ydyw o ddesgrifiad amgylchiad canol-nosawl : –

Ond daeth mellten yn fwy na'r cyffredin, nes bo'r cyfan yn wynias i gyd,
A gwelwn ddyferion y gawod ar 'u ffordd o'r awyr i'r byd.
Mi welwn fynydde Shir Benfro, a llafur i hochre yn wyrdd,
A'r teie yn wyn rhwng y coedydd, a'r gwlaw yn disgleirio'r ffyrdd.

Credwn nad oes un iaith fel yr eiddo deheu Ceredigion i fynegu meddyliau y Cymro yn ddarluniadol. Y mae llawer o ddadleu yn y byd llenyddol Cymreig parthed cyfreithlondeb defnyddio iaith llafar mewn cyfansoddiadau llenyddol. Tybiwn fod yr Athraw Morris Jones, Bangor, yn un o bleidwyr y symudiad blaenfynedol mewn traethiad llenyddol, ac nid yw Mr Gwenogfryn Evans yn hollol elyniaethus iddi, oherwydd darllenasom beth amser yn ol adolygiad o'i eiddo wedi ei ysgrifenu yn nhafodiaeth ei ardal enedigol fyddai yn fwy dyryslyd nag adeiladol i frodor anhyddysg mewn tafodieithoedd Cymreig.

Caernarfon yn Gwrthsefyll

Hydref 15 1903

Gyda golwg ar y cynhwrf presenol yn nglyn a'r Ddeddf Addysg Newydd, ac ymddygiad canmoladwy Cyngor Sirol Caernarfon a chynghorau eraill yn gwrthod cyfranu cynorthwy i'r Ysgolion Enwadol heb gael llwyr reolaeth arnynt, dyddorol ydyw sylwi mai nid dyma'r tro cyntaf i Gaernarfon "gymeryd y tarw wrth ei gyrn" neu "ysgafael yn nghyflegrau'r gelyn," a defnyddio diareb Lloyd George. Pan fyddai drwgweithredwyr, tua dechreu'r ganrif o'r blaen, yn cael eu crogi am weithredoedd anfeidrol llai na'r gosp, a pan ddedfrydid dyn i farwolaeth am ladrata papur punt neu gwerth dwy bunt o nwyddau o dy, ymddengys mai rheithwyr mewn brawdlys yn Nghaernarfon yn y flwyddyn 1817 oeddynt y "gwrthwynebwyr goddefol" cyntaf yn erbyn y cyfreithiau henafol ar gosp a ffynai yr amser hwnw. Y mater gerbron ydoedd cyhuddiad yn erbyn gwr am ladrata papur pum punt; yr oedd y tystiolaethau ei fod yn euog yn ddiamheuol, er hyny, er syndod i bawb, daeth y rheithwyr a dedfryd o "ddieuog" i mewn. Gorchymynodd y barnwr yn sarug i'r rheithwyr adael y llys, a galwodd am rai eraill. Y rhai hyny hefyd a wnaethant yr un modd a'u cyn-swyddwyr. Yn y flwyddyn ganlynol newidiwyd y gyfraith i'w chyflwr presenol. [sef, ym 1903, hawliau cyfyngedig rheithgor o "ddirymiad"]

Amddiffyn yr Aelodau Seneddol

Mawrth 3 1904

Pan yn amddiffyn gwaith yr aelodau Seneddol Cymreig, dywed eu cefnogwyr eu bod yn gwneyd yr oll a ellir yn rhesymol ddisgwyl oddiwrthynt. "Hawdd i chwi feirniadu" meddent, "ond beth yn rhagor a allasent wneyd tros eu gwlad a'u hetholwyr?" Ategir y dywediad yna wedyn gyda chyfeiriad at restr yr ymraniadau er profi eu ffyddlondeb, ac fel rheol safant yn bur barchus yn y rhes o'u cymharu a'r gweddil. Ar yr un pryd, bydd eu difrawder neu eu hesgeulusdod ar yr ymraniad diweddaf ar bwnc y Chineaid i'r Transvaal yn sicr o dynu sylw y cyhoedd, a disgwylir am eglurhad oddiwrth y gwyr oeddent yn absenol ar yr amgylchiad pwysig hwn. Llwyddodd y Weinyddiaeth i sicrhau mwyafrif o 51, ond yr oedd 92 o Rhyddfrydwyr yn absenol o'r Ty ar y pryd, ac yn eu mysg yr aelodau Cymreig a ganlyn: – W. Abraham (Mabon), Rhondda; Vaughan Davies, Aberteifi; Frank Edwards, Maesyfed; Syr W. Harcourt, Mynwy: J. Herbert Lewis, Fflint; Charles Morley, Brycheiniog; Sam Moss, Dinbych; J. Wynford Phillips, Penfro; Syr Edward Reed, Caerdydd; Samuel Smith, Fflint; Abel Thomas, Caerfyrddin; Syr Alfred Thomas, Morganwg; J. Aeron Thomas, Gower. Sef triarddeg allan o'r wyth ar hugain Rhyddfrydwyr, a hyny ar un o'r amgylchiadau pwysicaf i'n gwlad. Gwyddom am rai o honynt nas gallent fod yn bresenol oherwydd gwaeledd iechyd, ond yn sicr y mae ereill yn y rhestr hon y disgwylid iddynt fod yn eu lleoedd pan mae tynged y Senedd yn y glorian. Bydd yn ddyddorol gweled pa esgusodion a wna eu cefnogwyr yn awr?

Maddeuant

Ebrill 14 1904

Pwy yw y paganiaid?" gofynwyd i fachgen bychan mewn Ysgol Sul un tro. "Pobl nad ydynt byth yn cweryla yn nghylch crefydd," ydoedd yr ateb.

* * * *

Gipsy Smith (yr efengylydd enwog), yn ei hunangofiant, a edrydd am ddyn oedd yn feddwyn ac ymladdwr wedi cael ei argyhoeddu, a'i droi at grefydd. Yn fuan wedi hyny cyfarfyddwyd ef gan un o'i hen gymdeithion, gan yr hwn yr oedd wedi benthyca sofren.

"Wel, Jack," ebe'r benthyciwr, "clywais dy fod wedi cael tro."

"Do mi gefais, ac yr wyf wedi ymuno a'r eglwys."

"Wel, a wyt ti yn cofio i mi roi benthyg sofren i ti beth amser yn ol?"

"Ydwyf."

"O'r goreu, byddaf yn disgwyl i ti ei thalu yn ol. Pan fydd pobl yn troi at grefydd byddwn yn disgwyl iddynt wneud yr hyn sydd iawn."

"O," ebai Jack, gyda thawelwch hunanfoddhaol, "mae yr Arglwydd wedi maddeu fy holl bechodau, ac y mae hwn yna yn un o honynt."

Cymry dan y Tuduriaid

Mai 26 1904

Ysgrifenasai Dante ei lyfr "Ar Iaith y Cyffredin" [*Ar Huawdledd yn yr Iaith Frodorol* (1302-05)] er mwyn amddiffyn defnyddio yr Eidaleg fel iaith llenyddiaeth; a rhoddodd enghraifft ardderchog honi yn ei gogoniant yn ei weithiau ei hun. Arwyddair yr oes oedd peidio cyfyngu a chaethiwo bywyd i ryw linellau neillduol, ond ei fyw yn ei holl arweddion gyda'r mwynhad a'r calondid mwyaf. Ceisid myned yn uniongyrchol at natur ei hun er mwyn enill y profiad dyfnaf ac helaethaf a ellid o ystyr bywyd. O ganlyniad, nodweddir y cyfnod yn y gwahanol wledydd, ar rai adegau, gan awydd am brofiad helaethach, ar adegau eraill am brofiad dyfnach, o fywyd. Ceir yr un ysbryd, er o bosibl, nad oeddynt hwy yn hollol ymwybodol o'i, ym marddoniaeth beirdd Cymreig fel Tudur A!ed, a William Lleyn, mewn ymdrech i fyned tuhwnt i eiriau ac ymadroddion ffurfiol at ysbryd y peth byw. Yr oedd i'r Cymry hefyd y pryd yma, fwy o ysbrydiaeth at fywyd arddiad, am na lethid hwy gymaint gan y cywilydd hwnnw eu bod yn Gymry a fu yn fagl ac yn rwystr cyn hyn i gynnifer o'n cydgenedl. Hanai y teulu brenhinol ei hun o linach Gymreig; ac nis gellid yn hawdd daflu anfri ar y Cymry heb ddifrio yr orsedd hefyd. Nid rhai i gellwair a hwy oedd y Tuduriaid. A pha golliadau bynag oedd yn perthyn iddynt nis gallai neb eu cyhuddo o ddiffyg nerth ewyllys a phenderfyniad. Nid oedd y byd wedi dysgu hanner tosturio wrthynt hwy drwy geisio arddangos eu nodweddion neu eu gwendidau "Celtaidd". Dan gysgod yr hyfdra yma a gaffai oddiwrth y ffaith fod Cymru yn ffasiynol oherwydd ei chysylltiad a'r Orsedd, daeth y Cymro y pryd hyny, yr unfed ganrif a'r bymtheg, yn anturiaethus ei ysbryd, a chawn ef yn ymgodi i sylw mewn llawer cylch megis yn y Llys, yr Eglwys, y Fyddin, a'r Llynges. Rhaid cadw yr ysbryd effro, anturiaethus a phenderfynol hwn yn y Cymro yn wastad o flaen ein llygaid.

Richard Cobden

Mehefin 9 1904

Dydd Gwener diweddaf ydoedd can-mlwyddiant Richard Cobden. Rhyfedd fel y mae can-mlwyddiant y gwr nodedig hwn hefyd yn adeg ymosodiad ar yr athrawiaethau Rhyddfrydol y bu ef, ynghyda John Bright yn foddion i'w sefydlu. Chafodd Cobden ddim addysg athrofaol; iddo ef ei hunan yn unig yr oedd yn ddyledus am bob diwylliant a gyrhaeddodd. Nid oedd ganddo na golud na gradd uchel mewn cymdeithas, etto, trwy rym ei alluoedd a'i gymeriad, gyrodd ei wlad ar y fath hynt o welliantau a chynydd cymdeithasol nas gwelwyd ei debyg o'r blaen. Gellir adgofio bob amser gydag hyfrydwch ddarfod i Cobden gymeryd ei ochr yn ddeheuig gyd a rhengau Cristionogaeth. Dywedai yn aml "ei bod hi'n anobeithiol disgwyl unrhyw dda oddiwrth ddynion nad ydynt yn coleddu syniad cryf a bywiol o grefydd, nac yn gwneuthur datguddiad yr Efengyl ac addysg

Crist yn gychwynfan pob ddyledswydd ddaearol."

Tibet

Mehefin 16 1904

Hyd yn ddiweddar ychydig a wyddai y cyffredin am fodolaeth y wlad feudwyol, fynyddig ac offeiriad-lywodraethol hon, yr hon sydd yn nghanolbarth Asia, ac o dan amddiffyniad China. Am fod y Tibetiaid wedi tori y cytundeb masnachol a wnaethant a Prydain Fawr tua deuddeng mlynedd yn ol, penderfynodd llywodraethwr India anfon cenhadaeth filwrol i alw eu sylw yn gyfeillgar at y pwnc hwn, ac i geisio dyfod i gyd- ddealltwriaeth a hwy. Hon yw y wlad fwyaf mynyddig ar wyneb y ddaear; ac er fod ei harwynebedd yn fwy bedair gwaith nag arwynebedd ymerodraeth Germani, nid ydyw ei phoblogaeth uwchlaw tair miliwn, a hyny o herwydd uchder ei mynyddoedd, y rhai sydd o dan eira oesol. Mynegir fod mwy na haner y wlad yn uwch na Mont Blanc, heb goed na math yn y byd o lysiau yn tyfu arni, eithr gwyntoedd cryfion o'r gorllewin, ac ystormydd o genllysg a gwlaw trwy y flwyddyn yn crwydro ar hyd iddo.

Preswylia y bobl ar ddyffryn cul y Sanpo, neu Brahamputra, yr Indus, a pharthau uchaf y Mekong, ac y mae un rhan o dair o honynt yn offeiriaid, y rhan arall yn llwythau crwydrol fel yr Arabiaid, a'r rhai sydd yn byw mewn aneddau yn lled gyffredin yn amlwreicwyr. Nid yw holl gyllid blynyddo1 y wlad uwchlaw $75,000, ac y mae yr offeiriaid yn rhydd oddiwrth bob treth. Yr unig ffordd y gellir myned i'r parthau a breswylir o Tibet, ydyw trwy fylchau y mynyddoedd, o India o'r tu deheuol, o China ar y tu ogledd-ddwyreiniol, ac o Kashmir, ar y tu gorllewinol. Nis gallai byddin o Rwsia byth fyned i'r wlad hon ond naill ai trwy India neu o China. Rhaid i Cyrnol Younghusband fyned yno yn awr, gyda'i wyr o Calcutta, trwy fylchau uchel yr Himalaya. Gwelir yno camelod gwylltion, cyflawnder o asynod gwylltion, ceirw ac antelopes yn porfau yn finteioedd.

Ceir rhai rhanau o'r wlad yn meddu hinsawdd ddymunol, yn cynyrchu ffrwythau fel gwinwydd, peaches, afalau, eirin ac apricots. Gwelir pentrefydd bychain o gwmpas llyn Dangra yn yr uchder 15,000 o droedfeddi uwchlaw lefel y mor, a'r bobl yn gallu codi ceirch a haidd yn yr uchder hwnw. Ond tybir fod cyfoeth mwyaf y wlad, cyfoeth anhysbyddadwy, mewn mwnau, ac yn enwedig mewn aur. Tibet, medd un teithiwr, fydd California y dyfodol.

Bwdhiaeth ydyw ei chrefydd; offeiriad yw ei brenin, sef Dalai Lama, a chredir gan ei ddylynwyr ei fod yn cael ei eni drachefn, neu fod ei ysbryd yn ail ymgnawdoli ar ol iddo farw. Lhasa ydyw ei brif ddinas; yno ceir 15,000 o bobl, yn priodi ac yn rhoddi i briodas, a 18,000 o offeiriadon nad allant briodi; yno y mae y brif deml, yr hon sydd mor hardd ag eglwys St. Peter yn Rhufain. Dywedir fod y seremoniau crefyddol yn dra thebyg i seremoniau Eglwys Rhufain. Pan y concrodd y rhyfelwr glew Gengis Khan China, Tibet ac India, a phan yr oedd ei olynydd, Kubola Khan, yn chwilio am y grefydd oreu, galwodd ger ei fron, meddir, gynrychiolwyr o wahanol grefyddau, ac yn eu plith gynrychiolwyr y Pab ac offeiriaid Budhistaidd. Pan y gofynodd am wyrth methodd y Cristionogion Pabyddol gyflawni un, ond llwyddodd y Budhistaidd i wneyd hyny, trwy beri i gwpan o win godi o hono ei hun at ei enau ef. Penderfynodd trwy y weithred hon i fabwysiadu Bwdhistaeth fel crefydd; ond nid ydyw ond cymysgfa o'r grefydd hono ac o ddewiniaeth Affrica.

Ceir yn y wlad 3000 o fynachlogydd ac yn mhob un o honynt o dair i ddeng mil o fynachod. Gwelir pererinion o China, Corea, Japan, Mongolia, Manchuria, ac o India yn crwydro yn flinedig i ddinas sanctaidd y wlad anhygyrch hon, gan ddwyn offrymau gwerthfawr i'w canlyn. Ond nid yw yn beth tebyg fod Dalai Lama yn eu gwerthfawrogi, oblegid nid yw ond glaslanc o 18 i 19 mlwydd oed. Lleddir ef cyn ei fod yn ugainoed mewn rhyw ddull, a chredir gan ei ddysgyblion ei fod yn ail ymgnawdoli. Y bod hwn, Dalai Lama, ydyw Pab Bwdhistaeth – crefydd Burmah, Ceylon, Siam, Japan, Cochin, China, Corea, Manchuria a Mongolia.

Oliver Cromwell

Medi 8 1904

Dydd Sadwrn diweddaf ydoedd pen blwydd marwolaeth Oliver Cromwell, yn 1658. Efe ydoedd un o'r Prydeinwyr mwyaf mewn hanes; rhaid ei alw yn Brydeinwr, oherwydd yr oedd gwythien o waed Cymraeg [sic] ynddo, ar ochr ei fam. I'w ddylanwad arhosol ef y mae Anghydffurfwyr i ddiolch i raddau helaeth am eu rhyddid presennol ac oddiwrtho ef hefyd y mae gan Anghydffurfwyr, a Chydymffurfwyr, lawer eto i ddysgu o'r ysbryd goddefgarol hwnnw a'i nodweddai yn yr amserau anoddefgarol hyny.

James Russell Lowell

Tachwedd 10 1904

Fel yr oedd gan dywysogion yr hen Gymry bob un ei fardd i ganu ei glodydd, a thanio ei ddewrion i'r gad; felly y mae gan bob achos da, neu pob symudiad pwysig yn hanes y ddynoliaeth, ei fardd, amcan bywyd yr hwn ydyw ymladd dros yr achos gyda'i awen. Un felly ydoedd James Russell Lowell y bardd Americanaidd. Pan oedd cri wylofus y caethwas du yn esgyn i'r nef am waredigaeth, tua canol y ganrif ddiweddaf yn America, cawsant gydymdeimlad parod y beirdd Whittier a Longfellow; ond James Russell Lowell ydoedd yr hwn a ymgyssegrodd ei awen gref i'w hachos, pan oedd gwneyd y cyfryw yn tynu anathema y cyhoedd ar ben y neb ai gwnelai.

Y Geninen am y Flwyddyn Nesaf

Tachwedd 17 1904

Dyma fydd rai o'r pynciau yr ymdrinir a hwynt yn ystod y flwyddyn, a rhai o honynt eisoes ar ganol cael eu trafod ynddo:- "Llenyddiaeth Gymraeg y Ganrif Bresenol: Pa un ai Gwella ai Dirwyio y mae?" Yr Iaith Gymraeg: Pa un ai Mantais ai Anfantais i Foes a Chrefydd Cymru fyddai ei pharhau?" "Pwlpud Cymru: Pa un ai Cryfhau ai Gwanhau y mae ei Ddylanwad?" "Enwadau Crefyddol Cymru: A ydynt yn Gweithredu'n gyson a'u Credoau?" (Y mae llenorion o fri, Eglwysig ac Ymneillduol, wedi ymgymeryd a thraethu eu llen, bob un ar ei eglwys a'i enwad ei hun).

Hefyd, yn y rhifynau dyfodol fe barheir yr erthyglau ar "Fywyd ac Athrylith Enwogion Ymadawedig."

Llongfarchwn gyhoeddwr *Y Geninen* ar ei ragolygon i allu cynysgaeddu ddarllenwyr y cylchgrawn yna a thrysorau llenorol a deallol, henafol a diweddar, y flwyddyn nesaf, gwerthfawrocach nag erioed. Parheir yn, ac ychwanegir at, yr ymdrechion i gasglu a chyhoeddi "hen weddillion pridwerth," yn hanesyddol, hynafiaethol, chwedlonol, beirniadaethau, llythyrau oddiwrth enwogion at eu gilydd, etc. a'r cyfan yn dwyn perthynas a Chymru, Cymro, neu Gymraeg. Bydd *Y Geninen* hefyd yn parhau i fod yn "gronfa o gynyrchion eisteddfodol" gwerthfawr a dyddorol, fel nad elo llawer o'n trysorau llenyddol mwyach ar ddisperod.

Yn y rhifyn nesaf (Ionawr), ymddengys erthyglau o eiddo'r awduron hyglod a ganlyn – Y Prifathraw John Rhys, M.A., D.Litt.; Hugh Jones, D.D. (W.); Waldo; Y Prifathraw D. Rowlands, B.A. (Dewi Mon); John Hughes, M.A.; Berw; Gwydeddon; Cadvan; Eilir; Evan Davies (Trefriw); Elfed; W. Llewelyn Williams, M.A., B.C.L.; Gwynedd; D. Stanley Jones: T. J. Humphreys; Gwylfa; David Griffith; Anthropos; Iolo Caernarfon; Spinther; Ifano; yr Athraw J. E. Lloyd, M.A.; Elphin; R. Jenkin Jones, M.A. (Aberdar); Gwili; Watcyn Wyn; Tafolog; Rhosynog; y Parch. D. Lloyd; yr Athraw Anwyl, M.A.; Alavon; L. J. Roberts M.A.; W. J. Nicholson; J. T. Job; Dunodig; Dyfnallt; Brynach; yn nghyda'r enwogion ymadaweig Nicander, I D. Ffraid, Hiraethog, Cynfaen Cynddelw, Eben Fardd, etc.

Hefyd yn ystod y flwyddyn parheir y gyfres o ysgrifau ar "Gychwyniad a Chynydd y Gwahanol Enwadau Crefyddol yn Nghymru," a rhai a ysgrifenir gan lenorion profedig, perthynol i bob un o'r cyrff crefyddol, Eglwysig yn gystal ag Ymneillduol, sydd yn allu yn ein gwlad.

Perthwyr Awstralia

Ionawr 26 1905

Dywed teithwyr ydynt newydd ddychwelyd o ganolbarth Awstralia hanesion rhyfedd am bobl yn byw mewn nythod yn ngwylltleoedd y gwledydd yna. Perthwyr Awstralia, mae'n debyg, ydyw y radd isaf o ddynion y gwyddys am danynt. Y mae eu gwybodaeth mor fychan fel nas gallant godi y math symlaf o fwthynod i fyw ynddynt. Casglant frigiau coed a glaswellt, ac adeiladant nythod fel eu tai. Y mae'r nythod yn ddigon mawr i ddal y teulu; yn wir, gwneir hwy yn ol rhif aelodau y teulu. Welthiau bydd y dail yn tyfu fel gorchudd uwch eu pen; ond ni wneir byth un cais i ddarparu nodded rhag ystormydd.

Y Byd a'i Ieithoedd

Chwefror 9 1905

Afrad pob afraid.
Nwyfus pob gobaith.
Nid cywir ond cyfiawn.
Y llaw a rydd a gynull.
Diogel pob tangnefgar.
Am y tywydd goreu tewi.
Niwl y gaua' arwydd eira.
Niwl y gwanwyn gwaeth na gwenwyn.
– Hen Ddiarhebion.

Yn ol ystadegaeth y Gymdeithas Ddaearyddol, y mae poblogaeth y byd yn 1,503,290,000.

Dywed un Mr. J. Collier fod pum mil o wahanol ieithoedd yn cael eu llefaru gan ddynolryw. Y mae nifer y canghen-ieithoedd yn fawr. Yn Brazil siaredir triugain a wahanol dafod-ieithoedd; ac yn Mexico, y mae yr iaith Nahua wedi ei thori i fyny i saith gant o wahanol ganghen-ieithoedd. Yn Borneo y mae canoedd o dafod-ieithoedd. Nis gellir rhoddi trefn a dosbarth ar yr ieithoedd yn Awstralia; ond hyn sydd yn ffaith, fel y cynydda addysg y bobl, y mae nifer y tafod-ieithoedd yn lleihau.

Dywed un Proffeswr Andre Gambin fod ganddo gynllun sydd yn debyg a greu chwyldroad yn y byd morwrol. Y mae ganddo, meddai, ddull o wneyd llong all deithio drwy y mor ol pum' cant o filldiroedd yr awr. A chaniatau fod y pellder o Loegr i America oddeutu tair mil o filldiroedd, yn ol cynllun y Proffeswr gall teithwyr gymeryd eu boreu-fwyd yn Llundain, a chiniawa yn Efrog Newydd.

GLEANINGS ['LLOFFION']

The Harvester

July 9 1903

The hay harvest, which draws so much anxious attention of the farmer these days, has its own legal literature in England, says a correspondent in the

Daily Post. In ancient times there was a compulsion on the tenants to cut and cool the hay of their masters. A tenant at Badbury, for example, was obliged to ctop his lord's hay for one day, for which he received a meal of bread and cheese twice in the course of the day; then he had to gather the same hay, and received a bale of hay for his trouble. The harvesters also received between them twelve pence, or a sheep, which they were to choose from their lordship's pen by sight only. In other places, the harvester had what they called 'haveroe', that is as much grass as he could lift on his pitchfork without breaking one of its tines; another payment to a harvester for a day's work was as much hay as he could gather in his arms. In one manor house, when the tenant had cut the lord's hay he was deemed worthy of a "knitch" of hay, namely, as much as he could lift between his finger and his knee.It would be interesting to have some Welsh folklore about the hay harvest. – IVONFAB ['Son of Ivon']

William Ellery Channing

July 16 1903

A short time ago, the centenary was celebrated of the birth of Emerson – America's greatest thinker who grew up in the previous century; a few weeks later, the centenary of William Ellery Channing's ordination to the Unitarian ministry was celebrated. Who was Emerson? "A friend and helper of those who wish to live in the spirit," was Mathew Arnold's description of Ralph Waldo Emerson's work and message; "His greatness lay in his sublime personality, and when reading his works our spirits ascend to a new atmosphere," says another.

What, then, was the message of Channing, his contemporary? It can be said that he was a philanthropist in the highest and broadest sense of the word; and the dignity of human nature was the favorite theme of his conversation and writings. This is what an American paper, the *Christian Register*, says of its distinguished compatriot, "Outside Unitarian circles his influence is felt and liked by many in Europe and America who do not know him as the leader of a religious revolution, but as a sponsor of universal freedom – of the rights of man and the principles on which the American republic was founded. His writings have come to many patriots as holy scriptures, addressed to all who strive against oppression; and to those who work for the elevation of the human race; because Channing searched for the truth; in some measure he grabbed hold of it and trusted it completely. His sayings endure and his praise increases. His perorations on slavery were realised at last when the slaves were freed and his sermon on world war will be read in a time when war is no more."

There has never been a better example of talent and poverty combined in the same person than that of Robert Burns, the world-renowned Scots poet. His was a turbulent life; and yet, last week a copy of the first edition of his songs was sold for a thousand pounds.

"Without labour, no rest is won; without battle, there can be no victory" – Thomas A. Kempis

The Dialect of South Ceredigion

July 23 1903

In the midst of the many Welsh poetic products – excellent, so-so and bad – published continuously in the Welsh press, I cannot help but notice "Gan Shacci'r Gwas" ['By the Servant's Shack'] by Sarnicol in the excellent *Ymofynydd* ['The Enquirer']. Besides its excellence, what attracts the reader's attention is that it is written in the South Ceredigion dialect, which gives it a certain novelty and attractive naturalness. We do not propose to tell the story, because it is impaired in the translation. The following serves to show the illustrative power of its author, it is part of the description of a midnight setting:

> But the lightning came greater than usual, until all is white,
> And I see the shower-drops on their way from the air to earth.
> I see the mountains of Pembrokeshire, and the tillage to the edge in green,
> And the houses white between the trees, and the rain shining the roads.

I believe there is no language like that of south Ceredigion to picturesquely express the thoughts of the Welsh. There is much debate in the Welsh literary world regarding the legitimacy of using colloquial language in literary compositions. I would assume that Professor Morris Jones, Bangor, is one of the supporters of the progressive movement in literary narrative, and that Mr Gwenogfryn Evans is not completely hostile to it, because we read some time ago that a review of his written in the dialect of his native area would be more confusing than constructive for a native unversed in Welsh dialects.

Caernarfon Resists

October 15 1903

In view of the current uproar concerning the New Education Act, and the commendable behaviour of Caernarfon County Council and other councils in refusing to aid the Denominational Schools without having full control over them, it is interesting to note that this is not the first time for Caernarfon to "take the bull by the horns" or "capture the enemy's weapons," to use Lloyd George's proverb. Towards the beginning of the last century, when a wrongdoer would be hanged for actions infinitely lesser than the punishment and when a man was sentenced to death for stealing a pound note or two pounds worth of goods from a house, it seems that jurors at the Caernarfon assizes in 1817 were the first "passive opponents" of the ancient punishment laws that flourished at that time. The matter at hand was a charge against a man for stealing a five pound note; the evidence that he was guilty was indisputable, however, to everyone's surprise, the jurors came in with a verdict of "not guilty". The judge gruffly ordered the jurors to leave the court, and called for others. Those also did the same as their predecessors. In the following year the law was changed to its current state. [namely, in 1903, a jury's limited right of "nullification"]

Defending the MPs

March 3 1904

When defending the work of the Welsh Members of Parliament, their supporters say that the MPs are doing all that can reasonably be expected of them. "Easy for you to criticize" they say, "but what more could they do for their country and their electors?" That statement is then supported with reference to the list of divisions [votes in the House of Commons] that prove their loyalty, and usually they stand quite respectably in line when compared to the rest. At the same time, their indifference or negligence towards the latest division on the subject of the Chinese into the Transvaal will certainly attract public attention, and an explanation is expected from those who were absent on this important occasion. The Administration managed to secure a majority of 51, but 92 Liberals were absent from the House at the time, and among them the following Welsh members: – W. Abraham (Mabon), Rhondda; Vaughan Davies, Cardigan; Frank Edwards, Radnor; Syr W. Harcourt, Monmouth; J. Herbert Lewis, Flint; Charles Morley, Brecon; Sam Moss, Denbigh; J. Wynford Phillips, Pembroke; Syr Edward Reed, Cardiff; Samuel Smith, Flint; Abel Thomas, Carmarthen; Syr Alfred Thomas, Glamorgan; J. Aeron Thomas, Gower. Which is thirteen out of the twenty eight Liberals, and that in one of the most important circumstances for our country. We know of some who could not be present due to ill health, but there are certainly others in this list who were expected to be in their places when the fate of the Parliament was in the balance. It will be interesting to see what excuses their supporters will make now?

Forgiveness

April 14 1904

Who are the pagans?" a little boy was asked in a Sunday School once. "People who never quarrel about religion," was the answer.

****

Gipsy Smith (the famous evangelist), in his autobiography, reported about a man who was a drunkard and a fighter and been converted to religion. Shortly afterwards he was met by one of his old companions, from whom he had borrowed a sovereign.

"Well, Jack," said the lender, "I hear you have been converted."

"Yes, I have, and joined the Church."

"Well, do you remember some time ago I lent you a sovereign?"

"Yes, I do."

"Very well, I shall expect you to pay it back. When people get religious, we expect them to do what is right."

"Oh," said Jack, with a self-satisfied serenity, "the Lord has pardoned all my sins, and that is one of them."

The Welsh under the Tudors

May 26 1904

Dante wrote his book "On the Common Language" [On the Eloquence in the Vernacular (1302-05)] in order to defend the use of Italian as a language of literature; and he gave an excellent example of it in the glory of his own works. The motto of the age was not to limit and enslave life along certain lines, but to live it in all its aspects with the greatest enjoyment and heartiness. The attempt was to go directly to nature itself in order to gain the deepest and most extensive experience possible of the meaning of life. As a result, the period in different countries is characterised at some times by the desire for a wider experience of life, at other times for a deeper experience. The same spirit, although possibly they were not fully aware of its origin, can be found in the poetry of Welsh poets such as Tudur Aled and William Lleyn, in the effort to go beyond formal words and expressions and into the spirit of the living thing. The Welsh also had more of an enthusiasm for life at this time, because they were not so overwhelmed by that shame of being Welsh which had hitherto been a trap and an obstacle for so many of our compatriots. The royal family itself came from a Welsh dynasty; and it was not easy to disrespect the Welsh without discrediting the throne as well. The Tudors were not people to jest with. And whatever their deficiencies, no one could accuse them of lacking willpower and determination. The world had not learned to half pity them by trying to display their "Celtic" characteristics or weaknesses. In the shadow of the boldness to be had from the fact that Wales was fashionable, because of its connection with the Gorsedd, the Welshman of the sixteenth century became adventurous in spirit, and we find him coming to the fore in many circles such the Court, the Church, the Army and the Navy. This alert, adventurous and determined spirit in the Welshman must be kept constantly before our eyes.

Richard Cobden

June 9 1904

Last Friday was Richard Cobden's centenary. It is strange how the centenary of this distinguished man is also a time of attack on the Liberal doctrines which he, together with John Bright, was instrumental in establishing. Cobden had no academic education; he was indebted to himself alone for all the culture he acquired. He had neither wealth nor high rank in society, yet, through the strength of his character and abilities, he drove his country along a course of social progress and improvements the like of which had not been seen before. It can always be recalled with delight that Cobden sided adroitly with the ranks of Christianity. He often said "it is hopeless to expect any good from men who do not cherish a strong and living idea of religion, or make the revelation of the Gospel and the education of Christ the beginning of all earthly duties."

Tibet

June 16 1904

Until recently, the ordinary person knew little about the existence of this hermit, mountainous and priest-ruled country, which is in central Asia, and under the protection of China. Because the Tibetans had broken the commercial agreement they made with Great Britain about twelve years ago, the Indian governor decided to send a military mission to call their attention to this issue in a friendly manner. and to try to come to an understanding with them. This is the most mountainous country on the face of the earth; and although its area is four times larger than the area of the German empire, its population is not above three million, and that is because of the height of its mountains, which are under eternal snow. It is said that more than half of the country is higher than Mont Blanc, with no trees or any kind of vegetation growing there, but strong winds from the west and storms of hail and rain wandering across it throughout the year.

The people dwell in the narrow valley of the Sanpo, or Brahamputra, the Indus, and the upper reaches of the Mekong, and one third of them are priests, the other part are nomadic tribes like the Arabs, and it is quite common for those who live in dwellings to be polygamous. The whole annual finances of the country are not above $75,000, and the priests are free from all taxes. The only way to reach the inhabited areas of Tibet is through the mountain passes, from India on the south side, from China on the north-east side, and from Kashmir, on the west side. A Russian army could never get to this country except through India or China. Colonel Younghusband must go there now, with his men from Calcutta, through the high passes of the Himalayas. Wild camels, an abundance of wild donkeys, deer and antelopes foraging in groups are to be seen there.

Some parts of the country have a pleasant climate, producing fruit such as vines, peaches, apples, plums and apricots. Small villages can be seen around Dangra lake at an altitude of 15,000 feet above sea level, and the people can raise oats and barley at that altitude. But it is assumed that the country's greatest wealth, its inexhaustible wealth, is in minerals, and especially in gold. Tibet, says one traveller, will be the California of the future.

Its religion is Buddhism; its king, the Dalai Lama, is a priest, and his followers believe that he is born again, or that his spirit reincarnates after he dies. Lhasa is its main city; there are 15,000 people there, marrying and given in marriage, and 18,000 priests who cannot marry; there is the main temple, which is as beautiful as the church of St. Peter in Rome. When the brave warrior Genghis Khan conquered China, Tibet and India, and when his successor, Kubola Khan, was searching for the best religion, he called before him, it is said, representatives of different religions, and among them the representatives of the Pope and Buddhist priests. When he asked for a miracle, the Catholic Christians failed to achieve one, but the Buddhist succeeded in doing so, by causing a cup of wine to rise up by itself to his mouth. He decided through this action to adopt Buddhism as a religion; but it is only a mixture of that religion and African witchcraft. There are 3,000 monasteries in the country and from three to ten thousand monks in each of them. Pilgrims from China, Korea, Japan, Mongolia, Manchuria, and India are seen wandering wearily to the holy city of this inaccessible country, bringing valuable offerings to follow. But it is not likely the Dalai Lama appreciates them, because he is only a youngster of 18 to 19 years old. He is killed in some way before he is twenty years old in some way, and it is believed by his disciples that he is reincarnated. This being, the Dalai Lama, is the Pope of Buddhism – the religion of Burmah, Ceylon, Siam, Japan, Cochin, China, Korea, Manchuria and Mongolia.

Oliver Cromwell

September 8 1904

Last Saturday was the anniversary of the death of Oliver Cromwell, in 1658. He was one of the greatest Britons in history; he must be called British, because there was a vein of Welsh blood in him, on his mother's side. Nonconformists largely have his enduring influence to thank for their present freedom, and from him also Nonconformists and Conformists still have much to learn from the tolerant spirit that charactised those intolerant times.

James Russell Lowell

November 10 1904

As the princes of the old Welsh each had his poet to sing his praises, and fire up his braves for the battle; so every good cause, or every important movement in the history of humanity, has its poet, whose aim in life is to fight for the cause with his muse. One such was the American poet James

Russell Lowell. When the tearful cry of the black slave ascended to the heavens for salvation. about the middle of the last century in America, they had the ready sympathy of the poets Whittier and Longfellow; but James Russell Lowell it was who dedicated his powerful creativity to their cause, when doing so brought public anathema down on the head of any person so doing.

Y Geninen for Next Year

November 17 1904

Here are some of the topics to be dealt with during the year, and some of them are already in the midst of discussion:- "Welsh Literature in the Present Century: Is it Improving or Deteriorating?" "The Welsh Language: Would its Continuation be an Advantage or a Disadvantage to Morality and Religion in Wales?" "The Welsh Pulpit: Is its Influence Growing Stronger or Weaker?" "Religious Denominations in Wales: Do they Operate According to their Beliefs?" (Eminent writers, both Church and Dissent, have taken it upon themselves to tell their story, each about his own church and denomination).

Also, the articles on "The Life and Genius of Departed Celebrities" will be continued in future issues.

We congratulate the publisher of *Y Geninen* ['The Leek'] on his prospective ability to endow the readers of that magazine next year with literary and intellectual treasures, ancient and modern, more valuable than ever. The efforts to collect and publish "old precious relics", historical, antiquarian, legendary, critiques, letters from famous people to each other, etc. will be continued and extended, all sustaining the relationship between, Wales, the Welshman and the Welsh language. *Y Geninen* will also continue to be a valuable and interesting "repository of eisteddfodic compositions", so that many of our literary treasures are no longer dispersed.

In the next issue (January), there will be articles by the following esteemed authors – Principal John Rhys, MA, D.Litt.; Hugh Jones, DD (W.); Waldo; Principal D. Rowlands, BA (Dewi Mon); John Hughes, MA; Berw; Gwydeddon; Cadvan; Eilir; Evan Davies (Trefriw); Elfed; W. Llewelyn Williams, MA, BCL; Gwynedd; D. Stanley Jones: TJ Humphreys; Gwylfa; David Griffith; Anthropos; Iolo Caernarfon; Spinther; Ifano; Professor JE Lloyd, MA; Elphin; R. Jenkin Jones, MA (Aberdare); Gwili; Watcyn Wyn; Tafolog; Rhosynog; the Rev. D. Lloyd; Professor Anwyl, MA; Alavon; LJ Roberts MA; WJ Nicholson; JT Job; Dunodig; Dyfnallt; Brynach; together with the famous departed Nicander, ID Ffraid, Hiraethog, Cynfaen Cynddelw, Eben Fardd, etc.

Also during the year, the series of articles on "The Origin and Progress of the Different Religious Denominations in Wales" will be continued, along with those written by experienced writers related to each of the religious bodies, Church as well as Dissent, who have the capacity to do so in our country.

The Bushmen of Australia

January 26 1905

Travellers who have just returned from central Australia tell strange stories about people living in nests in the wilds of those countries. Australian bushmen are probably the lowest rank of men known. Their knowledge is so small that they cannot build the simplest type of cottages to live in. They collect tree tops and grass, and build nests as their houses. The nests are big enough to hold the family; indeed, they are made according to the number of family members. Sometimes the leaves will grow like a covering above their head; but no attempt is ever made to provide shelter from storms.

The World's Languages

February 9 1905

> Everything needless is waste.
> All hope is lively.
> None sincere but the just.
> The hand that gives will gather.
> The peaceful are safe.
> Best be silent about the weather.
> Winter mist is a sign of snow.
> Mist in spring is worse than poison.
> – Old Proverbs

According to Geographical Society statistics, the world's population is 1,503,290,000. A Mr J. Collier says that five thousand different languages are spoken by mankind. The number of branch languages is large. In Brazil sixty different dialects are spoken; and in Mexico, the Nahua language has been broken up into seven hundred different branch languages. In Borneo there are hundreds of dialects. The languages in Australia cannot be ordered and classified; but this is a fact, as the education of the people increases, the number of dialects decreases.

A Professor Andre Gambin says he has a plan that is likely to create a revolution in the maritime world. He has, he states, a method of constructing a ship that can travel through the sea at five hundred miles an hour. Allowing that the distance from England to America is approximately three thousand miles, according to the Professor's plan travellers can take their breakfast in London and dine in New York.

David Ivon Jones was actively involved in this former Unitarian Chapel in Aberystwith, which developed into a hotbed of religious and political unorthodoxy.

2

NOTES AND LETTERS

(1904-1915)

Florrie Anwl [chwaer]

Accounts Book
December 14 1904

Florrie anwl, rym ni'n meddwl
Pob ryw awr am danoch chi.
Maith yw'r ffordd, a maith yw'r cefnfor
Sydd yn llifo rhyngtom ni
A dywedyd y gwir,
Y mae'r amser yn hir
Heb glywed oddiwrthych
Ers cetyn go hir.

Shwt mâ'r brodyr, shwt mâ'r morwyr,
Shwt mâ'r milwyr yn dod ym mlaen?
Mae rhyw hiraeth ac anobaith
Yn cael effaith arnai'n lan.
A dywedyd y gwir
Y mae amser yn hir
Heb glywed o'r brodyr
Ers cetyn go hir.

Nawdd Duw arnoch pan dramwyoch
Eto hyd eyraidd estron wlad
Mewn peryglon mae E'n ffyddlon
Byddwn foddlon arno'n Dad.
A dywedyd y gwir

A byw yna'n hir.
Nes cwrddon weithian
Yn Ei wiwlan dir.

Dear Florrie [sister]

Dear Florrie we are thinking
Every hour about you.
Great is the journey, and wide the ocean
That flows between us.
And truly,
It is a long time
Since hearing from you
Quite a spell indeed!

How are the brothers? How are the sailors,
How are the soldiers getting on?
There's a deep longing and despondency
Affecting me greatly.
And truly
It is a long time
Since hearing from the brothers
Quite a spell indeed!

God's blessing on you as you travel
Once again in the golden, foreign land
In troubled times He is true!
Be contented with Our Father!
And truly
Live long
And we will meet at last
In His pure land.

A Sonnet to Buddha

SS Omrah, Letter to George Eyre Evans
March 3 1907

Here in the star domed temple of mankind
Despite strange forms of thought in me and you
Brothers are we who's birthright is the true.
Here in the Indian sea I joy to find
Men are made comrades by the might of mind.
Hence doth thy face for ever bring to view

The Universal Church – Immense and New
That men of old and now have 'pined.
It was my wish to speak with you upon
The ancient cults and glories of Ceylon.
I'd loved to hear from you oft and again
Of Buddha's pure and spirit-builded fame?
And during life whatever be your quest
May you find his Nirvana of the Blest.

Two Russian revolutionaries

SS Omrah, Letter to George Eyre Evans

March 12 1907

We have two Russian revolutionaries on board. One is in the open berths, 3rd class and the other in the second class. The one in the 3rd is Jacob, a simple fellow, that is harmless; but he seems very well read although he cannot speak more than a few words of English yet. He seems to know the socialistic theories of Karl Marx minutely. The other revolutionary – Moses Blank – spends most of his time down on the 3rd class deck. And every day we have a chat on deck. He can speak fair English. And also good German it seems. Moses is a most refined fellow, coming from a good family. Rather tall. Very fairly proportioned. Delicate face. The hands of an artist. And legs of a statuary. When Jacob can't make us understand, he says it to Moses, who gives it to us. When something of a twisty nature has to [be] said, Jacob gives it to Moses, Moses gives it to an English fellow who can speak German, who is also of the company, and he gives it to me. But for ordinary conversations, soon Jacob can manage with a little difficulty. He tells me that he was a bit of a public speaker in Russia. As all of the revolutionaries have to do a little of it to instruct the peasants. He was going one night to a secret congregation of 20 peasants in a cottage; to speak to them on socialistic ideas and the rights of man. Presently there came a rat tat at the door, and in came six secret police. He was bound and taken to a prison where there was only a small window of about six inches high. From there he was sent to Siberia with 46 other prisoners. He was put in a prison then. One of four in a small cell. From there the four of them made their escape by digging a hole beneath the foundations out into open air. He escaped to Smolensk, Moscow, St Petersburg and from there to Finland. Here he lay hid for three weeks until a ship was found for him for London. Jacob puts his thumb to his nose and his tongue out to describe his attitude to the secret police as the ship was leaving the quay. Whatever the difference of languages there may be the expressions of contempt and defiance are the same the world over. Both Moses and Jacob took part in protecting the Jews in Odessa from the Black Hundreds when the last great pogrom took place there. He says that all the young men are revolutionaries. He said that 1,000 Jewish young men and 1,000 Christians joined in a secret committee to protect the Jews from being massacred. The Jews are massacred because they are the prime movers in the revolution. He tells how the Governor of the place instituted a pogrom. His son, a student, was of the revolutionary committee to protect the Jews. So when the Governor sent his mercenary Black Hundreds out to massacre, sixty student protectors were killed with the Jewish men and women, old and helpless people.And of that sixty, one was the Governor's own son. A more tragic retribution was never told in a novel.

"Where even woman has her vote"

New Zealand, Letter to George Eyre Evans

January 10 1909

Not long ago I had my first experience of a New Zealand election. It was very interesting, and if I can (save) any of the relics in the shape of election leaflets, from the archives of my bulky coat pocket, hurriedly deposited there for you. I shall send them along. New Zealand elections are carried on model lines. The election saw the New Second Ballot Act first brought into practice. When one compares New Zealand with the old country in the matter of electoral rights, the latter comes out very unfavourably.

Every man and woman above 21 votes here, even though he does not own so much as a pig sty. Here, where even woman has her vote as a matter of course, the suffragettes' agitations at home seem strange to say the least of it.

The women's vote has done a lot of good here. Not so much in the Parliamentary election, but in the licensing poll that accompanies it. General elections occur every three years in NZ. And at every general election the local option question is put to the referendum.

A man goes into the polling booth and gets a ballot paper to vote for "Jones" or "Jenkins" according to his taste.. That much over he gets a much more important one (in some people's opinion). On this he records his choice:

I. That liquor licenses shall continue.

II. That liquor licenses shall be reduced.

III. That liquor licenses shall cease.

Local Option or No Licenses [i.e. Prohibition] as New Zealanders call it, was carried in about a dozen electorates this election. In Dunedin, the Liquor Interest made frantic efforts against the No License Movement.

Feeling rose high on occasions. Debates were held between advocates of both sides, at one of which two or three thousand people were present. In the result the Dunedin electors voted for reduction to the great relief of the publicans.

3

AFRICA CALLING

(1911-1921)

Dutch, Afrikaans and Basuto

Letter to George Eyre and Kitty Evans

January 1 1911

I don't know exactly where to begin with particulars. The *winkel* as the Dutch call a store here is situated close to the railway siding, past which two passenger trains, one up and one down, run every day. Behind is the broad Veldt, a broad, undulating expanse of relatively green upland, dotted here and there with Dutch farms. The personnel of the *winkel* is composed of my brother, myself, an assistant who goes out "smousing." "Smousing" means hawking or bartering goods on a large scale, round the country. Here we "smous" country which is beyond the reach of the *winkel*. Say fifteen miles away. It is done by a cart of 4 mules and another of 2 horses. The rest of the crew is composed of three K* or Basuto boys. Two work the "smous" and one remains round the store. The goods sold vary from "a needle to an anchor." To use an extreme expression. All the necessaries of a Dutch farmer, not to foget the Basutos. Ironmongery, drapery and grocery. Dutch farmers go to bed early and get up early. Considering the distance some of them come, they must get up before dawn even at this time of the year. They bring their cream to send away with the down train at 7 o'clock, and they are here to do their shopping long before, continuing all day more or less. A little later, after the first batch of Dutchmen, come the Basutos clad in their bright shawls and coloured head linen, bare feet, arms and shoulders, adorned with numerous beaded ornaments. These wait until the Dutch folk have finished their purchases, sitting outside on the green in chatty circles, conversing now soft now vehement, in their strange, weird language.

I am gradually picking up knowledge of the Dutch. The "Afrikaans" as they call it, is a *patois*, a degraded Dutch, used only in speaking.

Correspondence and newspapering is carried on in High Dutch, with as far as I can see, slight concessions to local whims.

The Basutos trade through the medium of the Afrikaans. Some of them possessing a slight smattering of English. They, like the Dutch, trade by Barter, sometimes cash. Eggs, eggs, eggs, they are the great medium of exchange, then fowls, wool and skins. The last including skins of goats, springboks, sheep, Westbuck etc. but eggs are the great fallback. In baskets of deftly woven straw, or native pottery, they bring this fragile cash, adroitly balanced on their heads whatever is needed, say 6d worth of sugar they draw out six eggs, which are placed by the seller in boxes under the counter. The styles of dealing are very different between a K* and Dutchman. The latter one has to humour, very much the same as the time honoured method of serving a customer in other parts: with the exception that, here at any rate, both buyer and seller are on a par: if any they the latter slightly superior. But no "cheek" is taken: and it is a reflection on the Dutchman when a row as sometimes does occur, wherein complimentary epithets are bandied about, where an Englishman would never out of self respect show his face again, the Dutchman will return the next day as if nothing had happened (as you will note by the numerous blots I am not very facile in my expression today which please excuse).

On the other hand with the K* one deals as if with an inferior; if docile, treat him as a child; if otherwise, which is seldom, order him outside till he learns manners. The Basuto language, to one who has been accustomed to listen to Europeans is a strange collection of sounds. I like to hear the Basuto women talking together. Their expression is infinitely gentler and more considerate than any European way of conversing. They have the *ll* sound of the Welsh language and a click also, which is produced by the same mode as the *ll* but in a condensed form

The methods of affirming and negating are so expressive that they are often adopted by white people. When a decisive "No" is meant, they defiantly say "Icona" but a pleading "No" is expressed by two sharp jerks of the larynx, reminding one of a patient's protest under a surgeon's incision, something like "agh-agh".

Oosthuizen's Siding, Kroonstadt District, Orange River Colony

The "Dutchman" and the "K*"

Letter to George Eyre Evans

January 31 1911

The best Dutchman as a rule is the least strict in religious matters. So that one is not environed by such an object of admiration and study as is presented by a class or community deeply sensible, according to his own perceptions, of religious truth. So far as I can see the Dutchman attends "kirk" to keep the sabbath purely for the same reason as he ploughs with oxen, and reaps with a sickle. Simplybecause his father did so. Of course this might be very cursory criticism, and be modified on closer acquaintance.

It is curious how silent they are on the controversies of the war. I do not see any bitterness shown. they seem to take it as a matter of history, "time that aged nurse" having rocked them to patience.

I am gradually picking up a few words of the vernacular, and can now serve, and carry on scraps of conversation with the customers. It is my ambition, if I shall remain here, to try and learn the High Dutch, which is slightly different to the Cape Dutch. However, all correspondence and newspapers are carried on in High Dutch.

I should like to tell you a little about our dark neighbours. Perhaps it will afford material for another letter. If I could only describe some as I find them, the impression they leave on me, I think I might interest you. Anyhow the K*s constitute a problem that it is difficult to solve. In many cases the proper and most polite method of treating K*s, as interpreted by most Colonials, unfortunately involves the forswearing of all those attributes of good behaviour which mark a gentleman. According to my tutors, I must forget all feelings of compassion and humanitarian ideas in dealing with a K*. It remains for me to find out how far this is true. If honesty, trust and fidelity count for anything, the Basuto is in the main a credit to his maker.

Or to take the first mentioned virtue, if as Burns maintained, an honest man is God's greatest handiwork, then many of our dark customers are greatly superior beings to some of our whites.

Oostingen Siding, Kroonstadt District, Orange River Colony

"Dance of the death's heads"

Letter. *Reynolds's Newspaper* September 14 1913

In 1907 there was a strike of miners here [Transvaal]. The miners appointed a Strike Committee. Here are the after-fates of the men of that body. In alphabetical order they were :-

1. J.H. Brodigan – Dead. Phthisis.
2. G. Clough – Still on the Rand.
3. Jas. Coward – Dead. Phthisis.
4. H. Cowan – Dead. Phthisis.
5. S. Crowl – Dead. Phthisis.
6. F. Crean – Killed. Mine accident in Canada.
7. J. Flanagan – Dead. Phthisis.
8. A. Flynn – Dead. Phthisis.
9. J. Johns – "Compensated". Bad with Phthisis.

10. Tom Matthews – Living. Has phthisis.
11. T. Shadwell – Dead. Phthisis.
12. R. Taylor – Dead. Phthisis.
13. J. Thompson – Dead. Phthisis.
14. M. Trewick – Living. Has phthisis.
15. T. Willis – Dead. Phthisis.

There were two other, possibly three, members whose names are not available. These men, however, are all dead … No public meeting of indignation has ever been held by the much needed public pn this scourge.

One of the Transvaal Miners' Association organizers, in a speech to the men the other evening, dropped the remark, "I've got it; we've all got it" – "it" being the spectre of the unnamed scourge which lays low all miners. About the same hour General Botha was addressing a gathering of the elite at Johannesburg, and while venturing the assertion that Labour was a very valuable asset to the country, deprecated anything that might injure the "credit" of South Africa and prevent the necessary influx of capital, &c., &c.. Poor Labour donkey. His load is a trifle heavy. Well, give him an extra carrot. What a dance of the death's heads!

Under Martial Law

Illicit propaganda during the 1914 General Strike in South Africa
Letters to George Eyre Evans

January 1914

These are the kind of messages we used to get when supplying authentic news for the Manifesto [pro-strike bulletin], to counteract the manufactured reports of the Censored press.

The difficulties of getting these manifestos printed and then circulated over the extensive area of the Rand were enormous. But we had several Jews who stinted no money, and had Russian experiences, and against their organization no Martial Law restrictions could avail.

The printer was known to myself and two others (George Kendall,who escaped to Australia being one). The printer took them hot to an isolated room as they came out of the press. From there they were taken to a dust heap in another part of Johannesburg by another set of chaps.there they were picked up by fellows with motors and bikes carrying official permits, some even being conveyed in unwitting police cars!! To all parts of the diasaffected area.

"GETTING DESPERATE": Note re to be careful in not giving our printer away. So wary was he that when the police [came], though a few minutes previously he had been hard at it, they could find no trace of form or manifestos. They were reasonably sure he being the last printer searched and arrested him on suspicion. Hence our caution in referring to him.

"THIS HOUSE UNDER ARREST". This was a message scribbled by Cresswell which he asked me to convey to the men at the Braamfontein [strike] centre. He made himself personally responsible for them after the arrest of the other leaders.On this occasion he subsequently decided to go. He and I went in cab together. From there we drove round to printer to arrange about second edition of his leaflet (for which he was arrested the following day and copy of which I have lost) stopping cab a couple of blocks away, we walked down. On gaining the house we were stopped by detective, saying "This house is under arrest," and Cresswell's sardonic temperament became grimmer and more set than ever. Half the government's operations were directed at destroyng his political influence. He is the Randlord's arch enemy.

Ymgom a Chymry

Press cutting in letter to George Eyre Evans

May 24 1915

Ar hyd yr oesau edrychasom ni y Cymry arnom ein hunain fel gwyr o asgwrn cefn, yn hoffi herio'r byd er mwyn egwyddor. Cawsom y gair o fod yn freyddwydwyr, yn arwain y byd o fyllni arfaeliaeth i feysydd eang diwylliant: gogwyddem glust y gwledydd i wrando cân melys Adar Rhiannon ynghanol mwstwr materiolaeth: cynnysgaeddwyd ni yn nidwyll laeth y gair, ac yn y llais ddistaw fain; a hoffem feddwl mae ein hannibyniaeth yn ngwyneb trais a thrachwant ein meistriaid oedd ein priodoledd penaf; ffermwyr Ceredigion yn cael eu taflu o'u tyddynoedd yn 1868 am wrthod pleidleisio gyda'r meistri tir, a rhyfeloedd y degwm, a chyffelyb ddigwyddiadau oeddynt bennodau hanes yr ymfalchiem ynddynt. "Y gwir yn erbyn y byd."

Ond y mai enw da gan Gymry'r Rand ymhlith y meistradoedd heddyw. Ac y mai si ymhlith y rhai ymladdant yn erbyn gormes fod Cymro yn air cyfystyr a Scab. Dynion ydynt, meddir, a'u hofn pennaf yw colli gwên perchennog eu bara beunyddiol. Y mae egwyddorion bellach wedi peidio ein denu. Ymgrafwn yn ngulgelloedd tywyll y caethwas ordeinir i ni gan dreiswyr y "Ty Cornel."

Ha, Gymrodyr hoff, cofiwn enw da ein hendadau. Mynnwn ran yn y gwaith gorfoleddus o ryddhau gwlad ein mabwysiadaeth o drais y cybydd a'r gormesydd. Naddwch enw Cymru yn y graig yn dragwyddol; ac yn y rhyfel fawr dros hawliau Llafur, moesoldeb, hedd a diwylliant, byddwch flaenaf yn y gâd, O chwi, feibion grug y mynydd.

DOLAU GWYRDDION

'Dialogue with the Welsh'

Through the ages we the Welsh looked on ourselves as men with backbone who liked to challenge the world on matters of principle. We were called dreamers, leading the world out of the narrowness of monopoly to the open fields of culture: we guided the ear of the nations to listen to the sweet songs of the [mythical] Birds of Rhiannon in the midst of the clamour of materialism. We were endowed with the genuine milk of the word, in its small quiet voice; and we liked to think that our independence in the face of the violence and greed of our masters was our chief quality; the farmers of Ceredigion expelled from their smallholdings in 1868 for refusing to vote as their masters demanded, the wars against the tithe rents, and suchlike events, these were the chapters in our history that we were proud of. "The truth against the world."

But now the Welsh of the Rand are well regarded by the masters. And amongst those who fight against oppression the name Welshman is now equivalent to Scab. They are men, it is said, whose major fear is losing the smile of those masters who supply their daily bread. Principles no longer appeal to us. We scrabble in the narrow dark cells ordained for us by the oppressors of the "Corner House" [Johannesburg headquarters of the Rand Mining corporation].

Ah, dear Comrades, remember the good name of our forefathers. Demand a place in the ranks of those who work to free our adopted homeland from the violence of the miser and oppressor. Carve the name of Wales eternally on the rock; and in the war for the rights of Labour, morality, peace and culture, be foremost in the battle, Oh you, sons of the mountain heather.

DOLAU GWYRDDION ['Green Meadows']

Sorrow and Profits: War in Miniature

Letter with leaflet to George Eyre Evans

May 25 1915

We have had most awful riots here. The German community is a large one, and a full dress pogrom was brought off resulting in the smashing of about half a million [units?] of property in Joburg alone.

Enclosed leaflet written by myself gives one our attitude towards the whole thing.

SORROW AND PROFITS

War in Miniature

You have been told that the War on War League should cease propaganda after the sinking of the Lusitania.

We give way to none in the sincerity of our sorrow and indignation at that brutal act of war, for we feel that warfare must become more and more brutal in this age of commercialism.

Reader, not Britain merely, nor France, nor Germany is in peril, but humanity.

We denounce this and every other act of war as murder. The ruling classes of Europe are driving humanity headlong to disaster, and it is for humanity we care.

Woe be to those who cause it, and to those who say that human reason has no deliverance for us from our present state, except for mutual slaughtering of countless thousands of the best and noblest of the sons of men.

They set up bogies like [Friedrich von] Bernhardi and [Heinrich von] Treitschke [German historians and warmongers], but we say that neither the people of Britain nor the people of Germany were in any real peril one from the other, or were animated by anything but the desire for mutual goodwill.

But the capitalists of Germany and the capitalists of Britain considered their interests in danger, in their scramble for spheres of influence and trade.

During the ten years that preceded the war this scramble of the commercial and financial interests of both countries inevitably impelled the two peoples,unwittingly and with the best of goodwill, towards a fratricidal war, until, despite the frantic efforts of diplomats to retrieve their insensate policies on the eve of the struggle, the holocaust burst forth, and the kind common folk of both countries have to pay the awful blood penalty of their rulers' greed and pride.

Those who think war is caused by other than commercial interests we would ask to think over the recent anti-German eruptions in South Africa.

In Johannesburg and other towns in the Union you witnessed an uprising not merely at the callous sinking of the Lusitania, you saw the causes of war in miniature.

Certain commercial interests in Johannesburg banded themselves into a "Patriotic Traders and Consumers Alliance". (The only "Consumers" in the concern appear to be the wives of of the "Traders.")

This alliance has been persistently endeavouring to profit by the country's need and peril to grasp Trade from its competitors, – German traders this time, because they are bottom dog.

Some time ago an adjunct to the Alliance appeared in the shape of a Petitioners' Committee, whose business it was to get the government to intern these competitors and sequestrate their property.

A golden opportunity presented itself in the Lusitania outrage. They seized upon the indignation and sorrow of the people to organise a pogrom for the destruction of these competitors. Lists were issued, and very few mistakes were made by the "demolition parties" as the pillagers were called.

Just as the ruling classes and financial interests through their press exploit the patriotic sentiment of nations to grab new spheres of trade, so was the indignation of the Johannesburg crowd exploited through the Rand Press and otherwise to eliminate the German competitors of the Alliance.

Apart from the income from the sale of Alliance certificates to display in the windows of those who will pay for such protection, the members of the

Alliance will profit immensely from the great increase in trade. The *Rand Daily Mail* has already warned the public that increased prices will follow.

For the men who fall in Flanders or go down with the Lusitania we can sorrow without despair, for they went down as men, with many touches of human affection and bravery.

But for us and our people who remain, and are made by the Consumers' Alliance to stalk like wild beasts hunting down innocent citizens, our sorrow is unredeemed by hope.

We ask you to consider, not only the degenerating influence of the Alliance and its kindred interests upon our own people, but also the fact that in a so-called Christian community the wives and children of hundreds of interned Germans are left unprovided for and faced with starvation. Their relief Store was smashed up in the general destruction of May 13th, and the whole organisation for their succour scattered. Many women whose husband's names happen to be Teutonic were turned out of their houses with their children to sleep the cold night through on neighbouring kopjes, spurned by all, despised and rejected of men.

Humanity we say is in peril. Our goodness and honour as freedom loving citizens are blighted by commercial interests and Consumers' Alliances whose one thought at all times, whether of sorrow or joy, is how to increase their profits.

In the present history of humanity, we plead with all reflecting people to contribute to save mankind from barbarism, and to lead men to the returning paths of reason, justice and fraternity.

South African Labour Party, Rissik Street, Johannesburg

The New International

The International, September 10 1915

Here we plant the flag of the New International in South Africa. Like all pioneer banners, it cannot be an elaborate one. Let us briefly trace the journey hither.

The East London Conference of the Labour Party, with a view to preserving working class unity, adopted a resolution on the war leaving the question to the dictates of each member's individual reason and conscience. At that Conference the Internationalists were in an overwhelming majority. Not, let us admit, that that majority represented the exact feeling of the rank and file on the war; but the passions of war and the electioneering virus had not as yet clouded the sense of the branches to the value of the Internationalists to the Party.

On this compact the Party worked for seven months. Then, with the approach of the General Election, the growing agitation to define the Party's policy on the war resulted in the Special Conference held at Johannesburg on August 22 last.

At this Conference the Party adopted by a majority of 82 to 30 the Bezuidenhout War Policy which pledges it wholeheartedly to support the Imperial Government in the prosecution of the war.

We need not refer to the domestic provisions for the succour of the disabled and the destitute contained in the subsidiary clauses of that resolution. They comprise the ordinary duties of a Labour Party at all times; and the only effect of their inclusion in this war policy is to throw a lurid light on the so-called "destiny and liberties" of our country so flamboyantly heralded in the principal clause.

The "see it through" policy has imposed upon a movement of revolt against Capitalism a pledge to support Capitalist Governments in the prosecution of their supreme crime War.

Militarism is the instrument by which the Masters impose their will upon the Workers. The pro-war majority have enthroned militarism as the first essential of a working-class representative.

Part of a movement based on the recognition of no boundary other than the boundary between exploiter and exploited, the Party now demands Labour representatives to range themselves on the side of one set of exploiters in this inhuman sacrifice of working class blood.

Up to the Special Conference all that the Party pledge implied was a guarantee of devotion to working class interests. To paraphrase the words of the Hebrew sage slightly, the Party in effect said:

> This is the pledge that I have chosen: To loose the bonds of wickedness, to undo the heavy burdens, to let the oppressed go free, and that ye break every yoke.

The Bezuidenhout Policy commits us, and its rough-shod supporters insist upon it, to what we hold to be a policy of aggravating the heavy burdens, to let the oppressor go free, and that we place the yoke heavier and heavier on the neck of the workers. That the workers, educated by their masters, demand it, makes not the slightest difference to our Responsibilities in the matter.

The adoption of this policy left the Internationalists torn between their allegiance to the necessity for working class unity and to the fundamental working class interests which it violates.

To compose the two necessities is the object of the formation of the International League within the Party, to propagate the principles held by us to be the very essentials of working class emancipation. These are the principles of lnternational Socialism and anti-militarism.

The International will be the organ of the League. In its columns the point of view of the Internationalist wilt the presented in its manifold phases. Like all young conceptions it is never fully told. Karl Marx, in his Eighteenth Brumaire, strikingly remarks that the literary expression of middle class revolutions were always grander than their actual content; but that the working class ideal struggles through to as yet inadequate expression. The substance of it is infinitely finer than the articulation.

ln the conception of the Working Class International, however, there emerges to unawakened earth the trumpet of a prophesy. Even in the hour of its numerical supremacy we see the national sentiment fading before our eyes, and slowly re- forming into the vaster constellation of International working class unity. This is now the only way of advance for Labour. The other way presents a vista of interminable despair with bayonets and cross bones stacked on either side. By this way of the New International alone can mankind hope for a release front the toils of the brute, end rise to that higher plane when men shall scorn all conflict other than the conflict of mind with mind in the realm of intellect.

"Peace in a Month". If Labour did its Duty

The International, September 17 1915

This is not a caption. It represents the firm belief on which we base our attitude, a belief worth all the howling down at meetings we are ever likely to get. Peace in a month if Labour did its duty! Of course there are many men to whom the war is a fine spectacle. They do not want the show spoilt. They howl down Internationalists just as they would an obstructor at a magic lantern show. There are others who own the "Star and other Capitalist papers who refer to the Internationalists in terms of ancient twaddle, making fine profits out of the business. They also are not appealed to. There are "see it through" Labour Parties out to win elections. They are not likely to respond at present. How inept are all these for anything more than to yelp like noisy pups behind the real combatants!

The Labour Party, or its present dictator, which is the same thing, is obsessed with the dogma that Labour policy must always be shaped on the assumption that the Party might win power to-morrow. Let us admit the soundness of that doctrine for the tine being.

Apart from any policy which we might consider peculiarly right for a Labour Party, let us not forget that we in South Africa live 7,000 miles away from the scene of carnage. What higher and nobler office, then, could be conceived for this country at the present juncture in the world's history than that of a mediator in European conflicts, a repairer of the breach between nations? Were the people of South Africa not besotted and debauched by Imperial Capitalism, and by those vultures of trade and finance who profit by the blood and misery of the common peoples of Europe, South Africa might have been united long ago for this magnificent end and a page of glory written in her history in place of the harrowing one of the year that is past.

The same thing applies to other neutral nations. Why is there no loud and insistent demand from these that this colossal inhumanity should cease? Why? If not because golden harvests are being reaped by the profiteers of all countries from this vast and purposeless slaughter.

Failing this work of mediation being undertaken by a nation so well fitted for it as the South African, what then do we propose? We propose the solution that has always been implied in the Labour Party's foundation principles, the solution of The International.

What did Lloyd George tell the Trades Union Congress? "With your help we can pull through; without you we are lost." The German workers are told precisely the same thing.

Now, the Trade Union Congress might reflect that there are two ways of saving England.

There is the one urged upon it by Capitalist Governments – the "see it through" way.

By throwing every ounce of moral and material support into one side of the conflict, for perhaps another year, to be modest, at the expense of two million British lives, there would be a chance, a fighting chance, of "saving England."

The German workers simultaneously come to the same decision.

What is the other way? Governments have found that not silver bullets, but the workers alone, can win the war. The British workers desire peace. So do the German workers. Seven hundred officials of the Social Democrats have issued a manifesto demanding peace with no annexations. For them and for us there is no "premature peace." That is the jargon of the Stock Exchange.

The first duty of a Labour Party is not towards the Government. The SALP show that. Its main election cry is still attack of the Government. To that extent there is still hope for it. The "see it through" policy is an academic abstraction only only to be pulled out at Conferences. The first duty of a working class party is towards the working class parties of other countries. Its place in this world conflict is to respond to peace influences from the German Party and to send them, like the cumulative polar currents of an electric dynamo.

The way of the International is to bring about combined pressure by the Labour Parties and Trade Unions of the world on the belligerent Governments to discuss terms of peace. The Trade Union Congress of Europe could dictate peace in a month. This is the most immediate, the most practical, the most humane and the most sure way out of the present catastrophe, and of saving England.

Why is it not possible? Why was Jowett prevented by the British Government from attending the Berne Socialist Conference. Why have we censorships of the Socialist Press? Let the workers ask themselves these questions. Why?

Because greater catastrophe than the loss of millions of lives, more to be dreaded by Capitalist Governments than the invasion of England, than the subjection of England, than the total dismemberment of England, more to be dreaded than all loss of territory and trade, is the taking control by the workers of the making of peace and the ending of war. Once the workers of the world do that, there is no concession they will not be able to wrest from Capitalism. That is why Jowett could not go to Berne.

Just yet, the workers do not see it. The twaddle of the "Star," "Mail," and "Chronicle" is supreme wisdom. But when the smoke of war rolls away they will perceive – beneath the glory and paeans, the grime and the slaughter of the physical conflict – evidences of that other conflict proceeding underneath between the Young Will of the Workers to exercise power over the issues of war on the one hand, and the determination of Governments on the other to keep them supine, blind and ignorant. We are fumbling in the dark for a way out of a charnel house. The door of the International is here waiting for the workers of the world to open.

The League's Message to Europe: A World Party

To the Secretary of the British Section of the International Socialist Bureau
The International, September 17 1915

The above League, which has just been formed, consists of branches and individual members of the SA Labour Party who refuse to accept the pro-war resolutions adopted by a large majority at a recent conference of that Party under the title of the "See it through policy." I enclose copy of a reply to that Policy published a few weeks ago by some of our members, also a leaflet entitled "Noblesse Oblige," reproducing with comments the manifesto of Karl Liebknecht and his 700 followers, and of the first issue of a weekly paper now being issued by our League throughout South Africa.

The result of the majority's vote has been to cause a serious, perhaps a final, split in the SALP, although none of us have so far seceded from the Party except two, who to vindicate our principles, are standing for Parliament in the approaching general election against the Party's official pro-war candidates, and who have thought that their continued membership of the Party in these circumstances would place them in a false position.

From the Socialist papers, such as the *Labour Leader* and *Forward*, which reach us, it seems clear that a more or less similar state of affairs has arisen in most of the other Labour Parties of the world, and not least in the German Social Democratic Party.

What we have looked for so far in vain, however, is news of any attempt to link up these antimilitarist minorities of the world into one New International Organisation to replace the old one which must be admitted to have failed.

Speaking in all humility from this remote corner of the globe, we venture to think that not only does the future of the whole working class movement in every land turn more than ever on the formation of a well-knit, united, executive International Socialist Organisation, but that the brightest hopes of an early peace with honour for all countries concerned in the present war depend upon action being taken at once to that end by such an organisation. We further feel convinced that the minorities above mentioned, together with parties like the Italian Socialist Party and the Russian Social Democratic Party, which we read have throughout remained true to their principles, form the obvious and for the time being the only suitable foundation for such a structure.

No doubt the difficulties of communication between the various countries are enormous, but we notice that news does from time to time leak through, and we feel, therefore, that with skill and pluck these difficulties should not, even now, be entirely insuperable.

We therefore desire to appeal to you who are more closely in touch with different centres of the movement than we to give your most earnest consideration to the proposal above made, and if satisfied, as we are, of its enormous and immediate practical importance, to take steps forthwith to carry it into effect. In particular, we would ask you to do your utmost to place it before the corresponding sections in Germany, Austria, Russia, Italy, and the USA. We would even suggest that you invite Dr Karl Liebknecht if possible to take the lead in the whole matter.

Many of us here feel considerable compunction at the idea of seceding from the official Labour Party of South Africa unless and until we can step from it into the larger International body whose formation we have above put forward. The same consideration, we should imagine, must weigh with similar groups in other countries, whose adhesion to such an organisation, when formed, will almost certainly be immediate and enthusiastic; and will, we feel sure, be followed by that of many others at present blinded by the call of patriotism, but nevertheless filled with that misgiving which no true Socialist can ever entirely suppress on the subject of war.

The ultimate effect, we believe, will be, not greater disunion in the ranks of Labour; but, on the contrary, a far more powerful and united, because world wide, movement than has ever been attained.

D. Ivon Jones
Secretary of the International League of the South African Labour Party

The Parting of the Ways

The International, October 1 1915

OUR JUSTIFICATION

As was announced in last week's issue of *The International*, the anti-militarists have definitely seceded from the South African Labour Party, and have formed a separate organisation called the International Socialist League (SA). The first step was the formation of the International League within the Party. This was done in the lingering hope that the Party might relent considerably in the application of its "see it through" policy, and afford some prospect of winning it back to what the Internationals consider its native principles. But it was not to be. Drunk with its newly-found ascendancy, the majority rode rough-shod over all finer sentiments of old associations, comradeship, freedom of thought, or working class qualifications; And, with one eye on the pledge and the other on the Capitalist Press, insisted upon the imposition of its Imperialism on that pledge, and on its signature anew by every candidate for public office.

TWO POLES MUTUALLY REPULSIVE

With the anxiety of the one section to protest its loyalty to the Empire by constant public dissociation from the Internationals, and the impatience of the Internationals at the growing flag-wagging propensities of the majority, the antagonism within the Party soon created an impossible situation, and the link finally broke. In addition to the inevitable estrangement, the secession was helped by other considerations. The Party has become definitely tainted with militarism and Imperialism. The alternatives were to remain silent within the Party, (an unthinkable attitude), or loudly to proclaim true working class principles; which latter inevitably made for expulsion in any case.

THE TWO UNITIES

It was a case of duty to the International as against the obligation to working class unity. It soon became evident however that unity for us meant unity with the anti-war minorities of Socialism all over the world. It was even felt latterly that the best answer to those who wished to "bore from within" was that no reclamation of the party to Socialism after the war will have any virtue unless a section of it have unmistakeably rebelled against its capitulation to capitalism. We claim that in the present conflict our best service to South Africa will be rendered by considering the claims of humanity at large. We have applied the same principle here. The best way to secure local unity is to make International unity our guide. Whether or not the present Labour Party will ever desire or deserve any working affiliation with the League on its return to sanity, the imperative duty of the hour is to give adequate voice to the International spirit in South Africa. If that has made secession inevitable -well and good. The fact that the final break was preceded by some lingering hesitation, not to say vacillation, is a guarantee of earnest consideration.

GREAT RESPONSIBILITIES

And now the principles of International Socialism in South Africa are in our keeping. We have undertaken great responsibilities. Every member of the League must feel the need for concentrating all available energies on making the organisation well worthy of the principles which it is to enshrine. We have the whole of South Africa to organise; and if we do not make the International Socialist League the most effective and best organised Party of the workers in South Africa, we hope to at least deserve that success.

NEW METHODS

We trust the League will draw new lessons from the spirit of the time. It will endeavour to ascertain from the experiences of the past year the pitfalls in organisation which should be avoided. The Provisional Constitution of the League appears in another column. It is purposely simple and embracing, insisting firmly on the one principle which accounts for our existence. We have learnt something of the dangers of too elaborate constitutions and pledges. Greater freedom of action will undoubtedly mark the Labour movement of the future. The War on War League has done magnificent work on a constitution of two lines only, proving that hard personal service in the Branches, and not constitutions, will do the work.

LARGER BRANCHES

There was a case not long ago of an electric plant working of itself all night through, after the attendant had been electrocuted. The Labour Party is very much in that position. Most of its Branches are now mere skeletons kept in being by persons interested in getting nominated for public office. The League will not follow the old method of forming Branches often in every constituency. Running candidates for public bodies will only be one of our methods, and not perhaps the most important one. Strong central Branches therefore rather than many small and scattered ones, is the securest organisation.

APPEAL TO SOCIALISTS

In this connection we would appeal to the Socialist Societies of Durban, Capetown, Pretoria, as well as other kindred organisations, to link up into one International Socialist Organisation for South Africa. Most encouraging response is being given by isolated Socialists in all parts of South Africa, to whom the Labour Party has not been able to make any appeal. The Socialists of the Transvaal have given sufficient guarantee of fidelity to the cause which they now espouse to give them the right to urge upon the organised Socialists of the other Provinces to link up at all costs. The Conference of the League which it is hoped to call in a few months time should be representative of the whole of South Africa. We look with confidence to them to rise to the greatness of the occasion, and form in South Africa an organisation worthy of the International.

THE OUTLOOK

We have glorious tasks to perform for South Africa and Socialism during the coming years. The nature of these tasks will happily prevent our being spoilt by overmuch public applause. A dilettante and exclusive Internationalism will however have to be guarded against. The International Socialist League will have the more significance the more it tends to pull the working class of South Africa with it. This involves a corresponding interest in industrial organisation with a view to giving it an International outlook.

THE REAL PROLETARIAT

Moreover, an Internationalism which does not concede the fullest rights which the native working class is capable of claiming will be a sham. One of the justifications for our withdrawal from the Labour Party is that gives untrammelled freedom to deal, regardless of political fortunes, with the great and fascinating problem of the native. If the League deal resolutely in consonance with Socialist principles with the native question, it will succeed in shaking South African Capitalism to its foundations. Then and not till then, shall we be able to talk about the South African Proletariat in our International relations. Not till we free the native can we hope to free the white. Is militarism to be destroyed, capitalism to be chained, and the lust of conquest "dragged captive through the deep" by the immeasurably finer order of the Great International that is to be? then SOCIALISTS OF SOUTH AFRICA UNITE!

"The quarrels of diplomats ..."

Letter to George Eyre Evans

December 11 1915

... England must be one armed camp now. Do you think there was no solution for the quarrels of diplomats and any other means than the sacrifice of five million lives? Do you think that it is any other revenge for the sufferings of unhappy Belgians to bereave some more million unhappy German women? What a huge swindle is the washing of Capitalists greed and avarice in the simple idealism of the Common People. Adverse bank balances, international credit, the demands of profit, the exhaustion of commerce, and not the consummation of justice or the destruction of Kultur, will end the war, for they have made the war. How well entrenched and how well disguised is this prodigious ruse on human nobility and human credulity. All we like sheep have gone astray. The *Inquirer* [*'Yr Ymofynydd'*] has disgraced itself in the same way by singing the same song of gore as the war lord. farewell, old enthusiasms. Welcome new light, however, weak and struggling.

Kind regard to Miss Evans and all friends. Write soon.

Affectionately yours, David

The Control of the Schools

The International April 7 1916

No question affects the working-class movement more vitally than the care of the children's education. The curricula of our elementary schools today largely decide the intellectual bent of the working-class tomorrow. The authorities know this. They are continually endeavouring to remove primary education from the influence of local movements. They are

Darwinian enough to know that local initiative develops variation, "sports," and that "sports" are the tendrils of evolution.

Thus there is a constant process towards centralizing control of the child mind, not in the School Board, not in the Municipal Council, not even in the Provincial Council, but in the Ministry of Defence. The Provincial Council has only nominal control of the schools. The Provincial Executive, which is and ever must be in the bosom of the Smutsian regime, it controls Adamson, the sole Director of your children's mental development.

Teachers Conference

For instance, at the Teachers Conference held this week, (and by a Teachers Conference is meant for all practical purposes a Head Teachers' Conference) Mr. Adamson, the teachers' master was present. The chairman, a Pretoria schoolmaster, urged for the abolition of all School Boards on the score of expense, and for other vague reasons; again with the object of increasing the monopoly of Adamson as sole dictator of what is to be construed as education in the Transvaal.

Is Mr Adamson then such a heaven-sent expert as to merit this slavish adulation, even from Labour Provincial Councillors? No degree of expertness should justify making a mandarin of the expert. Experts are good only as servants to carry out general principles. Perusal of the proceedings of the 1914 Select Committee on education gives an impression of his expertness mainly in withholding from public gaze that wealth of constructive imagination for which an expert must have a reputation, while expertly keeping it all to himself.

The authorities seem to realize the importance of educational institutions, not so much to educate as to pervert the mind of the coming generation. The manner in which centralized control is being misused for the pollution of the minds of the children with the debased clap-trap of jingoism has been already dwelt upon in these pages. At the Teachers Conference, Handel Thompson read a paper on "Patriotism," Adamson likewise urged that every opportunity should be taken to "teach to the children the righteousness and Justice of our cause" in the war. Howard Pim talked on "Courage," and found that element deified in the British Navy. School inspectors are learning that ability to make patriotic stump speeches to the children is the most important step to gain favour. Indeed, we are told that much of the school literature of the Transvaal is concocted by Handel Thompson, who is said to have the right of sale to his own Department, owing to the dearth, presumably, of English classics.

Apart from any conspiracy of central authority to train children into habits of servility, think of the dreary, jelly-mould education which is likely to flow from the ideas of one pedestalled but unimaginative collegian aided by inspectors suited to his taste. But that the conspiracy to centralize is in intention a conspiracy against enlightened methods of education is also becoming increasingly evident.

Labour and the School Boards

There are two proposals a-foot by which this process can be combatted. One is Colin Wade's draft ordinance at present before the Provincial Council aiming at the reform of School Board electoral machinery. The vicious device of voting by post is to be abolished. The franchise to be the same as the Municipal, and the elections to be held simultaneously with the Municipal Elections.

The working class, in order to achieve the great work of human emancipation, is compelled to seize upon every of avenue of power which controls directly or indirectly the means of emancipation. Under capitalism it is hopeless to expect an education that is not predominantly commercial in its aim. But in the School Boards we have a means, inadequate though they be, by which we may prevent this deliberate process of softening the brain of the children who are to carry on, and perhaps mainly accomplish, if rightly educated, the social revolution from capitalism to commonweal. In the School Board we have the communal unit as opposed to centralized tyranny. Given a keen interest in the School Boards by working-class organisations and lovers of true education, there is nothing to prevent the usurpation of primary education by the State for its own ends being checked by joint School Board action, and diverted towards liberal and humane ideas of education.

School Boards Congress

Primary education is getting more and more under the control of officials whose training knows only of rule and rote. Under the guize of this pedagogic rule and rote, and expert mandarinism, the children are made the sport of capitalist scheming through State control. The organisation of School Boards in a congressional body for the Rand, or with rural co-operation, is the only power that can guide the expert from Smutsian forms towards a free people's education.

Local Cash, Local Control.

Working-class organisations would be the most potent lever to compel home rule in education say, by a Rand Council. But an immediate means of power for School Boards may be found in the second proposal referred to – the demand for local taxation for primary education, which the agitation over inadequate school accommodation is bringing to the fore. In any case, means will be found, if the workers will realize the tremendous importance of wresting the child's young mind from the toils of the self-same serpent that also clasps the life of its father.

MANIFESTO. Against Economic Conscription

The International, 14 April 1916 (reprinted as a pamphlet)

TO THE WORKERS OF THE RAND AND SOUTH AFRICA

The International! Socialist League of SA (whose sole concern is the welfare of the working class movement) has hitherto studiously refrained from interfering with men who have sincerely and freely volunteered for military service. We have respected their courage though regarding it misplaced. We have instead endeavoured, in spite of manifold suppressions, to proclaim the international unity of the working class across all frontiers of race and country.

But the time has now come to record a most emphatic protest against the methods adopted by the self-elected Recruiting Committee which, with the connivance of the authorities, is conspiring with employers to force men to enlist against their will, by a system little removed from blackmail.

According to the orders of this inquisitorial committee, employers are *"to bring pressure to bear upon their employees as will be best calculated to ensure their immediate enlistment,"* and to *"refuse to employ single eligible men of military age after 30th April, 1916."* In other words (words evaded in the buccaneer politeness of this Committee) employers are to SACK THEM.

As a result of this Committee's activities hundreds of young men are today faced with the alternative of either walking the streets hungry or enlisting.

Enlisting for what? For an expedition that cannot by any stretch of imagination be regarded as a measure of defence.

What did the expenditure £15,000,000 and considerable blood and tears in German South West [Africa] bring to the people of South Africa? Are mothers and widows of fallen soldiers to be consoled by the reflection that De Beers have gained control of German West [African] diamond fields?

And now economic conscription, brutal and unashamed, is being brought to bear on young men to compel them to take part in another business of butchery, at an expenditure of human life that is scandalous to contemplate. *Is this again for the expansion of the interests of the Corner House in German East Africa?*

The workers are told of the freedom they enjoy in their immunity from legal conscription. Legal conscription on the continental system falls on the rich as well as the poor. But the conscription now in vogue in South Africa enables the employers and the well-to-do to go scot-free, while effectively compelling wage earners to enlist or to starve. This is the free choice that the workers enjoy.

K*s and Indians are fighting in this war "for liberty and justice," (which the masters, *sub rosa,* pronounce "markets and dividends"). What do these men get for it? Are they really honoured for their sacrifices? They are subjected to the same indignities. the same restrictions, the same exploitation as before,

So it will be with the white workers who have sacrificed themselves in this conflict.

The workers are contributing everything to the present war. While their masters are waxing fat in war profits, the workers give their life-blood on the field, and are forced to sustain the relief funds at home.

Furthermore, under the cloak of patriotism, employers are everywhere imposing extra burdens, in longer hours and more distracting labour, burdens which are becoming hard to bear, and are sapping the life of the people. Postmen, Railwaymen, shop assistants, office men and girls are compelled to take on increased work, and get scant attention when incapacitated by overwork. In all spheres the war and patriotism are made the excuse for levying an increased toll on the life and labour of the unorganised workers, in order that greater profits may be reaped by their patriotic masters.

Not only are the workers sacrificing while employers wax fat, but their rights are meanwhile being filched from them one by one. "The outbreak of peace" will find them domineered by police rule. Freedom of speech is being suppressed and all publication of views distasteful to the Government throttled. Detectives swarm the swell recruiting meetings to nip heckling in the bud, and arrest men who express dissent from the speakers of the Recruiting Committee. The high-flowing language of recruiting speakers only hide[s] the stage management of deceits and shams by which the mailed fist of conscription is covered.

Your children are enrolled in Boy-Scout regiments, so that in early youth they may be impregnated with the virus of militarism. They are marshalled in recruiting meetings to initiate the clapping, the applause, and "the spontaneous enthusiasm," at arranged signals from their scout-masters. These meetings do not bring recruits. They only gather the harvest of young men that economic conscription throws into the street.

We therefore protest against the swindle perpetrated on the wage-earners. We protest no less because the generous impulses of the workers are being exploited to their own undoing; misled and deceived by a Press whose sole function is the hoodwinking of the people and the clothing of capitalist schemes in patriotic terms.

We protest against the Christian Church bathing her hands in the blood of the peoples.

We protest against the Federation of Trades and the Labour Party, called to lead in the great movement of the liberation of humanity, abusing their position of trust to betray the workers at this time, acting as unholy procuresses for the enemies of the workers; and taking sides with the employers in this conspiracy of wholesale victimization.

We would urge the workers to organise themselves in store, workshop and mine against this latest attempt to treat them as helots to be driven to the trenches by intimidation and the sack.

To all those who look for deliverance from the present evils we have a message. We again declare that it is the mission of the international working class, acting on its own authority, to free the world from the crimes of war and capitalism.

We proclaim the new Socialism rising fresh and strong. We stand side by side with the great Italian Socialist Party, with the brilliant anti-war minority of the Social Democrats under the heroic Liebknecht, with the Independent Labour Party of Great Britain, with the Socialist Labour Party of America, with the Socialists of Scandinavia and Holland who have so far been strong enough to thwart the militarist designs of their governments, with the militant Trade Unions of France and New Zealand, with the great International Socialist movement we declare uncompromising hostility towards this unjust world of violence, on capitalism and the warmongers who degrade the life of the people.

The Capitalist press may laugh the forced laugh of men who are afraid; but we declare that it is the mission of the organised working class to accomplish the work of human freedom. The earth is bountiful. There is enough and to spare for all without arduous toil. Yet the nations are tea ring one another to pieces over the disposal of the surplus wealth created by labour, which, though many starve in the midst. of plenty, the workers are not allowed to touch.

But the forces are ripening which will abolish the slavery of our times if the workers will but assert themselves in combination. This is the message of Socialism, based not alone on sentiment but on science, to the heavy-laden and the toilers today.

"Workers of the world unite, you have nothing to lose but your chains. You have a world to win."

For the International Socialist League (SA)
WH ANDREWS, Chairman. D IVON JONES, Secretary.

The Greatest Defeat of the War

The International, May 26 1916

Further light on the efforts of the International Socialist Bureau to preserve peace in the days of July 1914 is given in notes on a French book in the Socialist Review. The work is very partisan, pro-ally, and gives only grudging recognition even of Liebknecht's efforts. Yet the author, in an appendix, quotes Renaudel's account.

Renaudel is a pro-war Socialist Leader of the interview between the German and French Socialist Leaders at Brussels before the declaration of war, in which the following paragraph occurs:

> Muller assured us that the Social Democrats, at the voting of the war credits in the Reichstag, would vote against or would abstain from voting at all, *if the French Socialists on their side*

> *would abstain*. There were some amongst us who took occasion to impress on Muller that *if France were attacked or invaded not a single Socialist would abstain from voting for the war credits*. Muller declared that the question of who was the aggressor was one about which different theories might be held, and one very difficult to settle.

What the Socialists failed to grasp was that the International was an entity inviolate, supreme over national issues.

The move of the German Army towards the Alsace frontier was not primarily a march on France but a march on the working class International. The first point of attack was on the International unity of the workers.

The Russians were allowed to swarm over the border when they could easily have been stopped, as has since been proved, to give force to the cry of the Russian Menace. Simultaneously the troops marched on France to drive a wedge between the French and German Socialists. Muller was forced to go back and inform Social Democracy that their French Comrades were resolved to fight if war was declared.

"Let Saints on Earth in Concert Sing"

The International, August 4 1916

Again, as the second anniversary of the outbreak of war comes round, the Governor-General calls for a special religious festival to celebrate the occasion. If you won't enlist, you must pay obeisance to the war-god in some fashion. No one is allowed to be neutral. Today it is either capitalism and war or Socialism and humanity. The Church has long ago succumbed to the worship of Moloch. Its parsons have every one gone helter skelter to the side of the capitalist prostituters of humanity. *"Let saints on earth in concert sing."* This is one of the hymns we are enjoined to use on the day of celebration. Dance, ye sanctimonious ones, at the cannibal feast of the blood of the workers. Close the shops, not to petition mass murder to cease, but to celebrate the day it began. What matters is that more and more sons of the working class are required by the unappeasable monster of war, so long as he gives fat Contracts and Good Biz. Let there be no sackcloth and ashes; for to-day Trade and the Casualty Lists boom together.

The employing class have long since shown their moral bankruptcy. They are too involved in the profit system which breeds war to respond to reason and humanity. But the workers have nothing to gain by war. It is for them to refuse any longer to endorse this orgy of capitalism.

One by one the high flowing pretensions of the ruling class have been exposed in this world slaughter.

They started by calling us to avenge Belgium – for the violation of whose neutrality all the European powers were equally guilty. Today they themselves flagrantly violate Greece, and starve her people to do their will.

They spoke of the rights of small nations; and they have bled Ireland, ruled her by rifle and revenge, and executed her patriots in prison yards.

They spoke of crushing German militarism; and they have subjected hundreds of objectors against militarism to atrocious tortures in the barracks of England worse than the militarism they were called upon to crush.

They spoke of Justice and Liberty. And the Trade Union leaders of the Clyde have been imprisoned and deported for trying to safeguard the workers of England from the greed of their English masters. Why, even in South Africa there are men today who are denied the right to work because they have acted as good Trade Unionists.

They promise this to be the last war, and they are already at work hatching plots to capture trade and rig up tariff walls for further wars. Their Economic Conferences, their burning and looting of alien shops, their "Consumers Alliances," all prove out of their own mouths that the object and origin of the war is capitalist trade.

Workers! This is a war on behalf of capitalist interests; and a civil war of the world's workers. Capitalist interests do not concern the workers. "The working class and the employing class have nothing in common." The same evil that brings poverty and unemployment at home brings wars abroad. While the workers are robbed under the wage-system, and the profits derived from their labour must be invested abroad, so long will there be international quarrels and armaments to back up trade.

The hour has come in the history of the world when humanity can only be saved from these and still greater barbarities through the workers saving themselves by organising in their various industries under one class conscious banner, one Movement irrespective

of race, colour or creed, to substitute the Co-operative Commonwealth for the present plan-less and anarchic system of production. The Town Hall recruiters may foam at the mouth, but they cannot keep back the working-class movement from, sooner or later, pursuing this great aim.

Working men and women: the message of Socialism is today the same as ever: Unite, be loyal to yourselves, stand together, not to provide bloody entertainment and profit for the master class of this or that State, but to dash to pieces the tyrant of modern society, its profit system, its "Empire-building," its rattle of swords, – its bankrupt capitalist class run amok, – a society under which you have nothing to lose but your chains; and win for the world your own Co-operative Commonwealth.

Another Milestone

The International, January 12 1917

Next Sunday will be held the second Annual Conference of the International Socialist League. The mildly interested reader may ask: "Well, and of what importance is it to the working class at large? Your numbers are small, your movement is under an eclipse, capitalism and war have gained undisputed sway: who are you to trumpet about annual conferences ?"

We could answer in the words of Shelley, were we of that Promethean mould: "Alas for liberty, if numbers, wealth, or the unfulfilling years, or Fate could quell the free."

But for testimony to the importance of a Socialist Conference in these days of war, let us look to the dread which our militancy inspires, rather than to our numbers. All the spare energies of capitalism, its censors, newspapers, pulpits, platforms, and schools are to-day busy keeping the working class from becoming tinder for the Socialist spark.

Hardly a line of journalism but is employed in hiding up and postponing the struggle of Capital with Labour. On the other side are we, exposing that struggle, and pointing the way out if humanity is to escape universal shipwreck.

The capitalists know the importance of a Socialist vanguard, be it the most lonely of outposts. They know we are formidable, not by number, but by the might of a principle which all their armies cannot keep from coming to its own. They know that no design of theirs can be consummated except at the risk of that Socialist vanguard touching the hills with fire, and mustering the working class to its own war for humanity. The silence of their Press testifies to their fear of Socialism.

Viewing things partially to-day, the Socialist movement seems everywhere under a cloud. With the progress of the war, Socialism finds fewer and fewer breaches for attack. The removal of the small middle class from the stage by King Capital has meant the abrogation of those civil liberties which gave the middle class political elbow room. This is compelling the Socialist movement throughout the world to fall back on stronger ground; and Socialism is everywhere quietly waiting.

It is not the quiet of collapse. We know from our little movement here that it is the quiet of preparation for a greater advance. In all periods of defeat a live principle consolidates its own science. Thus did Marx retire after the proletarian reverses of 1848; and his "Capital," with its arsenal of more solid conquests, was the result.

The Socialist movement in South Africa is also thwarted of opportunities to deploy by the peculiar circumstances of the war. It behoves it therefore to occupy the lull of the struggle in the development of Socialist theory. It is our business to know the factors with which the working class will have to deal in its coming conflict with capital. To "weep barren tears" over the increasing crimes and miseries of capitalism will avail little, and requires no organisation. It is for us to know the secret of capitalism's power, and thus direct the means for its overthrow

The Good and the True are molten in the circumambient mentality of man. They have appealed to him "since the memory of man runneth not to the contrary." It is not for the Socialist movement to wring hands at their non-attainment, but to open the doors of those economic forces which alone can let them in. These are the objects of socialist research.

And let it not be supposed that by Socialist theory is meant the spinning of dogma. Theory and practice, method and aim, are closely interwoven in the movement of the working class. Differences on Socialist theory decide our actions to-day, NOW.

For instance, the salient point of theory and practice which Socialists have to fight out in South Africa is their attitude towards the native wage labourers. This question goes to the root of Socialist theory, and yet it is the burning question of the time for us. Until the white and native workers awaken to industrial solidarity, the working-class movement, no matter what its electoral statistics may show, can do hardly more than mark time.

Here we have a fight before us of a magnitude unexampled in any other section of the Socialist International. But a fight fraught with wonderful possibilities for the native, and for the movement which he must inevitably dominate. The ISL has already declared its policy on the lines of the class struggle, and there is a growing tendency to regard this phase of international working-class unity as the one thing which makes Socialism worth fighting for in South Africa. And it is involved in the movement towards the organisation of the workers on industrial as against craft divisions.

These are not technical details. They are rooted deep in the principle for which the International stands: that all divisions of nationality, of craft, of creed, of colour (and if of creed why not of colour?) must sink out of sight before the stern division of class.

Let us shout it again for the benefit of those who do not know, this Alpha and Omega of the movement: The emancipation of humanity from capitalism and war depends upon all the workers of the world coalescing as a class and capturing and administering *as workers* the productive forces of society for the good of all. From this gigantic but simple turnover inexhaustible, unimagined glories will flow to mankind,

Thus to-day more than ever the true spirit of the working class calls upon us not to relax our endeavours, though we may have to vary their character. We speak of "fighting for Socialism". Why, is not the fight at its grandest now, while it is sternest? When the working class is again in tune with the spirit of its own movement, there will be no more "fighting for Socialism." It will have become a joy ride.

Our Conference is called again, and the War God is still Mighty, – *Almighty*, but for our "refusal to share the shame of its ill tyranny." Ours then is a duty whose honour is its own reward. It is ours without rancour to wait calmly and bear witness to the working class that is to be. Ours to do for the Socialist principle at least a tithe of that endured by the noble Misguided in the trenches of the war god. For it only requires a few Socialists to remain firm, and all the forces of capitalism and war, and all their shifts and guile, can but add to the measure of victory of the Socialist ideal.

A Great Working-Class Triumph.

The Australian Coal Strike

The International, January 12 1917

A few particulars are now to hand by the mail papers of the great strike of Coal Miners in Australia. The strike ended on November 30, when the men's demand for an eight hour day bank to bank was conceded to the letter.

But the significance of the strike is not to be found in the actual terms gained, so much as in the working-class solidarity displayed by the men of Australia, And this is the main test of success.

The mine owners started off in high dudgeon with point blank refusals. And it is evident that the men on their side were also prepared for a prolonged strike. The actual number of men involved in the dispute was than 20,000; but large masses came out in sympathy, and many industries were put out of action for want of coal: until, on the eve of the settlement, it was computed that there were 300,000 men idle.

The State Coal Mines in Victoria stopped work although they largely enjoyed the conditions demanded by their comrades. In all parts of the country local strikes were precipitated through refusals of men to handle coal, and the consequent "down tools" of their mates in the industry.

Such was the case in the Government Small Arms Factory at Lithgow. Ten men were sacked for refusing to handle coal. As in all industries connected with the war, the management presumed on the patriotic stampede to wield the big whip. But in the Small Arms Factory there is a "factory union," in which all hands are organised except the ASE [Australasian Society of Engineers] men and another craft not named. Common action was therefore swift. Next day, the Management refusing to reinstate the ten men, all hands, except the ASE men, came out. The Melbourne *Argus* evidently regarded this as the most heinous offence of the whole strike. It headed the news: SMALL ARMS FACTORY DECLARED "BLACK" BY UNION.

Thus, not only the prosecution of the War, and the needs of the Navy, but the "public" – "the people" – cry was exploited by the capitalists to the top of their bent. Premier Hughes, presiding at an abortive Conference of the masters and men, having failed to browbeat the latter, pulled a holy face and talked about "the community", whose interests he alleged he had to safeguard. The joke of it was that the men he spoke to represented 20,000 miners, besides tens, even hundreds of thousands of other workers who were out in sympathy with them.

Power is gradually shifting over from the capitalists to the workers.

Look at the capitalist champions, what "small beer" they are! Hughes, with all the power of capitalism behind him, had to prevaricate meanly like a Jesuit priest. The delegates were wisely restrained in wielding their power. But one robust utterance shewed how small they could make Hughes and his capitalist friends look. After about an hour's wrangling over secondary matters, Mr. Pillans, a delegate from Lithgow, blurted out:

> This is all humbug as far as I am concerned. I have listened to all this twaddle round this table and you have never yet got to bedrock. The question is: is this a fair thing that the miners are asking?

The New Zealand Miners and the Federated Seamen's Union were splendid in keeping the ring clear. The Union Steamship Company, whose red funnels are to be seen in every Australian port, sent the Seamen's Union an assurance about scab coal, saying: "We have declined to carry coal to Australia for commercial purposes, and will not do so." Such is the power of solidarity.

The necessity for giving meaning to terms of speech was never better demonstrated than in this fight. The Miners wanted eight hours bank to bank. The Mine Owners were prepared to give eight hours bank to bank! The whole fight was over the reading of the term. The miners wanted the *first* man down at 7 o'clock and the *last* man up at 3 o'clock, including half an hour for meals. The coal owners' version was eight hours from the *last* man down to the *first* man up: a very different proposition. The miners' definition of the term prevailed.

What is most alarming to the capitalist in this strike is the lead taken by the rank and file. The great strikes of the war are all remarkable for that. At one of the Conferences Premier Hughes asked the men's delegates to go back and take a ballot on the question of resuming work pending consideration of the men's claim by a special tribunal. The men's delegates seem to have been greatly impressed by this offer. Ballot papers were printed with a recommendation from the delegates that the offer be accepted. But the aggregate meetings of the men would have none of the ballot, nor of Hughes' proposal that he, Hughes, should conduct the ballot. The men refused to vote. The Delegates were sent back to demand the full claim. A few days later a special tribunal met. There was a show of palaver for an afternoon, and the men's demand was granted: the faces of the coal owners being saved by a promise to recoup them for the loss involved by some means not made clear in the reports.

Thus in wondrous ways does the working class unite. Those who despond of the movement to-day are indeed blind. The working class is no movement at all if not industrial. And industrially the Deed of the working class is in advance of its Creed; yes, far in advance of our creed.

Those 32 Votes

The International, February 2 1917

Reverting to the result of the Troyeville election, last Friday, when Mr. [Frederic] Creswell, the Labour Party Candidate, came top of the poll with eight hundred odd votes, and the rest nowhere, a few points deserve attention. The Labour Party poll was about the same as at the General Election. What happened to the capitalist voters seems to be that they refrained from voting. Creswell was allowed past the sentry post with the capitalist watchword.

The poll of 32 in favour of Comrade Wade, the candidate of the League, is the lowest yet recorded for us. This came immediately after the League gained working-class rock-bottom at its annual Conference.

All political parties that have no economic basis, or express no growing economic power, are Utopian. The Labour Party is not Utopian. It represents the small property holder, the agent, and the Craft Unionist whose property is his craft vanity; – all fag-ends of quickly vanishing economic forces.

The ISL, if it is not to be Utopian, must find its economic basis in the growing mass of the propertyless industrial proletariat. It is a foreshadowing of their consciousness as a great emancipating and emancipated class. But this great mass of the proletariat, which was only represented by 32 votes in the Troyeville contest, happens in South Africa to be BLACK, and therefore disfranchised and socially outcast.

The ISL has no hope of looking to the Labour Party constituents, the small shopkeeper and the artisan, for any large backing. Consequently, it is poised like Mohammed's coffin between an economic basis which it has left to its fate – the craft unionist basis; and that other economic basis which it is its mission yet to develop – the great industrial proletariat

International Socialism in South Africa therefore is nothing if not a virile propaganda to awaken the native wage-earner, and with the native his white prototype, to a consciousness of his great mission of human reclamation. To the League is entrusted this work. This work alone saves it from being Utopian. And in this work we hope to enlist all sections of the workers, including those who realize the ephemeral nature of their artisan status.

This is what makes Industrial Unionism a live wire in South Africa, – the native worker. This is also why the political field becomes a sine qua non. It is an axiom of Socialist economics that all anti-political societies degenerate into conspiracies. That axiom becomes a fiery warning to us in South Africa. ALL PROPAGANDA AMONG THE NATIVE WORKERS CALLING UPON THEM TO COMBINE INDUSTRIALLY IS A CONSPIRACY AGAINST "WHITE SOUTH AFRICA", (that is, propertied South Africa). Only on the political field can that call be made as a matter of right. Whether it be 32 votes or 2 votes, this must increasingly become the political issue for us: FREEDOM TO COMBINE AND POLITICAL RIGHTS FOR THE NATIVE WORKER.

170 Million Recruits

The International, March 23 1917

The Socialist International has become a far more tremendous thing by the Russian Revolution. It means that a people of 170 million has swung into line with the great proletariat of all countries, on its march to the Revolution by the side of which this and all previous ones are but "shopkeeper"s riots" in immensity.

JMG [JM Gibson] ably explains in another column the economic factors which have made this revolution possible. But while it is necessary to warn the workers of the partial value only to them of the conquest of political rights, the importance of this step forward in the world's history can hardly be exaggerated. The rising capitalist class cannot achieve its political revolution without the aid of the workers, nor without sharing the fruits with them. The capitalist looks only to the immediate necessities of industry, no matter if his successors have to reap the whirlwind. The proletariat must look to the end; for in its fight the means and the end, the method and the objective, are at one. The Capitalist seeks a political railroad for his system. He cannot win it without providing a railroad to the working class revolution.

We see two streams in this, as in all previous revolution. The Industrial Capitalist cry is now "ORDER." The proletarian driving power cries "LIBERTY." But the workers having won their "Programme of the Day", and the Capitalist the control of the State, the two streams immediately disunite and the class war begins on the last lap to the Socialist Revolution. Now is the dangerous hour. Now the dominant capitalist cry will be "order," and it will be enforced at the cannon's mouth if necessary, "tearing the side of the proletariat," as Marx once said, if the workers are not organised independently and strong to bear the shock of the recoil.

But it seems to us that the Russian workmen are so organised in the industrial centres. The independent existence of a "Council of Workmen" dictating terms all night to the Duma; scotching the Regency scheme; sanctioning capitalist control meanwhile, knowing that it has not the material means at hand (namely highly organised industry and a highly organised industrial working class), to push forward yet to the Socialist Revolution; sending back troop trains bound to suppress the revolution- all this augurs a working class conscious of its mission, and recognising this as a half-way house to it.

Only Russians can feel the thrill of the wonderful deliverance involved in a free press, free speech, and political liberty. Note, however that the right to combine is won as a result of the workers combining.

This is a bourgeois revolution, but arriving when the night of capitalism is far spent. It cannot be a mere repetition of previous revolutions. It partakes infinitely more of a victory for the proletariat, as well as for the industrial capitalist. Now the two classes pursue their several ways; one "to prosecute the war abroad" and "law and order" at home; the other to pursue the class war at home and "the Socialist Republic in all countries." Let us look forward with great hope to the entry of the Russian elemental mass into the International class struggle for human emancipation. The day of its coming seems immeasurably nearer by this awakening.

The Stockholm Conference

The International, June 8 1917

When we made our notes on this matter last week it did not enter our minds to refer to South African representation at the Stockholm Conference. The main reason for this perhaps was that no member of the League was looking for a cheap trip. We are too busy carrying on the fight here. Moreover, ISL members have a sense of perspective, and realise that our contribution to the Congress at Stockholm is not to send a delegate there who will not be able to speak for the working class of the Rand, but to bring the workers of the Rand up to the class conscious level of our European comrades. The significance of the Stockholm Conference is that the Socialists who will deliberate there speak for the vast bulk of the European workers. Our contribution is to carry on the fight in South Africa and remain faithful – as enjoined by the Secretary of the Italian Socialists in his letter to us – remain faithful to the end. The idea of a cheap trip did not vitiate in the least our great joy at the coming together of the workers of Europe at Stockholm.

Further, it should be pointed out that this coming Conference is a Conference of action. It is an executive Conference called at comparatively short notice for immediate steps. For such purpose the British Dominions are lumped in with the British delegation. When the far ends of the earth are required in international conclave, a year's notice will be given, and that Congress will be a Congress on general policy.

However, the organised Socialist movement in South Africa (and by the organised Socialist movement is meant the movement that carries on the fight for Socialism day in and day out, and not a handful of more or less unattached individuals who only come out of their holes when overseas palaver is in sight), our movement is not unrepresented at Stockholm. We are affiliated with the International Socialist Commission at Berne. We are a section of "The Zimmerwaldians" who are leading the fight against war in Europe today. Comrade Grimm, the Secretary of the Zimmerwaldians, informed us not long ago that our ISL Conference resolutions had taken a prominent place in the agenda of the second Zimmerwaldian Conference held at Kienthal. This agenda, like many other communications from Comrade Grimm, never reached us. But the comrades can rest satisfied, knowing as we do that a quite recent report of ours has reached the Berne Commission, the Berne Commission will be able to speak for the ISL of South Africa at Stockholm, and speak with a full knowledge of the facts, of the conditions under which we labour, of the men who have been carrying on the fight, and of the state of the movement in South Africa and its strength. The letter from Con. [Constantini] Lazari published last week shows that *The International* has regularly reached him, and no doubt through him, the Berne Commission.

Therefore, comrades, let us realize that as far as South Africa is concerned, our duty is here. Let us not pluck up the seed to see if the plant is growing. Let us not hanker after cheap glory, and mislead the European comrades with a delegation that will represent more money than men. Here is the fight. The eyes of the fool are to the ends of the earth. Internationalism does not mean running away from insoluble difficulties at home to an international conclave of cranks, but summoning the workers here at home to international unity with our fellow workers elsewhere, aye, and at home too; and, to the extent that we succeed, collaborating internationally. Mr Arthur Henderson sent by the workers themselves is of far greater significance than the "purest" of pure Socialists representing no one but his own ethereal opinions. Let us produce the international class conscious working-class constituency that will send the delegate of its free accord. That is our job. Our best immediate message to Stockholm will be to return Comrades Andrews and Bunting at the head of the poll on Wednesday week.

* * * *

Since the above has been set up in type the cables announce that the Russian Socialists have sent a call to the Socialist parties and trade unions throughout the world to come to Stockholm to end universal slaughter by international action of the proletariat.

Thus the situation changes from day to day. So far we in South Africa have not received this call, neither has the Trade Union movement. Nor are we likely to. We live in a corner of the world where the censor has full powers, and can use them with impunity. Nevertheless our previous remarks still hold. We can act internationally without delegates if need be. The proletariat of all lands can unite without telegraphs, telephones, or elaborate network of Socialist inter-communication. Indeed these things may be barred to the Socialist movement as the fight gets fiercer. The proletariat is international because it has one common enemy, one common aim, one faith, one great goal, and one battle cry of emancipation.

The Russian workmen in the tremendous power of their Socialist solidarity are forcing the Governments of Europe to grant passports for the Stockholm Conference. The Governments of Europe are making the best of a bad job by getting reactionary delegates sent to sway the Conference their way. Similar influences are evidently at work in South Africa to swell the number of mugwumps or worse, and Colonel Creswell's name was mentioned in an inspired paragraph in the *Rand Daily Mail* yesterday as the most suitable delegate!!! The shedder of blood at the Conference of the Socialist anti-militarist workingmen of the world!

The ISL has been carrying on alone in South Africa the same fight that the Russian Socialists have waged – the international class war. Those who are endeavouring to manipulate the present "cheap trip" on the pretence of sympathy with the Russian Socialists are averse to the class struggle and, being bourgeois pacifists, have not been heard of in the War on War struggle in South Africa. Beware of the side-tracking designs of the bourgeois pacifist!

What does sympathy with the Russian Revolution imply, comrades! It implies the solidarity of labour irrespective of race or colour. That phrase may be hackneyed, so let us be precise. The Russian revolution in South Africa means the welcome hand to the native workingman into the fullest social and economic equality he is capable of attaining with the white workingman. This is the bedrock on which we split in South Africa. How farcical to manipulate international delegates to sit with those who have abolished Pales and call that Socialism which places the bulk of the workers of this country outside the Pale of working-class emancipation! Hands across the sea to the Socialists of Russia, their feet upon the neck of Czardom, from the "Socialists" of South Africa – their feet upon the neck of the n*. Given a mugwump delegate, money will be easily forthcoming, and newspaper publicity to speed him hence. But mum's the word from Bain, Lucas and Co. when the fight has to be waged here and now against war, and colour prejudice, and militarism and the industrial disunity of the working class.

The fight of the International is greater and more urgent than ever. Good were it to have a working-class delegate at Stockholm, but we are doing our duty by calling upon the workers to return to their international fealty at the present Provincial Council Election. Let us send Andrews and Bunting to victory at the present election, and then talk about sending them further. If we do send one let it be by the organised International Socialist Movement or the organised Industrial Movement of South Africa or both; but not delegate of a scratch meeting.

Stockholm Congress

The International, July 20 1917

The newspapers announce that this Congress, initiated from Petrograd [renamed Leningrad (1924) and St Petersburg again (1991)] will open on August 15. It had previously been announced for divers dates going back as far as May last, and it may be taken for granted that it, or something like it, will not have closed by the time our delegate, if any, reaches Europe. There is therefore no fear that by holding our conference on the matter on the 5th August we shall be "missing the bus"; and that is also evidently the view of the Socialist bodies at Capetown and Durban who have already arranged for representation at it, while other organisations are contemplating following suit.

We attach much importance to the presence of representatives of Socialist bodies outside our own. As mentioned in our last issue, the question of sending delegates to Stockholm has been the occasion for the re-union of the French Socialist Party; and the Leeds Conference, also reported last week, must have gone far in a similar direction. Difference of "attitude on the war" seems to become solved in a solidarity engendered by a union of Labour to enforce its dictation, as Labour, on the whole warring world, "transforming the national war into the class war."

We hope and believe that our conference may in some slight measure serve a like purpose. Hence we renew our urgent and solemn invitation to all Socialist bodies and sympathisers in South Africa, interested in the outcome of the Stockholm Congress, to attend. Indeed there must be many Socialist elements even in the ranks of non-Socialist organisations who by this time have come to recognise the importance and possibilities of the Stockholm Conference, elements which, if they can be grouped, might form a most valuable addition to the Conference; and it is hoped that they will seize the opportunity and communicate with us accordingly. The ISL will do all in its power to facilitate their representation. No cut and dried resolution, mandate or nominee will be foisted on the delegates. All communications and contributions should be addressed to the Gen. Secretary, 6 Trades Hall, Rissik Street (Box 4179), Johannesburg.

Wallerisms! Spoof for the Mine Workers

The International, July 20 1917

The mineworkers have sent a new set of demands to the Chamber of Mines, mainly for increases in wages.

"For the first time in his life," Mr. Wallers of the Chamber of Mines has rushed into print warning the miners to go *gahle* [carefully] in their demands. Fifteen low grade mines will probably shut down, he says. This of course to scare the miners and influence the shopkeepers against them.

This "closing down" cry is an old one. But it is now backed by a new wheeze. It is not the old cry of "wolf" any more, says Wallers in effect. It is the real "wolf" come at last. For why? Because gold is the one product in the world market the increased cost of which cannot be passed on to the consumer. While the Mineowners have to pay vastly increased prices for material and labour, the price of gold remains the same. Therefore, mineworkers should moderate their demands, so says Wallers. This trump argument against a rise in wages is suspicious.

Mr. Wallers says that the gold mining industry is in effect a munitions industry, and vital to the prosecution of the war.

Then if British workers continue to agitate for higher wages, and thus raise the cost of mining materials, fifteen low grade mines in this munitions will have to close down, whether the South African miners make a move or not. Why should we have a share in the rise?

The Mint price of gold is £3 17s. 11d. This is the fixed price to which Wallers refers. The Imperial Government fixes the Mint price, but also clamours for gold. Gold, gold, my kingdom for gold! But not a ha'penny more than the Mint price (if we can help it) says the Bank of England.

If, then, gold mining really is a "munitions industry," they dare not close down any mines, nor limit the output in any way. The controlled munitions establishments in England are reaping great profits just now. The Government has cancelled the restrictions on profits originally imposed upon them, "in order to provide an incentive to production."

Here is a "munitions" industry," gold mining, vital to the Empire, so Wallers says; moreover, of tremendous influence in the counsels of the State, holding the key to credit, Lionel Phillips himself appointed chairman of a British War Mining Commission. And yet we are asked to believe that this industry cannot extort the ordinary pre-war profit while far less powerful interests in the English munitions industry are piling up huge war profits with the open encouragement of the British Government.

Again. The majority of the gold mines of the world belong to Britain. Before the war only a minimum of gold taken from them was sent to England. Ten millions to the English banks as against 458 millions (dollars) to other countries. (Kautsky, 1911). When the war broke out the British Government ordered all South African gold to be shipped to England. The British Government has never, least of all during this war, ordered an important industry to do anything without giving substantial concessions in exchange. All the vast quantity of gold sent to foreign countries did not go at Mint price, 195 million to Russia, etc. It went as an international commodity (not as money) at a price, like all other commodities, relative to the average cost of production. We cannot believe that the gold mining industry was asked to forego that vast market for no consideration whatsoever.

Mr. Wallers bases his alarum on the assumption of an assumption. He assumes that you assume that all the gold we produce is taken to the Royal Mint by the Chamber of Mines and paid for at Mint price. But the gold goes to the Bank of England. It is shipped from South Africa, not as money, but as a commodity. In peace time a great influx of gold stimulates credit, loans are more easily floated, and prices and capitalist prosperity rise. In war time, effects become causes, and causes, effects. Loans are perforce issued, gold or no gold. Gold is then as Mr. Wallers states in tremendous demand. The Imperial banks have their tongues hanging out for gold. Mint price is secondary. Bullion, more gold bullion is required to make credit stable, to ship a hundred million to America, or a dozen million to Bombay, to bolster up a credit here, or correct an international balance there; gold they must have, even by flooding England with paper and withdrawing gold coinage. It is demand that regulates the price now. The Chamber of Mines has nothing to do with the Royal Mint. That is the business of the Bank of England principally. Then do you mean to say that in the middle of this insatiable demand for gold the Chamber of Mines is not able to get its fair profit? Or is all the talk about the Imperial importance of the gold industry only bunkum?

No, the Chamber of Mines are not patriotic altruists, otherwise they would concede the miners' Demands without a grouse. The Chamber of Mines, being a capitalist institution for the making of profits, will see to that part of the business. The Bank of England will look after the Mint price part of the business. Let the Mineworkers of South Africa see to their part of the business, that is to get a bigger wage if they are sufficiently organised, and fear no "closing down" scare of Mr. Wallers.

South African Delegate to Stockholm.

The International, July 27 1917

The date of the special Conference to consider the advisability of sending a Socialist Delegate from South Africa to the Stockholm Congress is drawing nigh. The various sections and branches of the movement as unattached sympathisers, need to get their delegates for the 5th ready. However the cables may shuffle the news, we are confident that the outlook for the Congress at Stockholm is as bright as ever. Russia is the storm centre. That is why we are compelled to devote to events there so much attention. There is no doubt that the comrades there are handling the situation magnificently from a Socialist point of view. But whatever befalls the Russian Revolution, it has applied a spark to the whole world-wide movement which cannot be smothered.

The Socialist movement in South Africa is therefore well up to time in its preparations for sending a delegate. Although the Stockholm Congress opens on August 5th, our delegate will be in ample time. It is not conceivable that any further cessation of International relations can occur. It is more likely that the Stockholm Congress will become the instrument of the proletariat to dictate terms of war and peace. It will probably sit in permanent session and resolve itself into a Constituent Assembly of the working class of Europe.

The Special Conference on August 5th promises to be the most representative gathering of Socialists yet held in South Africa. On Saturday evening, the 4th, a Social Evening will be held at West's Academy to welcome the delegates and Socialist comrades from other parts of the country. All comrades are cordially invited, no entrance fee. Songs and short addresses interlarded with refreshments will beguile the evening, and opportunities for comrades to cut off corners ready for the Conference.

We wish to repeat the invitation given in our previous issues to all supporters of the proposal to send a delegate to Stockholm to be represented at the Conference, no matter to what other organisation they may happen to belong. Around this central principle that the workers of the world should meet whether capitalist governments fight or not, and meet to announce their solidarity, on this common ground we wish to welcome all. For we know that this principle is gaining new adherents daily among the workers of South Africa.

The Tramway "Casuals". Another Nibble

The International, August 17 1917

You may not know what a "Casual" is. In the good old days when tramps were free to roam abroad in Merrie England without a care for Conscription Acts or Defence of the Realms, the "casual" was he, the gentleman of the road, who dropped in, quite casually like, at the workhouse of an evening and broke a heap of stones in return for bed and breakfast. The kindly Boards of Guardians, mostly farmers, helped him through the grey, uncongenial towns to the cosy barns and cheap jobs in the freer, greener farmlands beyond!

But our tram "casuals" have not that variety of scenery and employment. They are the new hands on the trams. They hang about the forbidding sheds reporting themselves at stated hours all day, trying to get a car to take out. They are not "casuals" really, so says the Department, because they are assured a minimum wage. But how lovely are all employments in theory! Woe betide our poor casual if he reports five minutes late. The wonderful minimum wage is his no more for that week, and always, if he wants to exceed his three pounds ten minimum he has to hang round 12 and 16 hours to put in eight hours work. This is the 8 hours day. You work 8 hours, you are the property of the boss for 16 hours!

Karl Marx had heard about this system in 1867. Fancy writing about Barry and his merry martinets so long in advance! But he called it the "relay" system. Karl Marx would not have written so harshly nowadays because he did not know then that we had a Labour Tramway Committee, and a full blown (not fly blown) Socialist chairman, and a real live, brass buttoned Sinn Feiner as Traffic Manager. WE have advanced a great deal. Says he: –

> During the 15 hours of the factory day, capital dragged in the labourer now for 30 minutes, now for an hour, and then pushed him out again, to drag him into the factory and thrust him out afresh, hounding him hither and thither, in scattered shreds of time, without ever losing hold of him until the full ten hours work is done... Thus the hours of rest were turned to hours of (enforced – KM) idleness, which drove the youths to the pot-house, and the girls to the brothel. (Indelicate man, this Marx)... They paid 10 hours wages for 12 or 15 hours lordship over labour-power. This was the … masters' interpretation of the 10 hours law! These were the same unctuous Free-traders, (Town Councillors) perspiring with love for humanity … (*Capital.*)

Now the "casuals" had better look after themselves. They have a Union in name, and a man speaks for them as President who suffers none of the "inconveniences" of the "casuals," therefore is not able to speak for them. Let the casuals strike against bad conditions, not against fellow workers, who are their best friends. Let the Bum President shuffle as he likes, these are what Tram "Casuals" should demand: –

Demand equality of pay!
Demand the abolition of overtime! (That is, don't scab on the unemployed).
Demand that eight hours work shall be done in eight hours time!
Demand privileges for none and equal rights and wages for all! Don't be spoofed by Hicks: a man with six children eats as much skoff whether he has worked on the trams one year or five years.
Demand the abolition of the grade system, so beloved by Hicks. The grade system is the curse of the service, and keeps the men from uniting.

WAKE UP, WHITE WORKERS! THE ONCOMING NATIVE PROLETARIAT

The International, August 24 1917

Never has there been such vindication of the class war fight of *The International* for the solidarity of labour irrespective of colour, waged insistently by us for the last. two years, as came from the mouths of capitalists this week. The South African National Union met on Tuesday at the Carlton Hotel, and in its ninth annual report appeared sentiments which might easily have been echoes from *The International*. This National Union is a body formed to encourage the growth of industries in South Africa.

The report said *inter alia*: –

> The public mind has been so concentrated upon the actual fighting of the whole forces in the field that it has been apt to regard the Indians, and our coloured and native men, as merely pawns on the chess board, who will fall back into their old position once the war is over. No idea can be more fallacious … The days of indentured labour are numbered.

Industrial Capital is always revolutionary in the days of its youth. Listen to its philosophic radicalism. It will hardly suit the purpose of the old boss, the Chamber of Mines, which has little to gain by the extension of civil rights to the natives: –

> A vital modification of the industrial situation in favour of the coloured people is sure to be followed by social and political changes in the same direction. (Been reading Karl Marx) The

> whites will more and more tend to become an "over-seer" class, (police boys), and Mr. Merriman's characterisation of the blacks as the real working-man will be on the road to realisation. It only needs the continued locking-up of the land and repression of local industries to make this situation acute, and to make South Africa take its place in the Empire alongside of India instead of beside Australia.

The report draws attention to another remarkable development affecting the "poor whites" (the "white trash" of like economic conditions in the Southern States of America, as Sen Yah has pointed out): –

> In other countries the unemployed and unemployables have flocked to the colours and have been made men thereby. The "poor white" has been left unaffected by the war. Even the educational revival … passes him by. Standard IV at 16 is the summit of the ambition which his surroundings will admit. Hence the danger is that he may recede behind the advancing line of the non-European population.

So we see that the ISL has not been a whit premature in its propaganda. In fact we have leeway to make up. The choice is even now being offered to the white workers of becoming police boys fer the capitalists or of standing shoulder to shoulder with the native proletariat in its emancipating march. So long as the Federation refuses to bring the native worker within its purview, gracious concessions to white mechanics from the Chamber of Mines are nothing but lures to. buy them out from the class struggle. The lavish interviews granted the Federation Secretary in the[[Johannesburg] *Star* columns indicate that Wallers has discovered that the way of concession to white mechanics is the way of safety to the Chamber of Mines; for thus is the Federation being lifted high and dry above the mightier, broader currents of the teeming myriads of the bottom proletariat.

The only hope is that the Conference of Industrial Workers, which we see is being called together by a few prominent Trade Unionists on September 2nd, will become another Leeds Conference of rank and file men. If so, it will save the white workers of this country from being degraded into a police boy class. It will ensure for them a place in the ranks of those, irrespective of race or colour, privileged to unite together for the emancipation of the workers in South Africa.

Tramwaymen Spoofed Again

The International, August 24 1917

The Tramwaymen put in demands for increases for all grades; and the

Council has replied with an offer that ignores the lower paid, and piles on more privileges on the top grades. How long are the Tramwaymen going to tolerate this mean conspiracy to split their ranks by concessions to the higher paid at the expense of the new men? The Executive of the Union, mostly men of top pay, have resigned in a funk, although not long ago a scratch meeting put them in office for the duration of the war. Meaner than all, the Council has endeavoured to put the tram riders up against the men by increasing fares. And the game of "suspensions" for petty offences on tale telling evidence is still rife on the trams. This is about the meanest part of the whole mean employ. The Tramwaymen should first learn that their self-respect is of more worth than all increases in pay. The first thing they should agitate for is the abolition of "suspensions," so that they may feel a bit more like men once again, instead of being the trembling slaves of every martinet inspector that comes along.

Let them ask why are they so defenceless against this "suspension" system, that strikes at their stomach, and "suspends" their manhood. Why? Because the grade system splits up their ranks and prevents them uniting. ABOLISH THE GRADE SYSTEM BOYS! and be self-respecting men once more.

What keeps back the Native Worker? Biology or Economics?

The International, November 2 1917

In discussions on the problems of organising the native workers in this country there are many factors lost sight of by the pessimists. "All men are born to liberty," said the philosophic radicals, "and most men are bred in wage-slavery" adds the Socialist. But many of those who endorse the right of every man to liberty make exceptions when confronted with the case of the native. The vast chasm of "biologic" difference nullifies that right and will prevent him from ever following the path of workingclass emancipation, they say.

Those who emphasize "biology" forget the many economic factors that bar the way of the native worker. Briefly, the great obstacle in the way of organising the native proletariat in this country is that it is not yet quite proletarian. Karl Marx, the intellectual emancipator of the workers, showed that what makes the proletariat the one revolutionary class is the fact that it has nothing to lose but its chains. Such a class must eventually be brought to the forked road when the only alternatives left are either to Do or to Die. "Of all the classes which stand at present in opposition to the Bourgeoisie, the proletariat alone is a truly revolutionary class. The other classes decay and go under before modern industry; the proletariat is its special product." (Marx). [*Manifesto of the Communist Party*, 1848]. The workingclass is the ascendant revolutionary class not only because it exists by the healthy principle of labour, but also. because it has been divorced from land and property, is, in fact, bereft of all hopes of acquiring individual rights in land and property. It is the sense of property in his artisan skill that vitiates the revolutionary vigour of the craft unionist.

The native workers have not yet been divorced from the soil. Even where they are constantly engaged in capitalist industry it is doubtful if any large number have given up all hope of ever acquiring individual rights in land. They are not land serfs, and they are not yet "compleat" wage-slaves. They are in a worse position than either. They get starvation wages on the industrial field, and periodical vacations of starvation without wages on the land. This relay system, whereby the native reserves are used as breeding grounds for native wage-slaves, prevents the whole-time occupation of the natives in industry, keeps alive in the native worker the lingering psychology of the land peasant, and prevents the growth of that sense of solidarity with all his fellow wage-slaves which must rapidly result from the whole time occupation of the native workers in industry.

Under conditions where where workers are employed in capitalist industry only for short periods alternating with periods on the land, the most enlightened white workers could hardly organise. These are conditions which create scabbery, and it is a tribute to the communal instinct of the natives that Corner House methods of recruiting have not made scabs of them.

The native worker is the typical revolutionist in this country. All manner of penal laws and regulations are brought in to keep under his nascent workingclass solidarity. Even in the compounds they class the natives according to races; yet faction fights get rarer. The institution of "Kitchen K*" prevents him learning the language of the whites and the whites from learning his. There never was a "lingo" better suited for keeping alive his slave status, and for keeping white and native workers apart while appearing to be a means of communication between them.

The work necessary to be done before the native can be industrially organised is to convince him that, whereas he has lost. his individual property, he has also lost all hope of acquiring any except as a class. Instead of looking backward to the land of his fathers, he has to acquire the wage-workers psychology of looking ahead, of knowing that his Redeemer liveth, not in his chief or his parson, but in the working class. That he is dispossessed for good: that the wheel of economic dispossession never turns back. That he must march on with the working class and, by solidarity, capture the capitalist artillery which has dispossessed him.

A Special Appeal to all Comrades

The International, November 9 1917

£100 Wanted Right Away

Legal Defence and Propaganda

The League is passing through a trying time financially, and the Management Committee has decided to take all friends and comrades into its confidence, with a view to calling upon all hands to give the ISL a good lift this month.

It may surprise some of our readers to know that the cost of running the League Office, Secretary's Salary, and publishing *The International* comes to £65 or £70 per month. To those who know anything about running a paper the surprise will be that it is not much more. In what we regard as a good month we can look for £20 towards this from sales and subscriptions to *The International.* The balance is made up by Branch affiliation fees, (the Johannesburg Central being a great help in this, respect) and by donations from a small – too small – ring of comrades. League Socials also furnish good contributions.

Now we are forced with extra expenditure. A conspiracy is afoot to smash up the League. The court cases against Comrades [Sam] Barlin and [H.] Barendregt involve a principle which make the expenses of legal defence a charge on the League. The League as a whole is involved in these cases. We have appealed against the the judgement of the Magistrate's Court, and this will necessitate further heavy legal expenditures.

The intrigues against the ISL have taken on another form. A "petition" has been hawked round the proprietors of public halls binding them not to let their premises to the ISL Such a paper was presented to Professor West at whose Academy the League holds its monthly dances. But he refused to sign it. The "Sons of England" and the Empire League and similar cliques are responsible. We are assured that this hooligan clique were in attendance on our last advertised dance, which was luckily postponed.

In addition to Legal Defence the Management Committee and the Branches have decided upon a campaign of leaflet distribution to take the place of the temporary closing down of our public meetings. This will also involve heavy expense, but the kind of expense which the League exists to incur. The distribution of leaflets on a large scale is the finest form of propaganda, and if adhered to will eventually result in such a modification of workingclass opinion that there will be no question of breaking up our meetings.

ALL THIS REQUIRES MONEY. WE WANT £100 RIGHT AWAY towards Legal Defence, Leaflet Distribution, and to wipe off a debit balance on our general account **ONE HUNDRED POUNDS** wanted this month, and we know that the comrades will fork out once they know the position. We know that they do not want it to be said that a hooligan clique can close down our little paper. Rally then to the aid of the League, and make up that £100 before the month is out.

Subscription lists will be issued immediately, and all friends who desire to contribute to **"THE LEGAL DEFENCE AND LEAFLET FUND"** should hustle round and get one filled up. All together comrades!

A Question for Diogenes

The International, November 9 1917

The great wail at the Municipal Election just past has been, "Give us men." Tennyson, the all-round handy man of the parsons, has been in great vogue. That extinct genius, "the citizen," has been appealed to from pulpit and Press to vote for that Dodo, the "disinterested candidate." And from a hundred beer-barrelled platforms, racing touts, land-agents, and Municipal vagabonds have all given the Messianic response: "Here am I, Lord, send me." The little fleas of the Labour Party have become too expensive to keep. So they have turned in anguish, parson and Press, to the Reform Ticket, the pure, lofty, disinterested men. "God give us men." Have they not full throatedly moaned? and God has placed the order with the Braamfontein Estates and the Transvaal Consolidated Lands.

"The bourgeoisie," said Karl Marx, "wherever it has conquered power, has destroyed all feudal, patriarchal, and idyllic relations. It has pitilessly torn asunder, all the many-coloured feudal bonds which united men to their "natural superiors," and has left no other tie twixt man and man but naked self-interest and callous cash payment. It has drowned religious ecstasy in the ice-cold water of egotistical calculation. It has transformed personal worth into exchange value …" [*Manifesto of the Communist Party*, 1848].

Workers of the Bantu Race!

Leaflet drafted for the Industrial Workers of Africa
Reprinted in *The International,* February 15 1918

WORKERS OF THE BANTU RACE!

Why do you live in slavery? Why are you not free? Why are you kicked and spat upon by your masters? Why must you carry a pass before you can move anywhere? And if you are found without one, why are you thrown into prison? Why do you toil hard for little money? And again thrown into prison if you refuse to work. Why do they herd you like cattle into compounds,

WHY?

Because you are the toilers of the earth. Because the masters want you to labour for their profit. Because they pay the Government and the Police to keep you as slaves to toil for them.

If it were not for the money that they make from your labour, you would not be oppressed.

But mark! You are the mainstay of the country. You do all the work, you are the means of their living.

That is why you are robbed of the fruits of your labour and robbed of your liberty as well.

There is only one way of deliverance for you, Bantu workers. Unite as workers, unite! Forget the things that divide you. Let there be no longer talk of Basuto, Zulu, or Shangaan. You are all labourers. Let Labour be your common bond.

Wake up! And open your ears. The sun has arisen, the day is breaking. For a long tine you were asleep when the great mill of the rich man was grinding and breaking the sweat from your work for nothing. You are strongly urged to come to the meeting of the workers and fight for your rights. Come and listen to the good news and deliver yourself from the chains of the Capitalists. Unity is strength. The fight is great against the many pass laws that persecute you, and the low wages and the misery of existence. Workers of all lands unite. You have nothing to lose but your chains. You have a world to win.

The Call of the Bolsheviks – International Socialist Manifesto

The International, February 22 1918

WORKERS OF SOUTH AFRICA! It is time you knew what game is afoot. It is time for you to realise that your fellow workers in Russia need your voice and help. The Capitalist Press hides the real state of affairs behind foul slanders. It hides the fact that the Bolshevik Government is only the Government of the workers by the workers for the workers. It hides the fact that Lenin and Trotsky are only the delegates of the Russian Federation of Labour, otherwise the Council of Workmen, or the Soviet.

It is your fellow workmen they are slandering. It is your fellow workmen who are calling upon you to hurl these slanders back into the teeth of your and their capitalist enemies.

What are they up to now, these International Capitalists? Labour having conquered power in Russia is occupied in quelling the rebellion of the "bourgeoisie class," that is, the capitalist class. The bourgeoisie are opposing the workers by force wherever there is a hope of saving their precious private interests from being captured by Labour for the common weal. In some cases they have massacred the working men by the hundreds. What will they not do when, with the help of German arms, they get all the workers of Russia under their heels again? They will massacre them by the HUNDREDS OF THOUSANDS. The tiger of capitalism will show no mercy when his hide is threatened by Labour. You know that. You found that out in Commissioner Street in 1913, when even your parsons took up arms against you. Consider then the position of your Russian fellow workmen.

You say: the Russian workmen should not have dissolved their army. We say: that the victory of Labour means the dissolution of all armies. You cannot have Labour triumphant and militarism on top at the same time. Make no mistake: this is not the crime of German militarism alone, this attack on the Russian revolution.

Lenin has declared that the Allied Governments are silently backing the German Government against the Bolsheviks. No matter what family quarrels International Capital may have, they are all united against the Bolsheviks, that is, the working men of Russia. And they will unite against you too when you dare to assert your rights as the producers of all wealth. Balfour the other day would not deny that the British Government had negotiated directly with Austria. What did they negotiate about if not to protect their common capitalist interests in Russia? A gathering of International Financiers was held at Switzerland last year from all belligerent countries, Germany and Britain, America and Austria, and all the family cats of capitalism were there to arrange how to stem the rising tide of working class revolution in all countries. Remember that once, only once before, have the workingmen held power as workers, – in the Paris Commune of 1871. Remember how Bismarck, at the very time he was imposing harsh terms upon the French Government, co-operated with that Government to crush the workers of Paris by releasing drafts of French prisoners of war for the purpose. And the greatest massacre in all history was the result. Remember that it was a massacre of the workers. If they can they will do the same with the Russian workers, but on a still vaster and more horrible scale. While the Capitalist Governments are quarrelling over the booty they have stolen from Labour, they are keeping alive a family understanding against any sign of working class unity. They are all united when Labour shows signs of coming into its own. What can we do? It is our part as workers to denounce these capitalist slanderers of the Russian proletariat. It is our part to help in the great class struggle of the toilers of all lands that is now beginning. The humbug of national wars is-being exposed. Behind it all the exploitation of the workers of all lands stands out as their chief aim, their dearest treasure. The great war of Germany versus the allies may go on. It is the only hope of Capital that it should go on. In any case it is only the working masses that are slaughtered. Capital thrives on it. But the class war of international Capital against the rising working class is also waging today. Workers of South Africa! Arouse from your submissiveness and lethargy, and show that you see through this foul conspiracy of International Capital against the Russian workmen. The cause of the Russian workmen is your cause. Workers of the world UNITE. You have a world to win.

Census on Labour Solidarity

The International, March 22 1918

The census returns give good arguments for the solidarity of labour irrespective of colour.

In the Transvaal the persons living in the towns are classed in the following proportions:–

White	… …	41.95 per cent
Bantu	… …	52.82 per cent
Coloured	… …	5.23 per cent

Hasty deductions might assume that the organisation of white labour meant the organisation of 41 per cent of the workers. But whereas practically the whole of the 52 per cent Bantu are working folk or wage earners, the white section contains practically the whole of the exploiting class and its hangers on, besides the white wage-earning proletariat.

But we have already hammered home that lesson – the futility of white labour organisation as white – and its futility is obvious without statistics. The noteworthy point about the above proportional statistics is one for the coloured workers. The coloured workers will realise from this statement of the proportion they occupy in the town population – 5 per cent – how utterly futile it is for them to organise, whether industrially or politically, purely as coloured men, even if the whole 5 per cent are workers.

The coloured workers hold mass meetings in the towns where they live. The enthusiasm may be great, but their only power lies in industrial solidarity. Industrial solidarity is only a power where it can stop industry. Mass meetings have no power. The mass meetings of coloured workers are composed of men from many industries. If they all went on strike no industry would stop. They would merely lose their jobs. Their hope then lies not in organising as coloured workers, but in organising with all the workers in the industries, first of all with the Bantu workers, because with them also "colour" is the excuse given for their special oppression. At every meeting of coloured men this "5 per cent" should be kept to the front.

All mass meetings are only so many ciphers, noughts, noughts, noughts (000,000). Solidarity with all the workers irrespective of colour is the figure one placed before their noughts (1,600,000) that will turn the noughts into millions.

In the Cape urban areas the coloured population is 35 per cent of the whole. And right well are the coloured workers acquitting themselves there. They too must beware of organising as coloured workers. Let them remember their special function of leading the Bantu workers on towards industrial solidarity.

Where Nationalism Helps

The International, March 22 1918

There is a need for correcting a tendency in socialist circles to denounce nationalism as wholly bad. The papers this week admitted that, while the "nondescript" army of Russia were fleeing into the interior, the Red Guard alone showed patriotic spirit and stood prepared, "in its socialistic way," to oppose the invader.

Socialism does not smother the emotional virtues. It strives to capture them for the service of the class struggle on the proletarian side.

In South Africa it is our rule to magnify the obstacles in the way of enlisting the black proletariat to the class struggle. They are undoubtedly great, these differences of custom, of language, and of human nature even. The barriers which the socialist movement has to break down, or soar above, are the primeval barriers between the Occident and the Orient. But let us remember that these barriers are only barriers against the conveyance of the. message, not against the understanding of the message. Indeed it seems now that international socialism is the one Western idea which the Eastern millions can respond to from their very soil and proclaim with tenfold intensity as their own.

Take our Indian fellow workers. There are thousands, even tens of thousands, growing up in this country whose only language is English. But though suddenly become English in tongue, the young Indian worker cannot renounce so suddenly the inherited instincts of thousands of years. He cannot so suddenly alienate from his blood that deep native philosophy, that throbbing in tune with the throb of the world's heart for surcease from social contradictions, expressed in the pantheistic thought of India. It is as well that he cannot.

In international socialism these contradictions are solved, and the young Indian sees his aspirations as an Indian nationalist embraced in the international class struggle.

Of course, the nationalism of the Indian trader will never find its triumph. For his is the battle, not of the ancient glory of the East struggling for survival, but the battle on the commercial plane with the white shopocracy. Except ye become as little children, that is, take the standpoint of the modern propertyless proletarian, verily your nationalism cannot be born again.

As for the native workers in this country, their nationalism, what exists of it, is almost wholly a disguised class struggle. Nearly all natives are wage earners. And they are all oppressed because of their labour being necessary to the capitalist.

The coloured worker has no nationalism, no family traditions, no ancient national heroes the sound of whose names are potent to summon the proletarian into solidarity, not with his class, but with the middle class elements of his own colour.

Colour alone is a very poor cement for solidarity. It was very noticeable during the recent agitation against the Railway Regulations that Dr. [Abdullah] Abdurahman ['Coloured' leader of the African People's Organisation] kept a discreet silence. He belongs to the class that has made snug. And soon may the coloured workers realise that their one rock of refuge is that solidarity of labour which puts the Abdurahmans and the Indian capitalist in the same class as their exploiters.

The Land of Linga Linga

The International, April 19 1918

Linga Linga point is not so far north as northernmost Rhodesia, yet its appearance, and that of the little town of Inhambane within its land-locked bay, seems as remote from the life of Johannesburg and Durban as the placid East is from the fussy West. Sailing boats with long tapering triangle sails dot about its waters. They are manned by natives, the natives of Portuguese territory, and they are catching fish – catching it for themselves. And they do not carry passes. And when they go home they squat on their own little plot of land, for the kind laws of this apparent paradise say that where a native

squats and works, that shall he own. His daily pay, if he cares to go and work, is 300 reis (three hundred reis)! His only needs are simple food and a fig leaf, and his only ambitions women and wine. His masters, the Portuguese officialdom and the shopocracy of Inhambane, are not as other masters. They wear pith helmets and duck suits and take life easy in this land of the cocoanut and the palm, where you cannot tell the spot where the waters meet the sky, and the cocoanut trees stand upside down in the bay of green and shining glass. No, these calm Portuguese are not after invention and enterprise, like their feverish brothers of British climes. The train leaves for some hamlet inland on Sunday, and waits until the first-class passenger goes for another drink. And if he cares for another, well, the guard and porter go with him for another. And although they do not go to the length of having a drink with the "n*" passenger who has just returned per boat from the Johannesburg mines, they do not mind more intimate relations with his umfasi, as the rich gradations of colour, from jet black, through olive tan, to undoubted white, testify in the faces of the passengers who throng the station platform, which is also the side street. And they all chat together, without distinction of colour. There is no refraining from talk because of colour. It is indeed the land of Linga Linga, and why not linger longer?

But alas! there is no real oasis within our capitalist system. Round the corner are several natives with the letters WNLA standing out brazenly on their caps. It is the Witwatersrand Native Labour Association. (Just as certain lotteries in Johannesburg are innocent Portuguese Government bonds, but here they plaster the windows with "Rufe Naylor's Lotteries, Limited!") Here, far away from trouble-seeking, middle-class democracy, where there are no shopkeepers and farmers jealous of the competing mines magnate in the grab for native labour – here there is no need to hide the name. For here evidently are preserved all the conditions for breeding labour.

We forget one thing which native worries about, and that is his hut and wife taxes. To pay them he must go and get recruited by the bold letters, WNLA.

When we put up at the little hotel one night, the landlady next morning presented us with a bill for seventeen thousand reis. The pallor did not leave our faces till a friend in the know, having computed the present value of the reis. told us it was barely two British pounds sterling worth. The "Linga Linga" Portuguee carries his un-bourgeois methods to the currency by turning out reams of paper whenever he is short of cash, with chaos resulting. Armed with that knowledge we found that the 300 reis of the n* boy's day's pay at Linga Linga is just about ninepence. Truly a happy hunting ground for the investing capitalist. Space does not permit to show the ramifications of the Chamber of Mines' influence discouraging any industry calculated to sponge up this labour in the Mozambique, although the land is rich and fair and fruitful. But it is apparent to the dullest how the Portuguese officialdom, from the new Governor, who drank wine with Wallers on his way through Johannesburg the other day, down to the WNLA recruiter, are all boss boys for the international capitalist looking after this precious little breeding-ground of reserve cheap labour. Capital stays his iron hand here; yet even unto this fair inlet of the Indian Ocean does its shadow come.

Why do Mozambique Natives Come to Johannesburg?

The International, September 13 & 27 1918

Why do Mozambique natives come to Johannesburg? Both Labourites and Socialists often ask the question. They wonder what influences are brought to bear to induce labour from Portuguese East Africa to enter the mines. The WNLA, as the sinister recruiter, comes in as the villain of the piece where capitalist production in general is more often the culprit. I shall try as briefly as possible to indicate what it is that entices a "Mahobo" or a "Mungez" or a lithe "Ngatateme" to leave his native shore to be baptised at Johannesburg as "Jim Fish" or "Bloody Fool."

A visit to one of the chief recruiting stations of the WNLA in South Mozambique dispels much of the vague suspicion of atrocities which one would so dearly love to smell out. The methods employed are apparently just the usual methods of recruiting, registering and compounding the all-too-eager boys who wish to try their fortunes on the Rand. When a few are turned away as physically unfit – made unfit by previous terms of work in the mines – we are assured by the courteous and amiable superintendent in charge that it is with regret on both sides. Why so often do they go the Rand?

Let us approach the question by a brief survey of the general economic condition of Portuguese Territory.

There prevails a vulgar of identifying capitalism as inhumanity. Cruelty and suffering are the consequences of capitalism – incidents in its march. Previous forms of exploitation are also inhuman. To Socialists nurtured in the school of Marx it is unnecessary to labour the point that capitalism, that is, large industry founded on surplus values, is the essential pre-requisite to the Social Revolution. Marxians therefore who say: "Speed the day of the Socialist Revolution," also say, in proper time and place, "Speed the day of capitalist appropriation."

That is how one feels in Mozambique. A Marxian in Portuguese East, if he is not careful, can become a red-hot Imperialist before he knows where he is. He longs for the day of big capital (which he fights in its full flower on the Rand); for the day when it shall invade this abode of bureaucratic petty bourgeoisdom and wrench the whole population – white and black – from its low existence of primitive squatting, hop distilling and trading in wives, into the quick and nervy issues of the great class struggle.

Portuguese East Africa is an anomaly. Nominally a dependency of Portugal, economically it is a dependency of Johannesburg. The exchange value of the pound sterling is regulated from Lisbon. Yet all the pounds come from the Rand. Unlike other countries, the rate of exchange is more of domestic than of international concern in Mozambique. Every time the price of the pound sterling jumps from 7500 reis to 8000 reis, all the storekeepers' needs must change the prices of their wares. The reis paper currency is the means of payment, but the English pound is the standard of value.

The resulting chaos and commercial uncertainty is the same as if the yard measure changed from day to day.

The hut tax must he paid in pounds sterling. For every hut one golden pound and a few hundred Portuguese reis. Natives when paying hut tax are discouraged from paying in the Portuguese equivalent of the pound. The Portuguese officials require sovereigns and these come from Johannesburg.

Portuguese East is administered bureaucratically – a governor-general governing direct through a hierarchy of district governors, administrators, and petty officials galore. All these are paid from Johannesburg via the mine boys. Creswell's agitation to stop the importation of native labour from Mozambique territory would stop the salaries of all these Portuguese officials. If by a fluke such a thing could happen, in a trice we should have Mozambique united politically with the South African Union as it is to-day economically so united. Speed that day too!

I am not forgetting, by the way, that Creswell's agitation resulted in the recruiting of natives for the mines being confined below Latitude 22 deg. It is a peculiar coincidence, however, that the Companhia de Mocambique – a powerful concern with English and French capital holding sovereign rights over more than a quarter of Portuguese East – peculiar, I say, that this Company's sphere of influence stretches from the Zambezi down to just about latitude 22 degrees South!! Thus there is no reform of the system which is not at once a sop to some vested interest as well as to the reformists.

Being 22 degrees South then, this hierarchy of Portuguese officialdom holds the land in fief from King Kapital on the understanding that they breed a plentiful supply of labourers for the mines and elsewhere. They acquire a vested interest in breeding labour. That is the dominant industry. And they exercise the restraint of petty feudal lordlings over any enterprise calculated to upset the breeding industry.

But labour is not only bred for the mines. When those who live below the 22nd parallel speak of Mozambique, they refer to that tract of tropics several hundred miles to the north, being the district of that name touching on Lake Nyassa, hence the name of Nyassaland also, where the natives are truculent and refuse to be bothered with the rate of exchange. At present and for some time past, commercial as well as military operations of an extensive character, needing much labour, are afoot there.

Thither are despatched all evil doers, and thither too many thousands who do no evil. Has a native killed his wife? He is sent to labour in Mozambique. Is he the most amiable and law-abiding? Let him happen to be in the path of the press gang and he also is sent to labour in Mozambique. "Mozambique" is a word to conjure up terror in the native breast. Many the native who goes to the "Componi," as they call the WNLA, as to a city of refuge from the terror of Mozambique. He also goes there to escape a debt very often.

When the order comes for more labour for Nyassaland, each *administrador* is required to furnish a quota. The means are left for him. He has about forty or fifty native policemen, *casadors* they are called, to enact his will. These are sent round the country with plenary powers to arrest every male native of fit age they can meet and bring them to be shipped off to Nyassaland. Many are the tales of cruelty and extortion practised by *casadors*, who are generally of the lowest type.

Of late however, the sight of a *casador* makes every native run; also the sight of the administrador, his entourage or his boat or pony and trap. Now therefore the casadors sally out at night, and like the cackling of a fowl pen disturbed by a fox is the commotion when the casadors ring around a kraal and manacle the male inmates off to the "commandant," as the administrator is called by them. These unfortunates are then regarded by their people almost as good as dead. Death is the punishment for him who tries to escape. Death is his most probable fate in any case, for it is only five per cent who return from Nyassaland, physical wrecks from fever and privation in the swamps of that torrid north. Can it be wondered at that for them Johannesburg is indeed the City of the Golden [Fleece]?

The Mozambique native is nowhere near being a proletarian until he sees Johannesburg. Not only salvation and medical advice are the sops which make a sponger of him, but he also gets land free. Wherever the native squats on open land, there he may abide. When a farmer buys land the native thereon cannot be turned off, although they can be made to work in a fashion for the farmer. To that extent they are serfs. They own the land; the "commandant" owns them. If the native lives near the sea, he can live on fish. What impels him to labour is the desire first of all to buy a wife. Having bought one to begin with, there is not so much further trouble about providing food. But then he has to pay the hut tax, and if two wives then tax for two homes, and so on. If he fails to pay the tax, the "commandant" takes him to forced labour. If he clears off, the commandant takes his wife, who is forced to labour in the "commandant's" fields until the tax is paid. But this is the crowning disgrace for a native, and if he is anywhere alive he raises the money to free his wife and will clear off to Johannesburg to repay the debt. He will also clear out to Johannesburg to escape the complicated penalties imposed by tribal customs. In young boys it is an undoubted desire to see the world and come back to buy a wife. In any gang of Mozambique natives, most have been to the Rand, and those who haven't are dubbed *momparas* [country bumpkins] by their mates (for here, too, the ubiquitous Kitchen K* is the black man's Esperanto).

Thus with land to laze upon, with few wants, yet not propertyless while he can still till, with *surra*, the juice of the cocoanut blossom, or *sopa*, the juice of the sugar cane, or the juice of the *caju* fruit, to intoxicate away the hours withal, his ordinary ambitions are satisfied, and he stagnates into a pilfering, petty trading black trash. Unlike his brother Bantu down South, he has learnt to trade and to haggle from the Indians, and the natives monopolise the buying and selling in the market places: prehensile shopkeepers, not embryo proletarians.

Until Johannesburg invades the Mozambique, good luck to the Mozambique native who invades Johannesburg. It is the only school that can make a man and a proletarian of him. The missions make him desire a stiff collar and tie. But a cry of despair goes up from the missionaries to-day. The converted "brothers" break into the Bible store and cart off the the holy word for small profits and quick returns (as in a recent case), mystic charms to extort *mali* [wealth] from the heathen.

Marxian Socialism discards personal righteousness as the prime factor in the Social Revolution. In the development of the large industry lies the hope of Revolution. One wonders when it is going to capture Africa for capitalism, and the Africans for Socialism. In the same week that the trial of our comrades for sedition opened in Johannesburg was opened at Pretoria a smelting furnace to treat the iron ore of that district. Both were events of great revolutionary significance.

From the point of view both of sentiment and of science, therefore, we Internationals can have no truck with Creswellian agitations for prohibiting the recruiting of native labour from Mozambique. The toll of native mortality in the mines is undoubtedly serious. But it seems to be a choice between the frying pan of Johannesburg and the hell fire of Nyassaland.

Suggested Explanation of the ISL Platform

The International, January 4 1919

The International Socialist League founds itself upon the principle of the class struggle.

The class struggle pre-supposes that modern society is based on the capitalist system of production, that is, the exploitation of wage labour by an employing class.

This system, first evolving in England at the close of the middle ages and spreading later to all the other countries of the world, tends inevitably to the destruction of the individual ownership of small industries and one-man shops, and to the concentration of all machinery and natural resources into large industry on a colossal scale owned and controlled by a small privileged class.

This concentration of capital in the hands of a few involves at the other pole, the concentration and forced mobilisation of labour into large armies of workers, and the conversion of the mass of the people into wage-earning proletarians – propertyless and utterly divorced from the control of the means of production as well as from the products of their labour.

The small tool develops into the big machine. The one-man shop into the great factory employing thousands of workmen.

The product of this development of industry and invention falls into the hands, not of society, but of the capitalist class, who by their ownership of the machinery of production control the Government and all other domains of social life, as well as the lives of the working class. Capitalism pollutes everything that it touches.

For the workers the result of this development of industry is unemployment and destitution for a large number, the loss of individual liberty, with massacre by the million in the stupendous conflicts which are the natural outcome of the competition of various national capitalist combines. The advent of machinery and the large industry creates a saving of labour by the hundred and the thousand-fold; not as yet in the reduction of the hours of labour, but in the reduction of the number of labourers required by the employers.

But the marshalling of the workers into large masses under single managements also generates among them the spirit of co-operation and solidarity as a class. With the result that, the people having learnt to labour in common, nothing now remains but for them to appropriate the fruits of their labour in common.

This will be done by transferring the capitalist means of production – the earth and its fruits, mines and quarries, raw materials, tools and machinery, means of exchange, etc. – from private to social ownership; and thus effect such a revolution that capitalist industry, which has hitherto been a source of misery and oppression to the classes whom it has despoiled, may become the source of the most comprehensive social harmony.

By becoming masters of the product of their toil, the workers will emancipate themselves from the slavery of wage labour.

To effect this revolution is the work of the proletariat in all lands, and by them alone can it be achieved, as all other classes have a common interest in the continuation of the capitalist system.

The working class and the capitalist class have therefore nothing in common.

The interests of the workers are identical in all lands; and all wage-labourers have a common aim irrespective of any difference of colour and race. It therefore follows that labour cannot emancipate itself in South Africa until it has conquered all race prejudice and antipathy of colour. The emancipation of labour is a task in which the workers of all lands have a share.

The economic domination of the capitalist class is maintained by capitalist control of the public power. The first step in the proletarian revolution will therefore be the capture of that public power by and on behalf of the whole working class: thus asserting the political dictatorship of the proletariat.

Whether the political dictatorship of the proletariat will be best effected in South Africa through the present representative institutions or by a Council of Workmen, will be decided by the degree of parliamentary representation enjoyed by the revolutionary proletariat when the hour of revolution strikes. The disfranchisement of the great bulk of the South African proletariat will in any case render necessary a Council of Workmen with local Soviets to control the situation. Meanwhile elections to public bodies shall be considered as part of the platform propaganda of Socialism, whenever expedient.

Under the shield of political dictatorship the proletariat will destroy the oppressive institutions of the capitalist state, the courts of law, the police, the prisons, the armed power and the bludgeon of Government.

It will organise the industry of the community, and nurture the proletarian control and management thereof in the whole and in its parts.

All repressive institutions having vanished with the repression of the proletariat, nothing will remain except the need to maintain and increase the productive power of industry by an ever-expanding development of machinery and natural resources and co-operation of labour forces.

Each individual plant will be controlled by its own Committee of Workmen. Each individual industry by its Association of such Committees. Industry as a whole by combination of these associations into one Industrial Republic, national and international, which will co-ordinate the industrial activities and supply the needs of all the people.

Thus, with the obligation of all to work, all classes will vanish, and the last act of the political dictatorship of the proletariat will be to abolish itself. The Class State will die out. Nothing will remain but the administration of things, leaving all men free to develop themselves according to their boundless possibilities.

To accomplish this revolution in South Africa is the aim of the International Socialist League. Already the path has been cleared by the glorious Socialist Revolution in Russia on November 7th, 1917. And although the development of capitalist industry already described herein has not reached general maturity in South Africa, the advent of the proletarian revolution in Europe makes imminent the destruction of capitalist domination in all countries.

It is the work of the ISL to educate, agitate and organise the workers for the great task that is ahead of effecting the revolution in our own land. It is especially its work to attend to the aspect of the struggle peculiar to South Africa, occasioned by the presence in South Africa of a large mass of unlettered native population, newly emerging from primitive manhood, and partially assimilated by the system of wage labour. To awaken and inspire our native fellow workers to grapple with their responsibility as part and parcel of the world proletariat must be our urgent duty. As part of this task the white workers must be encouraged to educate, organise and co operate with their native fellow workers at the place of work in mine, factory and workshop: in order that the Socialist Republic of South Africa may be inaugurated by the unanimous solidarity of all the workers.

[Proposed by the Benoni Branch, International Socialist League and adopted as a Declaration of Principles by the ISL in 1920.]

Illiterate Native Workers

The International, January 4 1919

What is it that constitutes for us the "problem" of the native workers? We put the word "problem" in quotation marks advisedly, because for the working class movement, as. Marx told Proudhon many years ago, "there are no problems to solve." Working class dialectic puts no conundrums. It studies what is, and what is becoming: and accelerates the becoming. The solutions appear before we have time to put problems.

Putting aside all thought of European developments for the moment; what is there lacking in South African industrial development to consummate the social revolution.

Firstly, the increasing development of large industry in all important departments of production. That is not our task, but that of the bourgeoisie, so far as they are conscious agents of the process of which they form part.

Secondly, the increasing development of the proletariat, their growing solidarity and unification. We read in the *Communist Manifesto* that the linking up of a whole country by railways also links up the workers.

But that assumes a common language, a common medium of communication. And that also implies elementary knowledge of reading and writing. That is lacking yet in the South African proletariat; and to accelerate its coming is our task as a movement.
The task requiring to be done before the revolution is the same as that which, if the Day finds it unfinished, will have to be continued after the Revolution. That the Revolution is impending elsewhere, and will precipitate ours, makes no difference to our course of action or to the nature of our task.

Fortunately perhaps for the native worker, the Government has not concerned itself overmuch with his primary education. Like the Russian worker, not having a vote, there has been no need to "educate" him in the right way of voting. The lack is supplied by religious bodies, and that will be found to account to a great degree for the attraction which these religious organisations have for the native. In small nationalities struggling to retain its vernacular against the imperial language, the religious Sunday school will be found to flourish best. For these supply elementary education in the reading and writing of the vernacular (as in the case of the Welsh language) which is denied in the Government schools. Thus the religious organisation gets the kudos for a success which is only half religious, the other half being a secular desire to attain knowledge.

This tuition of reading and writing it should be the function of the Socialist movement to supply. It will have to be its function for some time after the triumph of the proletariat. A solid proletariat is helped by a common language. I think it beyond question that there is a universal desire among natives to learn English. However that may be, the primary need is a knowledge of the printed word, let it be English or Zulu. But the tendency to a common language should be encouraged. Else how can we cope with the need which was felt in Russia from the Liberal revolution of March to the proletarian revolution of November, when the chief Bolshevik papers issued four and five hundred thousand copies daily?

Here is a way of approach to native propaganda, an approach which is "irreproachable," from the point of view of those who would bring down the mailed fist on us for "incitement." The main cause of the failure of Socialist Sunday Schools is that they supply no need of education other than Socialistic teaching itself – direct. With the full glare of the electric torch of Socialism; which makes it clear as day to us who hold the torch, but blinds the path to those whom we would show the way. The teaching of Socialism will be most successful when it is incidental, affords the atmosphere, to the teaching of something more elementary, such as music, dancing, or reading and writing. Then it comes with dimmed light into the mind. It also makes the movement comply with a universal law which seems to demand from movements as from men that it give before it shall receive.

For instance, in teaching a native to read and write, give him for dictation or for copying on his slate (for that comes first) Karl Marx's call "Workers of the world unite, you have nothing to lose but your chains, and a world to win." Say nothing to him of the sentiment which he "ought" to take to heart, or that he "ought" to remember the words of the great master, or that he "ought" to tell all his friends all about it. No! I only concern myself with getting him to write it down passably well, after he has got his ABC to heart. Teach him to write, which is palpably for his good. But let the objects, examples, instances and "discipline" (as Fluellen would say) be in the language of Socialism. The learner will imbibe them all the more readily because they are not obtruded upon his attention, but form the atmosphere of his schooling.

The Iron Heel. Is it Propaganda?

The International, January 10 1919

"Have you read *The Iron Heel?* You really should, you know!" Who has not been buttonholed by some comrade or other with this question? If you cannot say. "Yes" you are not much class in the Socialist movement.

There it is on the bookshelf! For the sake of peace and quietness let's read it through. Let us see! Chapter One, Two, Three: Love story, or story of young love, with Karl Marx as Cupid. Very charming and all that.

Peace to the soul of Jack London! This belated review reflects not on love, only on the propaganda value of the book. The first nine chapters, so far as we know anything about style and that sort of thing, are excellent reading. They weave into the love's awakening discourses and battles royal between the muscular Socialist hero, Everhard, and the various groups of bourgeoisie; with pathetic accounts of victims of the industrial machine, completing what we shall consider the first part of the book with two chapters describing, in Jack London's brilliant Americanese, the laws of capitalist accumulation. These two chapters are celebrated. They show how the countries of the world are developing capitalist industry at an accelerating rate and producing surpluses which they all want to dump in a world market that is ever dwindling to the vanishing point, culminating in a world crisis such as we are truly face to face with to-day.

Soon the inevitable conflict for the remaining world market breaks out between America and Germany; and this is not the only unverified prophecy to the credit of the book. To prevent the world conflict, Jack London proceeds to describe a complete General Strike of the workers of Germany and America, so complete that all communications are cut off and the whole of the people go on holiday – a rollicking time it was. The Oligarchy in both countries conceded the point, obeyed the Socialist ultimatum, stopped the war, came to heel – and went on with the exploitation of labour! Here was the Revolution; but Jack did not recognise it. Here the book should have closed triumphantly with the hero's wedding and the inauguration of the

Socialist Commonwealth, which latter could have been the only outcome of the events described in the chapter on the General Strike, as it amounted to a general lock out of the capitalist class. Instead of that Jack makes the proletariat go back to work, meekly to bend the yoke to the exploiters for another seven centuries. For no other reason, as far as we can see, than to do Karl Marx a shot in the eye for being so "peskily shrewd"! Or was it because there were no Socialist members of Congress to ratify the thing constitutionally?

After this there are eleven more chapters, a kind of an Apocalypse. So far Karl Marx, with Austin Lewis, has been a super in the drama. Now that Jack's proletariat has gone balmy Karl Marx disappears from the book. The plot now bedraggles itself through another eleven chapters without any guiding principle of art, history, or economics; other than a perfervid imagination visualising a horrible social nightmare. These eleven chapters are all right as a solemn warning to society, but not as a sequel to the Marxian ones; and the Socialist movement should have been kept out of its miasma. Mud sticks to the art that paints with it more than to the thing painted. There is a subtle boomerang in our lurid anti-militarist cartoons, if you will notice: Molochs sacrificing the young by millions in its eternal fires – or gigantic War Gods whose vast jaws draw in the teeming populations to death and despair, great ogres of militarism and monsters unnameable – these things need to be done with great restraint and art. They appeal to the reason of the converted, but the impression on the unreasoning psychology of the popular mind is that the party that paintg "them things" is itself an uncanny, Seventh Day Adventist kind of outfit. That is the effect of the association of the Socialist movement with the Oligarchic monstrosity in these eleven chapters.

Well now, in Chapters 13 and 14 the proletariat are back again starting their seven century night-shift. Although there is no longer any world market, the book hardly realises that it has killed the capitalist system. But it is troubled nevertheless about the surplus of production. So the Oligarchy sets about finding ways and means of consuming the surplus. It has a million or more mercenaries – to consume the surplus. A favoured labour caste – to consume the surplus. A vast army of satellites, art, "Great Art", wonder cities never dreamed of by man – all to consume the surplus, the "perplexing surplus!" The puzzle is: why the dickens didn't this Oligarchy, seeing that it was looking for means of consuming the surplus, dump some of it on the People of the Abyss, and then all the bother would be finished.

Barring its economics, this second portion of the book would have been all right placed before the other nine, as a not too overdrawn picture of the present system. And as for the economics of these eleven chapters, perhaps they are meant to infer that Socialism is indeed the only possible outcome. An Oligarchy whose incentive was to consume the surplus of production would very soon end up in consuming the productive forces themselves.

The Co-operative Commonwealth is therefore the only conception of society to-day that is not Utopian, the only system that can preserve the productive forces. The capitalist system is to-day itself Utopian, impossible. It stands overwhelmed by the force of its own tremendous backwash. And it survives only by the artificial oxygen of militarism.

But without going into much detail on economics, the main reason why the *Iron Heel* is bad propaganda is that throughout these eleven chapters the Socialist movement is presented as a marauding band of anarchists and terrorists, engaged, not in the Great Idea, but in espionage, trickery. legerdemain, capital executions, secret service, bomb manufacture and everything that is the antithesis of Socialism. It is a travesty of the Socialist idea, casting a lurid and uncanny gloom over the whole conception. Its eleven chapters of anarchism can be depended upon to annul its two chapters of Marxian teaching. It also spreads a healthy pessimism calculated to damp the ardour of any would-be convert. The suggestion of those seven centuries of waiting is worth a lot to the bourgeoisie. Hence the book can be bought in sevenpenny editions on Hoy's railway bookstall, while Marxian literature can only be produced by Socialist effort.

I should say: leave the *Iron Heel* out as propaganda. There is more humanity, beauty and truth, in fine, more Socialism, in Jack London's unsophisticated *White Fang* than in all his conscious propaganda efforts.

Right About! Demobilise

The International, February 7 1919

The new demobilisation plans are published. Rather we should say: this week's demobilisation plans came out last week end. What the plans for next week will be does not follow. A few weeks ago "Conscription" was the word. The abolition of conscription depended upon other Powers doing likewise. Demobilisation was to be at the rate of a few thousand per week. Lloyd George sat on the fence even before the general election and only promised repeal of conscription if the Devil would let him. Surely, we thought, after the election he will go the whole hog for conscription. But to-day he's sounding the "Dismiss" to beat the whole "No Conscription" band. What's the matter.

How oft did the fire-eating Imperialists not prescribe "Conscription" as the antidote for (militant) Trade Unionism and Socialism? Indade! Indade! They've gone clean crazy; lost their heads. The rains came and the winds came and blew upon that house of theirs. They did not know that conscription carried in the heat of "national peril" meant the armed people. And when the ghost of "national peril" has been laid they have seen what the armed people can do.

The working class with rifles in its hands spells Bolshevism. Russia revealed it, it was Light from the East to them. And Germany has put the matter beyond doubt. And, it may be, when their job of "fighting for Liberty" was over, the sobered British working man in uniform began to think "sominat" [to dream] along that left bank of the Rhine.

Indeed, we had hints of same, accompanied by ever-increasing daily drafts for home and blighty, but the British ruling class, as Marx said, is "peskily shrewd." When England and America embarked on conscription, they prepared the way by voluntary recruiting; that is, they prepared the way by forming an army of those most likely to be faithful to their cause, with which to bludgeon the rest to fall in.

They are falling back on the same tactic to beat the revolution. The armed people is the armed working class. At the eleventh hour they will save the burning building of capitalism with their time-honoured fire hose; demobilise the people, and raise a voluntary army of 900,000 for "Ireland," "internal order" (blessed word), the Russian Bolsheviks, the Rhine (which means German Bolshevism) and the Balkan revolution. The League of Nations' Guard of Gunmen.

Weel a weel, I do be thinking ye're closing the door after the horse is oot.

The Dangers of Lip Piety. Inoculating Bolshevism with Labourism

The International, February 14 1919

Bolshevism receives the most unexpected receptions. Where one would expect execration we hear half-hearted endorsement. Indeed, in South Africa, Bolshevism is becoming quite respectable with Labourites and petty bourgeois, gaining applause in quarters where the word International Socialism is still anathema and bad for trade. "Verily, verily," we might say of the pacifist reformists and the unreformed [Morris] Kentridges and [Henry] Sampsons [Labour Members of the Legislative Assembly], "ye white-wash the graves of the prophets and persecute their children."

Bolshevism is something like a bomb to draw press attention when you are laying about with a will on that marionette stage – the Johannesburg Town Council.

Let us beware of Labourite piety. Let us keep them to the issue. Let us hold fast to the meaning of it, the ideal which Lenin is so fond of holding before the eyes of the Russian proletariat to nerve them to the struggle – not "economic industrialism," not "Industrial Socialism," not "pacifism," but "International Socialist Revolution"! And in South Africa the word "International Socialism" has acquired a meaning from which Labourite lip piety to Bolshevism shrinks with terror. That meaning is solidarity of the proletariat irrespective of colour.

Why do the pacifist petty bourgeoisie sing paeans to Bolshevism in South Africa, while their prototypes in Russia under the Right "Social Revolutionaries" conspire by every means to wreck the Soviet Republic? For the same reason that the British capitalist class applauded [Karl] Liebknecht and persecuted John Maclean.

When the [Johannesburg] *Star* threw bouquets at Liebknecht in the early days of the war did we welcome a conversion to International Socialism? They only saw in Liebknecht a fighter against German capitalism, not a fighter for the proletariat. Likewise the militant petty trader class who are merely anti-capitalist without being pro-proletarian – they only see in Bolshevism an enemy of their enemy. It has not come near enough home for them yet to realise or care that Bolshevism is pro-proletarian, the movement of the industrial proletariat, and therefore anti- every other class that stands in the way of its advance, the petty bourgeois class not excepted. When our pro-Bolshevik Labourites realise this – that party of small agents and shopkeepers – their deeds of to-day, like their record on the war, assure us that they will be found conspiring against the proletarian revolution when the testing time comes.

This approval of all ranks for the time being answers well in restraining intervention campaigns; it keeps the ring for the revolution. But with us also the times are urgent. We are within measurable distance in South Africa, not of revolution, but of commercial and political collapse consequent upon the European revolution. And with our great black proletariat, and the great hatred against it by the white population with their machine guns and aeroplanes, the prospect demands serious study and preparation.

Just now, while the mining interest is dominant, it is easy to quell any anti-native pogroms, such as the incipient one at Benoni the other day. But with the collapse of international credit, will they bother to run the mines (assuming that America is too embarrassed to step in and control)? With the vanishing of that great economic interest which makes towards equality of the proletariat irrespective of colour, it will then become the ruling class motive (and the ruling class will be the Boer farmer class) to incite civil strife and bloodshed to keep down the ambitious native, to retain him, that is, in his place – the place of a good farm labourer. The economic forces will then have a centrifugal effect. They will tend towards race wars.

To avert this is the great task of the ISL To this matter we have devoted *The International*. In the beginning we fondly preached the doctrine that industrial unionism was an arm of power which could achieve the revolution without bloodshed. Although today we have to do largely with the military victories and defeats of the revolution, yet our preparations must ever be those of industrial solidarity. We are always to assume that the revolution will be bloodless. And the way to assume it here is to pin solidarity with the native worker as the *sine qua non* of [the essential pre-condition for] Bolshevism.

The great strategic factor in this work is the white trade unionist. The economic difference between him and the native is the same in kind as that between the skilled ASE [Amalgamated Society of Engineers] man and the "dilutee" in England. We remarked after the Troyeville election that in appealing to the white worker for solidarity with his black fellow worker we did a double work; for the echo of it reached the native too, besides being a guarantee to the natives that we are not looking after cheap "leaderships" among them.

The rigging up of skeleton "Workmen's Councils" like "bogus branches" is futile work, besides being a conspiracy, and outside our function as a party of political propaganda. Our task must ever be to sound again the clarion of solidarity, familiarising the workers with the Shop Stewards Idea, getting white workers to admit Jim Sixpence more and more, with a comradely cuff on the ear perhaps at first. They will do it! The generous idea is surely gaining ground among them. And when the hour strikes, the Workmen's Councils will spring into being overnight.

Republicanism: Whither does it Lead?

The International, February 28 1919

The Republican campaign may have more far-reaching consequences than we have yet imagined, and its effect on the revolutionary movement in South Africa needs to be taken into account. On the face of it, it seems absurd for a party seeking to accomplish its purpose by a majority to go outside and attain that purpose by intervention or some means not yet divulged. We are not told what the Nationalist deputation will ask for. Will it ask for Wilson's moral support, or an assurance from the Powers that they will not thwart by military intervention the expressed will of a majority here?

It has been demonstrated that the imperialist opposition to Nationalism, and vice-versa, although ruthless and bitter, does not rest on fundamental antagonisms. Nationalism is inconvenient and harassing to capitalist expansion, not to the capitalist system. When the capitalist system is imperilled by the proletariat, petty nationalism is then capitalism's Old Guard; it is unleashed to massacre the Social Revolution, as in the case of the Poles, Ukrainians, Czecho-Slovaks, etc. Lloyd George's objection to the Nationalists will be: "We don't want you yet."

We have Sinn Fein so far as an exception. But can the crowd of farmers, lawyers and small landowners who form the leadership of Nationalism in this country be looked upon as intransigeants to the bitter end? No! Their interests are bourgeois. We can only hope to sever from them their poor white and proletarian following – that following which when the hour strikes will be armed to crush the revolutionists and slaughter the native workers, if that same following is "loyal" to its masters.

An interesting item appears in a *Nieuwe Rotterdamsche Courant* of November last, in which the opinion is expressed that unless Smuts returns "with a handsome present of increased independence" a Dutch Government will appear in South Africa with a strongly marked nationalist tendency.

"Or would it be possible that President Wilson should see to it that the question of an independent Republican Government, at least in the late Republics, should be settled by a plebiscite? We remind our readers of a motion of Deputy Cary in the American House in April last year, expressing the wish that the Transvaal and Orange Free State should be restored to independence. This motion was accepted, and referred to the Committee for Foreign Affairs in the Senate.

That sounds interesting: America just waking up to the fact that there was a Boer War! Incidentally also American capital increasing its interest in South African industry! Traditions of Queen Victoria make it awkward to exploit our army of cheap labour properly, and pitchfork them off the soil. What more useful in this direction than a Nationalist Republic, whose chief mark to posterity will be its firm conviction that the "K*s" have no souls and are created in the Devil's image to be slaves for the Whites?

No one in the Nationalist or Imperialist camps has the sinister intentions of these possibilities But bourgeois psychology moves instinctively towards the attainment of bourgeois interests without formulating them too far in advance. It is the task of the Socialist movement to detect them and forestall their tendencies by propaganda.

That is to say, with a Nationalist Government, the Afrikander will become ripe for Socialism. And the sooner Hertzog resumes his pick-handle sceptre the better

"CINCINNATUS"

All Roads Lead to Revolution

The International, March 28 1919

Capitalism has come to the cross where all roads lead to revolution.

Allied capitalism continued the war as long as it could because war had become the world market, and it kept out an important competitor from the world's unexploited areas.

The war however ended by an accident unforeseen by the Allies – the "accident" of the German revolution; and the double danger menaced "us" of losing our chief market, war, as well as of allowing Germany to enter the already attenuated world market.

Nothing for it then but to keep up the blockade of Germany and throttle her industries by famine and a ring fence against raw materials.

Result: The rise of Bolshevism, menacing the very next door of the Allies. All appeals by the German bourgeoisie to dish the Soviet movement by allowing in food and encouraging employment were met by their Allied brothers with a knowing wink. Being sharpers themselves they weren't going to be taken in by any confidence tricks. It was the cry of "wolf" heard many times before.

But now the "wolf" of Bolshevism has really come, and the Allies are hastening to lift the blockade to give German bourgeoisdom a chance to restore industry and combat Bolshevism.

That means allowing the hated competitor into the market again, with a wry face. We have talked a lot about capital being international, but the revolution is hastened by the fact that the various national bourgeoisies are not conscious of their identity of interest until it is too late. Their internecine wrangle is socialism's opportunity, and now the only alternatives left to them are to hang together or hang separately.

The White Workers' "Burden"

Communist International 11 April 1919

There is a danger of allowing assumptions, to crystallise. How much harder is it to unlearn than to learn! It has often been repeated by us that the revolution is more backward here in South Africa than elsewhere, because of the "backward races." That may be so with regard to the consolidation of the revolution. But its effect may be the reverse upon the conquest of political dictatorship.

Here are two distinct phases in the revolution. Long after the November 7th Revolution, that is, after the conquest of political dictatorship by the Russian proletariat, Lenin warned the Russian people that they were yet a long way from being revolutionary.

In theory it is pernicious to divide the proletariat, and our propaganda is ever towards the idea of solidarity irrespective of colour. But the fact is, that as a result of the colour line, there is a sharp division of function between the white and black workers.

Contrary to common assumptions, skilled labour in South Africa can as a rule paralyse industry more effectively than in white countries because of the native proletariat. We will see how.

Industry today requires a high average standard of intelligence. In South Africa the skilled trades are in fairly good demand compared to the supply. In white countries the gradation from the highly skilled down to the lowest unskilled descends by imperceptible stages. Even among the unskilled there are large numbers of workers of high intelligence. In the ranks of these the employing class have a weapon against the skilled trades. There is no clear cut line as in South Africa. Hence the skilled trades in white countries are economically far weaker than in a country like ours.

We are too apt to think of the white workers in terms of mining. In the mines the white worker is generally a ganger [a foreman in charge of labourers]. But follow him to the other trades, carpenters, fitters, bricklayers – here the native labourer does about the same work as a fitter's or carpenter's labourer or hodman in Europe. But go further to tramwaymen and railwaymen. Instead of the proportion of ten to one as on the mines, here the native workers are about equal to whites, while on the running staffs there are hardly any natives.

The presence of this big gap in function (not in the interest) between the bulk of the white and the native workers renders the white proletariat master of the *political* situation, using "political" in the broad Marxian sense. This is the only section of the proletariat as yet politically articulate.

The position then is this: The white workers can themselves win political dictatorship for the proletariat. But, as has been well said, *unless within twenty-four hours after the revolution the whole proletariat experiences the joyousness of freedom* (even though hungry), the revolution fails. And the immediate work of the revolution must be to bring out in freedom the latent possibilities of the native workers, arousing their co-operation in the work of construction, and making them partners through education and emulation in the great work of consolidating the revolution and forming their very own Commonwealth of Labour.

To get the economic machine to run again the white workers are wholly dependent upon their native fellow workers. In the hour of collapse they will pretty soon realise the fact. And here our fact will fall in line with our theory – the working class becomes one, knowing no demarcation of colour.

It is only on this view that we can account for the fact, that Reform Socialism and Mugwump Labour, so strong yet in white countries, are so bankrupt in South Africa. We often say that the white worker is himself an exploiter. If this were essentially true, we should expect a strong middle party of Labour on the political field. But such a movement has only transient success simply because the white worker is only superficially an exploiter, only transiently conservative. The difference in industrial function makes him appear to be an exploiter only to hasty observers. An exploiter renders no service. Skilled wage labour that requires the aid of unskilled wage labour is exploited labour none the less for its supervisory duties.

There may be many accidents accounting for an economic interest being almost unreflected or badly reflected in the political field. But what is to account for the fact that no propaganda, no line of action except the revolutionary one seems to fit the bill in industrial South Africa? Where is the Single Tax, where Liberal Labourism? It has a town club provided by capitalist friends.

The only way to account for this is by the assumption that the white proletariat is a revolutionary factor, it is the engine of revolution in South Africa, just as the comparatively small industrial proletariat of Russia steered the big mass of the Russian people into the Soviet Republic.

It may also be said that the native workers are ultimately the true revolutionists, with potentialities undeveloped, and that the clarity of the class struggle here is really due to their mass psychology. Be it so. The working class is interdependent. And we have only put the matter in other words. The moral therefore is: while not abating our cry for unity of the proletariat, white and black, let us not slide into the false idea of Unity which sneers at either section of the proletariat. For that is to be anti-proletarian in the below-zero direction.

Reflections on Remand

The International, April 18 1919

Some of our contemporaries have a column of persiflage which they call "Tattle" or "Table Talk" or such like into which they throw all the odds and ends that are no earthly use otherwise. I propose a column like that "for this week only," not because we have odds and ends to throw in, but because this week I have really had occasion for "Reflections."

It started with the Bobby No. 20. New on the job, he was back in a sunny suburban street of Maritzburg. He seemed bored for something heroic to do when I turned up with my two little Indian boys – the three of us loaded with leaflets and on the job. Here was No. 20's chance. The heading was enough: "The Bolsheviks are Coming." In five minutes he paced away proudly with my name and address and visions of a distinguished career before him.

Next day (here's where Reflection number one comes in) I bumped against him and a 'tec in the main street. They politely requested me to come down to the CID [Criminal Investigation Department]. Not arrested, oh, no! Just for a friendly chat with the "Chief." He wanted to see me. I mildly refused, and reminded them they had my address.

Now why do (or is it "does") the CID do this sort of thing. Suppose I had been going along that sunny street burglarising. Would they have asked me down "for a talk"? We Communists (good word that) are either committing a crime or not. Then this desire for an "interview" looks dangerously like compounding a felony on the CID's part; and if acceded to, looks like bartering a principle, on our part.

They are so used to the fair-weather Labour leader who blows his tin whistle of Labour Agitation before the capitalist's house, not to rouse the workers, but to get a penny to shift to the next street – a job in the government service or in the Cabinet. They must think we are after a government billet too.

Well, next day saw me down there, under a more pressing invitation. The Chief, a genial old Major, could not refrain a verbal nudge and a twinkle: "You came down this time, eh!" Indeed, while the Sherlock Holmes and he were drawing up the charge sheet, you'd think I was a specially good customer, so courteous were they.

We'll pass over the magistrate, who took a very serious view indeed of the case, had, in, fact, himself issued the warrant. Luckily for these "Reflections," the hundred pounds required were not forthcoming till Monday, and here I was on Thursday looking at the big strong walls of His Majesty's Gaol, topped with broken bottles. Indeed, indeed,

I know not whether laws are right

Or whether laws are wrong.
All that they know who lie gaol
Is that the walls are strong.

Gaol is the pill of wage slavery without the sugar coating of "democracy." It is an epitome of the capitalist system.

But what struck me in gaol was the nonchalance of the native. He walked, or slouched about as if he owned the place. He worked less than his mate outside, simply because the only effective punishment is too expensive. His wants are so few, then how can you punish him. And herein I made a discovery, or rather discovered a discovery known long ago to Jim Sixpence.

Luther said: "I nothing have, therefore I nothing fear." Marx echoed: "Nothing to lose but your chains." That is, reduce your denominator, and your nominator also falls.

Put it algebraically, 5/9ths is a fraction. 9 is your denominator – your wants. 6 is nominator, your satisfaction thereof. Full happiness requires 9/9ths. Fully misery 1/9th. But reduce your Wants, your Denominator! Then, while misery may be nearer, satisfaction is equally so; until Jim Sixpence comes down to 4, the non-reducible Nominator and Denominator, impervious to the shafts of ill, but still open to a little more satisfaction. Do you see it? You don't follow that? Shows it's good algebra!

Take my example then. So few can grasp formulas without examples: "Waiting trial" prisoners have a scale of privileges, such as food from outside, if they like; newspapers, their own bed, see friends twice a week, write letters, etc., if they like. They must also observe all the prison regulations like any convict. Penalties for breaches thereof: loss of privileges!

But suppose, as in my case, you waive all "privileges." Then there can be no "penalties." You are a free man. One night I felt particularly happy, and started whistling in my cell. The night warder soon began to start, lifted the shutter in the big round Cyclops eye in the cell door and shouts: "Heigh, whistling not allowed." Between retorts I continue whistling. "Can't a man be happy?" "No," says he with great concern. Presently, after more altercation, he goes off, not so much in wrath as in consternation; as if a man and not a poor regulation was getting killed to the torturing strains of "Pop goes the King and God save the Weasel." He runs for the head warder. He is a long way off. But presently they both return at the double to save the poor regulation. Meanwhile I am wetting my whistle with the water of which the prison diet allows a liberal supply. They burst into the cell, the big Dutch warder craning over his superior as if he expected to see the strangled corpse of his poor regulation at my feet. There were warnings, solemn warning, and more warnings as the officer closed the door with the air of Jove going to forge his thunderbolts.

But the thunderbolts did not come! Simply because: no privileges, no penalties! I think this is one of the great discoveries, the honour for which is shared between Martin Luther, Karl Marx and Jim Sixpence!

I don't think the above Contempt of Court. Like the flowers that bloom in the spring, they have nothing to do with the case. The leaflet may be sub judice, but prisons, not yet. Though we never know how soon we'll have to turn them into cattle sheds.

THE BOLSHEVIKS ARE COMING!

Leaflet published in English, Zulu and Sotho. The conviction of co-authors DI Jones and LH Greene in April 1919 for defying censorship and inciting alarm and unrest was overturned by the Supreme Court.
Republished in *The International*, April 25 1919

To the Workers of South Africa – Black as well as White

A spectre is haunting Europe – the spectre of Bolshevism!

What is this Bolshevism that the ruling class is so much afraid of?

Why do they send British Armies to Russia to fight the Bolsheviks?

Have they not had enough killing? Or is it a thirst for righteousness that makes them pack Tommy Atkins off to freeze in the snows of Archangel, just when he was looking forward to Home and Blighty?

The Czar massacred half a million nomads in Southern Russia in one swoop. They did not send an army against him.

Why then are they so scared of Bolshevism? Why do they turn pale at its shadow as at the ghosts of murdered men? Why?

We will tell you why!

The Great War of Nations is over, and the Class War against Labour has openly begun.

Bolshevism means the rule of the working class! And where the workers rule, the Capitalists cannot carry on their Robber System any more.

A Campaign of Lies

Workers! Do not be misled when the Capitalist Press reviles the Bolsheviks. They slander the Bolsheviks because they have lost the fat money bags they lent to the Czar to crush the Russian people.

They slander the Bolsheviks because they have lost the rich mines and factories which the Russian workmen are now working for themselves; and the land, which forty million peasants are farming in common under the Soviet Republic.

They slander the Bolsheviks because they fear you will follow suit. They are afraid the workers in South Africa will also become free and independent.

They are losing their hair over Bolshevism because they see a prospect of losing their Profits.

Bolshevism Means Labour on Top

The workers of Russia and Germany are forming themselves into Soviets – that is: Councils of Workmen.

They are taking over the control of the country into their own hands – the hands of the great wage-earning proletariat. That means the end of the Profiteering System, the end of the Capitalist exploitation of wage-labour for profit.

Why have the workers of Russia and Germany to shed their blood?

Because the Capitalist Class of all countries will sooner tear the people to pieces with their cannon rather than let the people rule. The workers are the people.

Remember the massacre of the workers in Johannesburg in 1913 and in Bloemfontein last February!

Down with British Militarism! It is a weapon to crush the workers.

Down with Allied intervention in Russia!!

Down with the Capitalist Class in all countries!!!

The hope of the workers is coming from Bolshevism. The free commonwealth of labour is an actual fact in Russia today.

Bolshevism means the victory of the wage-earners. It will soon spread to Britain, France, America and throughout the world.

Get Ready for the World-wide Republic of Labour

The way to get ready is to combine in the workshops. Combine as workers, no matter what colour.

Remember that an injury to one is an injury to all, be he black or white.

While the black worker is oppressed, the white worker cannot be free.

Before Labour can emancipate itself black workers as well as white must combine in one organisation of Labour, irrespective of craft, colour or creed.

This is Bolshevism: The Solidarity of Labour.

WORKERS OF THE WORLD UNITE!
You have nothing to lose but your Chains.
You have a world to win!!

Syndicalism in Action

The International, April 25 1919

The Natal papers stigmatised the Johannesburg Board of Control as the first Soviet of South Africa. It is good to have it acknowledged that Soviet is only another name for Workers' Control of industry. But you cannot grow figs off thorns nor gain the Social Revolution until the political temperature is revolutionary. We have not yet locked out the capitalist class so long as we have to pay the takings into the masters' bank account.

The method of revolution taught us both by Marx and by events, still remains valid, namely to capture proletarian dictatorship as the first step.

All other methods lead to the quandary we witnessed the other day: The workers nominally on strike but working the services in the interest of the public, and paying the takings into the masters' bank account; thus relieving their masters from any responsibility in the matter, and saving them from coming to any decision.

Such experiments can only be successful by forcing the whole proletariat to capture control first of political power, preferably through Soviets. Nothing is premature if it succeeds. A drop of water put into the pump often makes the pump give water. As such, our Johannesburg Board of Control might have started the revolution. But in the absence of political dictatorship the difficulties of management are made ten times more difficult. The revolutionary discipline which is necessary to replace capitalist discipline is moreover not there yet. And a failure will be advertised by the capitalist press as a splendid argument against Bolshevism and Soviet Control.

A Municipal Commune might materialise managed by a Workers' Council, if the capitalist lion will consent to lay down with the Soviet lamb. But, that is a big IF.

The Workers' Rally. May Day Demonstration

The International, May 2 1919

Words almost fail us to describe the success of the May Day Demonstration. After the riot on Sunday night there was some apprehension among comrades regarding the wisdom of the ISL participating in the procession. This was not improved by a vote of 17 to 14 in the General Council of the Federation against our taking a certain place in the procession. But at the Conference of Shop Stewards on Monday our deputation composed of Comrades Andrews and Ivon Jones were given a favourable assurance, and arrangements for mutual co-operation were concluded between our deputation and the Executive of the Federation on Wednesday with the utmost cordiality.

At nine o'clock May Day morning the various Trade Union and ISL platforms lined up on the spacious Union Ground, the ISL being first in the field with its equipment, and with the major portion of the crowd waiting for the International speakers. Comrade WH Andrews took the Chair with a few opening remarks, and introduced the resolutions published by us last week.

The first, expressing the solidarity of the toiling masses in all lands, was moved by Comrade Tinker, seconded by Comrade Colin Wade. The second resolution contained a demand for the withdrawal of those Allied troops who are being used to crush the Revolution in the different countries. This was moved by Comrade SP Bunting and seconded by Ivon Jones. The third resolution urged as a means to the Revolution the industrial solidarity of the workers irrespective of race, colour, sex or creed, moved by Comrade CB

Tyler and seconded by Comrade Rodger, with Comrade Banks supporting.

The speeches were of necessity short, but terse and splendidly received by a huge crowd. The resolutions were carried with but two or three dissentients.

The Federation platform was surrounded by a big crowd and the following resolution was passed: –

> That this meeting expresses its satisfaction that after many years of effort by the strength of trade union organisation, May Day has now become a recognised Labour holiday, and pledges itself to maintain the 1st of May as a holiday in future years. Further, this meeting extends fraternal greetings to fellow-workers in all lands, and expresses the hope that a co-operative system of society, guaranteeing to all workers the full product of their labour, will be brought about in the near future by the development of industrial organisation.

The speeches concluded in a spirit of unanimous enthusiasm and the Federation and ISL marshalls mobilised the Trades Unionists and ISL members for the procession headed by the BWIU [Building Workers' Industrial Union] with the Masons' banner and the Federation Band and followed by a large concourse of Trade Unionists under their respective banners, including the time-honoured banner of the S.A. Mine Workers' IU. Then under the head of "Labour Organisations" came the International Socialist League with the "Socialist League" band, and carrying red banners representing Johannesburg, Benoni, Pretoria and the Jewish-Speaking Branches. Another beautifully designed banner with the crest of the Soviet Republic (a sickle and hammer crossed with a sheaf of wheat) and the words in bold relief, "Follow the Lead of Free Russia," was carried. "Down with Capitalism," "Long Live the Workers' International Revolution," "Workers of the World Unite," were the mottoes on the remainder.

The International was for sale, with the May Day Souvenir and a special publication for the day of Connolly's "Socialism made easy." We also had a leaflet for distribution, "May Day Appeal to Trade Unionists," reproduced in this issue under "The Rabble."

There was a most inspiring rally of Internationals, as if all were determined to give the answer to the hooliganism of the previous Sunday. An old Labour man who has watched the movement for many years said the procession was the finest in his 26 years' experience of the Rand, and the Internationals formed nearly the half of the lone line. Our band played at frequent intervals the old revolution song, "The Marseillaise," and as the procession wended through thickly packed crowds in the central streets, the Revolutionary Hymn and our own brave turn-out moved the comrades to frequent cheers. At the end followed the banner of the Industrial Socialist

League and a trolley bearing little children of the Socialist Sunday School, also with their banner and singing their Socialist songs. The closed shops along the route testified to the awakening of Labour to the significance of May Day. The Trade Union procession went along. Harrison Street towards the Zoo, and the ISL section wheeled down to the Palmerston Hall. There the band played the Red Flag to a huge concourse all wearing red badges with a sprinkling of coloured and native listeners. Further speeches were delivered from the balcony by Comrades Kessler, TP Tinker, Rodgers and Dunbar, then Comrade Andrews wound up with a speech on the constructive aspect, delineating the industrial organisation necessary for the purposes of the revolutionary movement. Comrade Andrews made especial reference to the regrettable absence of native and coloured workers from the procession, and assured them that he had found that the Federation Executive were not unfavourable to their participating, but that it had been mutually decided both by white and coloured organisations to refrain at this juncture, meanwhile making every effort to batter down the prejudice among the white rank and file.

The morning's proceedings closed up joyfully with the singing of the Red Flag

The Women's Industrial Union picnic at the Zoo lake and grounds in the afternoon was attended by huge crowds who in perfect weather thoroughly enjoyed themselves.

Bolshevism on its Trial

Statement to the Court

The International, May 16 1919

"I wished all workers, irrespective of colour, to read the pamphlet. The dictionary definition of militarism is government by military force. Tshaka drilled his troops on approved civilised methods and so became dictator. The Bolshevism I support does nor countenance murder, it will do away with murder, class distinctions and international conflict. I published the pamphlet in exercise of my political rights. I claim no special knowledge of native tribal customs. Our appeal is however to industrial workers, and being interested in the working class movement I have made a special study of conditions in industrial centres, where the great developments of modern society take place. The industrialised natives, breaking away from tribal connections, are not an unruly class, they are the hopeful element in the population. This breaking away and making a home in the industrial field is essential before the labour movement in South Africa can attain its object. The working class as a whole are the only class fighting to take control of the country (i.e., of themselves). The white workers may stop industry but cannot carry it on without the native workers. The movement is doing its utmost to develop the capacity to rule (i.e., for self determination). But the workers will not be divided into black and white: the majority, consisting, like the minority, of black and white, will rule by reason of the basic principle of the movement. The workers will never gain control until they realise that their interests are one. The natives are not yet prepared to rule the country, and that is why propaganda has to be carried on. It is most improbable that such propaganda will lead to any tribal uprising. Combining in the workshop does not mean inter-marriage. A Socialist Government of Maritzburg alone is an impossibility, but a Maritzburg Soviet would *inter alia* control judicial functions. The working class movement is not responsible for the violence which attends strikes; that is to be laid quite as much at the door of the employer. The majority is not responsible if its will is opposed. Colonel Ward's letter was written to please those in political power. "British Militarism" is exemplified in the Allied intervention against Russia, and the thanks of the Burgomaster of Coblenz to the British General for shooting down the local Soviet. Bolshevism in South Africa will mean disfranchisement of landowners and hirers of labour for profit. Bolshevism means world-wide brotherhood, without country boundaries ...

It is with this ideal in view, and not from any freak incendiarism, that we appeal to all proletarians to unite in fields, factories and workshops, in order that their voice may be articulate politically. But this working class unity which we ask for is not the unity of a section. One section of the workers can never alone appropriate the fruits of their labour, or the control of their particular industry.

The Communists hold that the emancipation of the working class must be the task of the working class itself, not of social welfare societies, charitable institutions or Native Affairs Departments: no matter how "expert" the latter may be in its "opinion" of people who mav have opinions of their own.

Creswell Sounds the Retreat. "Labour Party" but not a "Party of Labour"

The International September 5 1919

During the week, Mr FHP Creswell has addressed himself to the Labour Party's National Council in a letter occupying four columns of the *Rand Daily Mail* (to say nothing of the editorial pats on the back). There is no doubt that the letter is intended to force the pace of the party in the direction towards which Creswell thinks it ought to travel. By the welcome given to it in the Daily Press that direction may be very easily guessed at. It is a direction away from a "party of Labour" towards a "broad-based" amorphous party of the lower middle class, promising all things to all men, this year, next year, sometime, never!

The great war was fought in vain for Colonel Creswell. So far from bringing enlightenment to him it has fossilised him in his grandmotherly notions of middle-class democracy. This is no great concern of ours or of the working class. But it is our businessto acquaint the rank and file of the Labour Party whither they are being led by their *Daily Mail*-blessed leader.

Briefly, the letter may be summarised thus: First, a description of the evils of the present economic system, in language reminiscent of Creswell's more eloquent and more militant days. He sounds the tocsins of reform – tocsins undistinguishable from those which led ten million men to slaughter – all-embracing words like [British seafarers' leader Havelock] Wilson's – leading to love, or wrath consuming quite, according as "platform and other support" may decide.

Then follows a criticism of the orthodox political parties – the Labour Party included – in which he says that the Labour Party "has failed to fill the bill." Why has it failed to fill the bill? Because it is almost as bad as the SA Party, the Unionist Party and the Nationalist Party; while these parties are out to safeguard the "pecuniary interest of the landowners," etc., the Labour Party is out to back up the "pecuniary interest of the manual workers." (Note words quoted.)

In so far as Creswell objects to narrowing a party of Labour to certain sections of manual workers he is right. But that is not his complaint. Indeed he mentions the non-voting black worker. But he does not want to spread out in that voteless direction, otherwise we should have seen little of this Creswellian screed in the capitalist press. The thing to go for is a vote-getting political party, with the best vote-getting name and the best vote-getting platform. That is the sum and substance of this clarion call.

That is bad enough! But fancy a "leader of Labour" talking about the "pecuniary interests of the manual workers" in opposition to the pecuniary interest of the propertied classes. He seems to have forgotten what little he once knew: that the opposition is not a merely "pecuniary" one, but the opposition of vested interests of property to the demand of the toilers for life and for liberty. "Pecuniary interest of the manual workers"! There is the escutcheon of the Tory on the hindquarters of a Labour Leader. Let the workers pursue the spectacle "with loud.and irreverent laughter."

So scared is Creswell of the "manual workers" that he warns his party that sole reliance on them will lead to "continual intriguing and more coarse corruption in the ranks of the party of which we have had recent painful experience."

Therefore he urges his party to scrap its cumbrous platform and decide on six or ten planks such as "Land values taxation," "Municipal enterprise," "abolition of indentured labour," and so on, all very desirable if combined with the *sine qua non* of the political dictatorship of the proletariat.

But the means to the end is the acid test, no less than the end itself. We have had enough of "objectives," and the high-sounding slogans of reform. How you propose proceeding to attain them is the test of your sincerity. Creswell discards the proletariat as the power of emancipation. He gives the lie to that central assertion of the Labour movement – that the. emancipation of the working class must be the task of the workers themselves. The only place in the world where Creswell's Ten Points are pursued to-day is in Russia, under the regime of the manual worker whom Creswell, in his incorrigible blindness, so much despises as a political and moral force. It is only the intellectual stodginess and political stupidity of that lower middle class whose political ideas he represents that could produce the incongruity of a self-appointed Labour leader denying the political existence of those he is leading – or misleading. But for that stupidity, the obvious inference would he that to mislead is his direct aim.

But this is nothing to what follows. Having said in effect: "Don't base your party on the appeal to the manual workers, it will lead to intriguing and corruption," this political virgin proceeds to say:

> The party should require all its candidates to place these (ten points) in the forefront of their addresses as policies they are pledged to, and outside of these they should be free to settle with their constituents, and with those on whom they rely for plattiorm and other support, as to any particular views of their own.

If Auckland Park Sporting Club (or "other support") wants you to vote their way, you are free to bargain any "particular views" of your own so long as it isn't in the ten points. Chuck overboard the driving power of the "manual workers" with no bribes to give, and base your party on the "other support" – that immaculate middle class whose interests vary in every constituency, watering its milk here and sugaring its sand there to the tune of high Creswellian moralisings.

As for Creswell's complaint about the exclusion of "brain" workers," this is too thin altogether. None knows better than he that this distinction is never made in the Labour movement. It looks as if he were seeking excuses to quit. If there are any class conscious workers left in the Labour Party they should take this insulting document at its true value, not that of the *Rand Daily Mail*, and encourage its writer to go and form that middle-class "Democratic" party of his heart's desire outside the ranks of Labour.

"Captured body and soul"

Letter to George Eyre Evans
March 31 1921
Dear GEE,
Thanks for your letter. I was beginning to wonder what had become of you.

As it may make surprises as to my immediate plans I had better let you know by return of my immediate plans. But I am still pursuing a kind of doctor's regime which I shall see the back of in a week or so. It has done me a slight amount of good. As for the future, well the cardinal point is that I am captured body and soul by the Communist movement, and that is the burning interest in my life now. I hesitate to inflict myself on friends who are either antagonistic to the idea or are at least indifferent. Nay, perhaps the indifference I do not mind if we have other points of contact. But I cannot remain long here as my interest in the communist movement is a source of displeasure to one good friend, Mrs Evans. Although she would be the last to admit it.

It results in a lack of things in common, and for her burning interest in spiritualism I have nothing but aversion to. So that I cannot look upon Villa Via as a permanent biding place, although Mrs Evans' kindness has been very great, and she would like me to stay. But I am not yet superannuated. I still have something to do in the world given a little health. I must either get a job here soon or come to Wales and find something to do. I should like to stop here and improve my French. We live very quiet here, no friends, no visitors and always English in the house, so that I have very little practice, and we are in the suburbs, and a good way from the centre. The weather is simply perfect. Of course another point of worry is how the climate will suit.

I should like to go on a farm, ploughing and haymaking for a few months. I feel that would set me up, say in the Lampeter district, where it is drier. Ah, how the charm of the Teify draws the heart. But one is afraid of risking the pain of disillusionment. Old friends are gone from there. But the old Welsh spirit is always the same, I know.

And now that I have transcended the sectarian phase of my "infidelity" I should again love to attend the Gymanfa Ganu [Festival of Song], and hear the same good old Welsh sermons again, purely for love of the language and the symphony of its sounds. For of all the languages Welsh, I find after many wanderings, to be the most musical.

Of course that does not mean that I have conscientious objections to the Meeting House – of course not. I shall even be prepared to give a discourse – if you are prepared to listen to it – I should try to keep out points that would shock, but I fear that it would no longer be prayerful. I have lived two lives since I last left you, it seems so long ago, and one would need to be brainless not to have imbibed new ideas after so many wanderings, changes of scenes and occupations. And the world also changes – watchwords of emancipation of ten years ago, today become the slogans of reaction.

Unitarianism, once was alive, not afraid to take in the world, had a clue to the ills of the world – is it so today? Has it a way out other than death for the chaos of the world? Unitarians themselves are greater than Unitarianism – they love truth. The old order is bankrupt, from the point of view of an old pacifist idealist the world is getting worse – tyranny is raising its head higher and higher... the sufferings of the poor greater, the wars of the classes and the nations are getting more and more acute, more and more hysterical are the hatreds become, more and more feverish the hectic rush of the peoples struggling for a way out from some impending catastrophe – if all our idealisms are not to suffer more wreck, where is the clue to it all? Hence I am a Communist and a follower of Karl Marx – in very self-preservation!! You never told me that because of the Two Tommy's of the old days. Tommy Mann, what became of him?

I shall let you know when I am coming. But it does not matter if you don't know. I shall esconce myself in your chair till you come back. I may go to South Wales for a day or two to see Tom, and perhaps Aberdare where I have a comrade in the movement whom I knew a few years ago in Africa. I suppose I had better bring my books with me. I jettisoned a lot this time in leaving South Africa – but preserved the heirlooms such as "Cardiganshire and Lampeter" of course from the old days.

Well old pal, shall see you anon.

Au Revoir, as ever,

David.

Villa Vittoria, 14c Ave Capelle Besset, Nice

Communism in South Africa

Statement to the Executive Committee of the Communist International from the International Socialist League of South Africa

Communist Review, July & August 1921

The Third International has, of necessity, not given much attention to Africa so far, further than a passing recognition in the heat of the European struggle that the teeming millions of the Dark Continent are also to come under its wing. Africa may not cover such a vital part of the anatomy of Imperialism as India does, But a country's immediate contribution to the collapse of world capitalism is not its sole claim on our attention; we have to consider what positive dangers it may harbour for the movement as a whole. European capital, however, draws no mean contribution from South African cheap labour. "K*s" (as gold shares are appropriately nicknamed) are the mainstay of a large section of the bourgeoisie of Paris and London. Besides which the depressing state of the vast mass of K* labour from the point of view of proletarian development – illiteracy, generally low social and civil status and backward standards of life – is not a matter to which the Communist International can remain indifferent.

Africa's hundred and fifty million natives are most easily accessible through the eight millions or so which comprise the native populations of South Africa and Rhodesia. Johannesburg is the industrial university of the African native, although recruiting for the mines has been confined in latter years to parallel 22 in Portuguese territory.

South Africa, moreover, is an epitome of the class struggle throughout the world. Here Imperial Capital exploits a white skilled proletariat side by side with a large native proletariat. Nowhere else in the proportions obtaining on the world scale do white skilled and dark unskilled meet together in one social milieu as they do in South Africa. And nowhere are the problems so acute of two streams of the working class with vastly unequal standards of life jostling side by side, and the resultant race prejudices and animosities interfering and mixing with the class struggle.

South African Populations

The Union of South Africa, occupying the country South of the Limpopo River, comprises the old Boer Republics of the Transvaal and the Orange Free State, the old British Colonies of Natal and Cape of Good Hope. These now form one Government with their own local Provincial Councils. The more sparsely settled areas of Rhodesia and German West Africa are not yet in the Union. The white population of the Union is divided almost equally into Dutch and English extraction, with a large Jewish population in Johannesburg. The whites number about a million and a half. The feuds existing between the two main sections of the white population are matters of history, and animosities resulting therefrom are serious political factors at the present day.

The native population of the Union numbers about six millions. The native race is mainly composed of one type, called the Bantu, meaning "folk," divided into several tribes which have their remnants of tribal territory in Zululand, Basutoland, Swaziland, etc., nominally under the protection of the Imperial Government; in practice, however, the native peoples are governed by the Union's Native Affairs Department.

Between the black and white peoples there are shades. There is what is known as the coloured people. In South Africa "coloured" means "half-caste." The coloured population, inevitable accompaniment of a black and white society, numbers hundreds of thousands, mainly in the Cape Province, with large numbers in Kimberley, Johannesburg and Durban, and other industrial centres. They are a social link with the natives, though not socially intermingled. They are a section apart, aspiring to the social standards of the whites and invading the skilled trades. In the Cape Province coloured people enjoy the civil and political rights of the whites with a far larger measure of social equality than in the Transvaal.

In Natal is centred a considerable Indian population, originally indentured to the Sugar Estates. A large proportion of these people are South African born. They socially intermix with the coloured people. Further immigration of Indians is prohibited in the Union.

Industries

In a country of a million square miles, agriculture is of necessity a staple industry, though the old Boer farmers' methods are obsolete, and there are vast tracts of land held up idle by the landed syndicates in combination with the mining houses.

The Gold Industry of the Transvaal, with its Witwatersrand gold reef sixty miles long, is a world-renowned phenomenon. The Reef, with the town of Johannesburg as its centre, provides the economic stimulus for the whole country. The diamond mining industry of Kimberley and Pretoria, the coalfields of the Transvaal and Natal, the Sugar Estates of Natal, sum up such industries as affect the world market. The Railways are owned by the State.

Political and Social Currents

In such a milieu one may guess that the social relations are rather complex. After the overthrow of the old Boer Republics, the Boer political leaders, Botha and Smuts, proceeded to make friends with the mammon of unrighteousness, and fitted themselves to govern by acquiring interests in land and gold mining. By 1907 they were deemed sufficiently safe to be entrusted with self-government. There was a distinct subsidence of the animosities aroused by the war. After the Union of the Provinces in 1910 the Dutch Party was again entrusted with the Government. Hertzog, the present leader of the Republican Party, was at that time the left wing representative of the Dutch in the Cabinet as Minister of Justice, and, it may be observed in passing, the first to conceive the brilliant idea of arming the mounted police with pick handles to beat down the tramway strikers of Johannesburg. After his expulsion from the Cabinet in 1912, the Dutch Party split up into the present South African Party led by Smuts and the Nationalist Party led by Hertzog, who since the great war gives half-hearted homage to the republican idea, and Tielman Roos, the more thoroughgoing republican leader. Since 1912 those "heralds of ill will," Dutch Nationalism and British Chauvinism, further fostered and embittered by the world war, have sounded the slogans of Capitalist Imperialism versus petty bourgeois federalism. During the war the Dutch Nationalists broke out into open rebellion. It was, however, speedily suppressed. Latterly the Party has gained popularity at the polls with its republican and populist programme, appealing as it does to the increasing mass of disinherited Dutch Afrikanders. This has caused the consolidation of the British Unionist Party with the Dutch South African Party. The February elections showed that the Nationalist farmer recoiled before the consequences of the Republican propaganda, and the Government Party obtained a safe parliamentary majority for the Imperial connection.

Dutch Nationalism and the Native

The great festival of the Dutch Afrikander people and of the Nationalists in particular is Dingaan's Day. This day is made the occasion of political appeals on present issues, as well as a commemoration of December 16th, 1838, when the Dutch Voortrekkers crushed the power of the Zulus in a bloody battle fought on the Blood River, Weenen. On this festival the dual oppression bearing on the small Dutch farmer are inveighed against:

justifiable hate of British imperialism and of the British Chauvinist on the one hand, and hatred of the progeny of Dingaan on the other, his own hewers of wood and drawers of water. "Presbyter is only Priest writ large." More glaringly than in most Nationalist movements the freedom demanded from British rule is almost avowedly freedom to more fully exploit the native. As a concession to Nationalist sentiment, Dingaan's Day has now been officially declared a legal holiday throughout the Union. On these days, as on others, the rifle and the sjambok are invoked as the appropriate remedy for native grievances. In his personal relations the Dutch farmer adopts a quite friendly and patriarchal attitude towards his native labourers, provided of course they keep their proper stations. To the old Boer the native is a simple beast of burden. His religion is that of the Old Testament. It involves no contradictions, for his economic environment is primitive, though rapidly changing now with the advance in agricultural methods. General De Wet's excuse for going into rebellion in 1914 was that he had been fined five shillings for flogging a native servant – an unpardonable restriction on personal liberty! The Nationalist movement has a literary reflex. What there is of Afrikander literature is of course inspired by Nationalism. But the mania for isolation reaches absurd lengths. For example, Holland Dutch is one of the official languages of the Union. But the spoken language is a crude patois called Afrikaans. Previously the Dutch Afrikanders were content to let Afrikaans remain the spoken language, and used Holland Dutch as a vehicle of religion and literature. But now the Nationalist movement resents Holland's intellectual patronage as much as Britain's Imperial dominance, Though there are no fixed standards of grammar or style or spelling in Afrikaans, it is now being tortured into requisition as a literary medium, and the upholders of "Hollandse" [a derogatory term for the Dutch language] are stigmatised as the creatures of Smuts. The treasures, historical and literary, of the mother Dutch are thus thrown overboard; but the young Afrikander intellectuals cannot possibly endure such a self-imposed sentence of solitary confinement for very long.

Our remarks on this movement as the movement of a class must not be construed to apply to our Dutch friends as a race. They partake of the virtues of all good people. In the feud with the British it is they who have always held out the hand of conciliation, often spurned with insult by the British Jingoes.

British Chauvinism

Among the British section of the population there is a corresponding animosity towards the Dutch Afrikanders. The recent elections show that the Republican scare took away many votes which had previously been given to the Labour Party, although that Party blows the Imperial trumpet loudly enough. But this brand is too notorious to need any description here.

Franchise Anomalies

Only whites are qualified to vote in the Transvaal and the Orange Free State. In Natal the coloured people are qualified to vote, and even natives, but on terms so strict that only three or four individuals are able to avail themselves of it. In the Cape Province, besides manhood suffrage for whites and coloured natives are also qualified to vote on certain slight education tests, and the coloured and native vote is a serious electoral factor to be reckoned with. These disparities of franchise rights obtaining for the various provinces are inherited from the pre-existing provincial governments, and are the cause of the most amusing antics of electioneering parties operating simultaneously in the different provinces. The liberalism of the Cape is the legacy of the old Free Trade Governors of the Victorian period. In those days Manchester looked upon native populations more as buyers than as cheap labourers – people whose standards of culture and, above all, wants should be improved.

In the Transvaal, thanks to the slave-holding traditions of the old Boer voortrekkers, Imperialist Capital, with capital to invest rather than goods to sell, found cheap labour in a civil milieu to its liking for the exploitation of the gold reefs.

These political cross currents produced some curious effects during the war. The British workers cried down our anti-militarist declarations, while the Dutch approved. But coming to our native workers policy, it was then the turn of the Dutch to decry, while the British with their trade union traditions were prepared at least to listen. We were being repeatedly consigned to prison by the Johannesburg magistracy: and the judges, drawn largely from the older population, as repeatedly quashed the sentences.

The Indian traders, who are fast gaining control of trade in Natal and other parts of the Union, are the cause of much heart-burning among the white traders and anti-Asiatic movements, into which the workers are often dragged, are frequent.

Among the Trades Unions of the Transvaal, the wage-cutting effect of the coloured labour that swarms to the industrial centres is a burning question, aggravated as it is by the short-sighted policy of the Unions in excluding the coloured worker from membership. This time it is the turn of the employing class to sneer at Labour's inconsistency.

White Labour Movement

The white Trade Union movement in South Africa dates from the end of the Anglo-Boer war of 1899-1902, although such trades as the Typos., Engineers, and Building Workers were organised in South Africa previous to that. WH ['Bill'] Andrews, prominent among those who did the spade work of the Transvaal Labour Movement, is still to-day active blazing the trail of the Communist Movement. The growth of the movement was marked by the usual steps of the formation of unions in the different trades, the Trades Council of Johannesburg, from which sprang later the Federation of Trades and the Labour Party. After the Boer War, the gold magnates profited by their victory to introduce Chinese labour into the gold mines of the Rand. This created a White Labour Policy League, of which [Frederic] Creswell, then a victimised mine manager, was the head. This movement also mixed itself with the labour movement, and brought Creswell into the Labour Party, of which the capitalist press soon appointed him popular leader in opposition to the class leadership of Andrews. In 1910, when the four provinces formed a Union Government, the South African Labour Party was inaugurated out of the various Provincial parties. This party had a Socialist objective in its platform, as also a demand for the abolition of the indentured system of native labour and the prohibition of the importation of native labour from territories. outside the Union, The Party started in 1910 with four members in Parliament; it gained another four in by-elections up to 1915. The Party very soon became the accepted political expression of the white workers, its class-conscious elements rather than the White Labour Leaguers of Creswell being dominant. At that time "class-conscious" meant white class conscious, and the native as a fellow-worker and a comrade in industry never entered into any Labour calculations; neither did the idea of Labour enter the native mind, so well defined were and still are the respective industrial functions of black and white. Indeed, the wholly utopian proposal of segregation of black from white in strictly delimited areas, in accordance with the scheme of the White Labour League, and the withdrawal of the native from white industry, was the only Labour proposal for the natives up to the time of the war.

In 1913 a general strike of white workers broke out on the Rand, causing a complete stoppage of the gold mines for the first time in their history. This strike was a bloody affair. Troops were called out, and shootings by the regular troops resulted in 22 persons being killed and several hundred wounded. At that time the Chamber of Mines, which employs about 20,000 whites, had not learned the value of class collaboration – a wrinkle which Syndicalist [Archie] Crawford [Secretary of the South African Industrial Federation] taught them later. In 1914 another general strike broke out, this time forced upon the white workers by the Government, which spread to all parts of the Union. The massacres of 1913 had brought the workers an unexpected victory; but in 1914 the Government had prepared in a military manner. Martial Law was proclaimed, and 60,000 burghers from the veld were armed and put in possession of Johannesburg, having first been told that the English were making war again. The workers were driven back to work and leaders imprisoned by the dozen. Nine trade union leaders, and others who were by no means leaders, were deported by force to England.

The indignation against deportation found a vent in the ensuing Provincial Council elections, when the Labour Party obtained a majority of seats in the Transvaal. This resulted in a large influx of middle class elements into the Party. The outbreak of war found the Party divided on the question of militarism, but the Executive was anti-war, though few in a truly revolutionary sense. At a special conference of the Party held in 1915 the Executive were defeated by an overwhelming majority on the war issue, and were thereby forced to resign. The Creswell faction carried things with a high hand, and forced every candidate to give a written undertaking to "see the war through." The anti-war section broke away, and with the co-operation of what were called the SLP men (Comrades like John Campbell and Rabb who propagated the principles of Marxism as formulated by De Leon) formed the International Socialist League, which is today the South African section of the Communist International. The League started its career backed by the majority of the Labour Party Executive, including the Chairman (Andrews) and the Secretary (Ivon Jones), who took similar positions in the new organisations. It, however, soon shed its Reform Pacifists on the adoption of a revolutionary programme and the extension of the class struggle to include the native workers.

The Era of Collaboration

The Labour Party, thus rid of its anti-war executive, fought the elections of 1915 on the cry of "See it through," and for its pains got its Parliamentary representation reduced from eight to four. Up to the time of the split the Labour Party was composed of open political branches, and the Trades Unions affiliated or de-affiliated to the General Council, according to the fluctuating votes of their respective memberships. Up to the war the Party was largely composed of elements from the trades unions, the Engineers, Carpenters, Miners, Boilermakers, and Printers being affiliated. On the war issue the trades unions followed Creswell's lead, but they seem to have very soon got ashamed of their handiwork, for today there are no trades unions affiliated to the Party, which has deteriorated as a machine into a collection of electioneering committees trading on the name of Labour. This is partly due to the increasing number of Communist supporters among the active elements of Trades Unionism; and partly to the influx of Dutch workers into the towns for which the unions must "cater." To these workers the Labour Party is anathema, for it has by its beating of the Jingo drum violated their legitimate national sentiments.

Nevertheless, in the general elections of the early part of 1920 the Labour Party, by a judicious handling of the two issues of the Cost of Living and the Imperial connection, pulled off twenty-one seats. But at the general elections of the early part of 1921, when Smuts forced the issue of the Imperial connection against the Republican propaganda, the Labour Party, led by Creswell, though it jettisoned the "Red Flag," all its economic demands, as well as the Jonah of Socialism, and frantically protested on every platform that it was faithful to the Empire, only obtained nine seats, Creswell himself being beaten. This looks like its final decline. The factors are too complex in South Africa for a powerful Social Democratic Party.

During the war the White Trades Unions gained enormously in membership, and lost equally in fighting spirit. Crawford, at one time anarcho-syndicalist, is now the apostle of class collaboration, and as Secretary of the SA Industrial Federation, is the willing agent of the Chamber of Mines.

Labour Aristocracy

The failure of the anti-war Executive of the Labour Party to keep the workers to the class struggle was due to the fact that in the white worker consciousness of class is, so far, fitful and easily lost. He is used to lord it over the unskilled native as his social inferior. The white miner's duty is almost wholly that of supervision. With the fitters and carpenters the native labourer does no more than the fitter's or carpenter's labourer in European countries, But he is black, a being of another order, and moreover only has half a shirt on his back, more for ornament than for use, and sleeps in a tin shack. As workers whose functions are wholly different in the industrial world, there is hardly any competition involved; indeed, the white miner is as much interested as the Chamber of Mines in a plentiful supply of native labour, without which he cannot start work. They are therefore annoyed at any strikes of natives, and are prone to assist the masters in their repressive methods, although in the case of white strikes they are not behindhand in appealing to the natives not to go down the shafts; and the natives as a rule are unwilling to go without the white miners. For between white and native workers there is as a rule the best of good humour at the place of work. The native addresses the white worker as "boss," it is true, but this term has now become almost a convention like "sir," and there is no doubt that the native is animated by a large measure of respect for the white worker as his industrial educator, a respect which will find more generous play on both sides in a better economic order. One of the nightmares of the white miner is that he may lose his monopoly to the legal right of holding a blasting certificate. Under such conditions what wonder if consciousness of class among the mass of white workers is somewhat narrow and professional.

During the war, the capitalists, urged by the necessity of keeping up gold production, discovered that it paid them to regard the white workers as an unofficial garrison over the far larger mass of black labour, and that it was not bad business to keep the two sections politically apart by paying liberally the white out of the miserably under-paid labour of the black. The white workers were far more intractable to Communist ideas at the end of the war than in the second or third year when the colonial campaigns were in progress. The premium on the mint price of gold enabled the Chamber of Mines to keep up this policy of economic bribery till the end of last year. Now it seems as if it had come to an end. The bribe fund has petered out. The premium on the mint price of gold is being reduced, and under the threat of closing down the non-paying mines the white miners are compelled to accept lower pay. During the last few months there have been unofficial strikes against the will of the Union Executives and of Crawford, the Federation Secretary. The mines have retaliated by withdrawing the "stop-order" system. This system, introduced in 1916, was an ingenious bait to trade union officialdom. Every miner had his trade union contribution deducted at the mine office from his wages, and the mine offices handed it over to the union in a monthly cheque, thus making the Union an adjunct of the Chamber of Mines. Now this "privilege" has been withdrawn as a measure to weaken the non-too-pliant membership. The garrison is too costly. The mining industry can only save its profits by following the historic process, namely, to raise the black standard and depress the white, making towards a homogeneous working class.

Rural Movements

There is no white labour movement of any kind in the country districts of South Africa, excepting, of course, the attempts at organisation in the townships wherever cheap white, coloured and native labour are engaged in local industries. The natives do nearly all the farm labouring. The sons of the Boer farmers, no matter how impecunious they may be, are generally too race-proud to labour on the land. In any case the cheap native labour tends to drive all but white proprietors to the towns. The laws of inheritance are measures of disinheritance. The farms are divided up amongst the children, calling for most intensive culture, to which the Dutch farmers have not been trained, the old system of pasturage enabled the farmer to sit on his *stoep* [veranda] and smoke his pipe. Thus the farms fall to those who bring progressive methods of agriculture to bear on the land. There is a considerable class of landless Dutch Afrikanders. They eke out a living on the "bywoning" system, by which they are allowed to occupy a hut and pasture and cultivate a small corner of a farm in return for services to the farmer when called upon: a kind of servitude. But this system is falling into disfavour with the rich farmers. They prefer the "squatting" system, a species of sub-letting to natives on half shares. There is therefore a constant stream of landless Dutch to the towns. Large numbers are employed in gangs, called "poor white" gangs, on pay so miserable that they are in a constant state of semi-starvation. These cast-offs from the rural districts, spurned socially and economically by the very class of nationalist farmer whom they follow politically, help to make up the slums of Johannesburg. Vrededorp, the Johannesburg slum district, is a social cesspool where the Dutch, English, Indian, Coloured man, K* and H* all at last find equality in wretchedness, "equally of no account to the capitalist class." It would be hard to find a parallel for Vrededorp in any town in Europe. The rigorous anti-liquor laws, which make it a penal offence to give alcohol to natives in the Transvaal, find their victims in this class. Three-fourths of the white inmates of South African prisons are convicted of selling drink to natives;

that last tempting resort of the destitute and the miserable.

As a result of the migration to the towns, the urban workers are becoming increasingly Dutch. Before the war the Executive of the Mine Workers' Union was wholly of British descent. Now more than half are Dutch Afrikanders. The tramway systems and semi-skilled services are now largely run by Dutch workers, who soon develop into good trades unionists and loyal agitators for their class, always of course within the limits of their colour.

At a local strike on the Simmer Deep mine last year, when both British and Dutch miners stopped work as a protest against the dismissal of a German member of the Union, both sections tacitly dropped their respective nationalisms for the time being; and it was good to see the young Dutch workers, who a week before and perhaps the week after, sported their nationalist green and yellow, on this occasion proudly wearing their bits of Red as the only suitable emblem for such an occasion as a strike. The industrial system is also weaning gradually the Dutch workers from the most violent forms of colour prejudice. The traffic of Dutch workers to and fro is linking up town and country as never before; and the expropriated Dutch of the country districts will soon share in the inevitable change of outlook.

The South African Native

Speaking generally, the South African natives are a race of labourers. The bulk of the race is now found interspersed in white areas. Certain territories are still reserved for their tribal homes, such as Zululand, Basutoland, Swaziland and Bechuanaland. In these areas a sort of primitive communism exists as far as the land is concerned. What little government of local matters is required in a society where there is very little property is exercised by the chiefs, petty chiefs, and Headmen, always of course under the supervision of the police patrol. The perpetual sunshine renders maize the only prime necessity. Zululand, for example, is a land of free and rolling "savannah" with no property boundaries; dotted with the round straw huts of the Zulus, which are without windows or outlet for smoke, and with only a low hole in the structure to creep in and out. Round the huts are the small patches of maize chiefly dug by hand, or of *idombis*, a kind of Zulu potato. The natives in their tribal state live very closely to the soil, they and their habitations seem part of it, elemental in their simplicity of life. In Basutoland they are more affluent, owning horses and cattle; and of late an increase in cattle is to be observed in Zululand also, enabling their owners to plough at home instead of going to labour for the whites. In the Transkei, Cape Colony, a system of native small proprietorship was tried known as the Glen-Grey settlements. But this is an exception to the general scheme of things. A recent clamour from white settlers that Zululand should be opened up for settlement for white farmers was answered by Minister Malan that this was out of the question, as it would increase the cost of native labour for the whole country. This, then, is the function of the native territories, to serve as cheap breeding grounds for black labour – the repositories of the reserve army of native labour – sucking it in or letting it out according to the demands of industry. By means of these territories Capital is relieved of the obligation of paying wages to cover the cost to the labourer of reproducing his kind.

Between the territories and the industrial centres there is a constant traffic to and fro of natives. What draws the native away from his home? The marriage customs are a cause. Wives are worth so many cows, and money must be got to buy them. But the chief impulse is the hut tax specially levied for the purpose; besides which large numbers are allured to the towns by social instinct and the excitement of town life among so many of their own folk there, so that the first excursion from home in many cases becomes a permanent absence. For the native there is the prospect of learning to read and write; he has a keen desire for education. There is the native church in the towns, either as an adjunct of the white religious bodies or his own Ethiopian church, an institution frowned upon by the white Christians for its lack of respectable guidance in the interpretation of the gospels! There is the allurement of machinery. The native is captivated by a piece of machinery, and will seek out its inmost pulsations and tend it as a god. In the towns also there is freedom from the social interference of the chiefs, even if obtained at the cost of subservience to white society. For native women there is emancipation from the tribal marriage customs; tens of thousands of native women are detribalised by contracting free liaisons in the towns not sanctioned by tribal custom. The chiefs are benignant enough old institutions. But they bewail their disappearing authority, although they are useful to the capitalist for the recruiting of labour. In a prosecution in which we were involved for a Bolshevik leaflet addressed to natives as well as whites, the Crown Prosecutor continually referred to those town natives who no longer own allegiance to the chief as "the hooligan class of native," that is, they are no longer under official control. They have taken the step from tribesman to proletarian.

Outcast and outlawed the native may be, but no "hooligan." In the Transvaal and the Free State Province the native has no vote, no civil and political rights. A breach of labour contract is a penal offence. The natives on the mines work on a system of indenture, generally of one year's duration. They do not live in private dwellings, but are herded into "compounds" adjacent to the mines. Indeed, native housing in the towns is not fit for cattle. Most of the hundreds of thousands of natives who work in the towns are housed in backyards, tin shacks, stable lofts, the best way they can. Their level of existence is inconceivably low. Every native male must carry a passport: one to leave his tribe, another to seek work, a monthly pass while working, another pass when he wants to be out after nine o'clock curfew. A policeman may at all times stop a native and demand his pass. Hence most natives have been to jail at one time or another. That is a mere trifle to him with all the regulations that hem round his daily life. He is paid two or three shillings a day, with or without his ration of mealie meal, as the case may be. A rise of a shilling a day would create a panic on the gold market.

Yet in spite of it all, the Bantu is a happy proletarian. He has lovable qualities. "His joy of life and fortitude under suffering," to quote Lafargue's words on the negro: his communal spirit, his physical vitality, his keen desire to know, despite his intellectual backwardness, make him an object of lurking affection to the whites who come in contact with him.

Moreover, he is no fool. He has a certain naive wisdom which goes to the root of things. It was the questionings of the Zulus that led the celebrated Bishop Colenso to change his religious views. Arrested development of the native mind has been a theory very much resorted to by the negrophobes. To the exploiters, the less a man has the more must be taken from him. Some bourgeois negrophiles, like Loram the Natal Educationalist, have even gone to the pains of disproving this meaningless theory. To us it suffices that the native workers are the producers, and are robbed of the products of their labour. The truth is that a radical difference in psychology exists. The native bends to capital, but capital also bends to his primeval instincts. See a gang of natives working on the roads or railways! On every possible pretext they will work in unison, raising and lowering the pick, with rhythmic flourishes thrown in, to the tune of their Zulu chants. Ever and anon the tune or the time changes, in an endless variety from the ancestral repertoire, in perfect harmony and rhythm – impromptu choruses of the wild, charming even the dullest. No gaffer can speed up such a gang. And when the same gang tries to sing a simple Christian hymn it makes a most discordant mess of it. Such is arrested development!

The Native Labour Movement

A formal statement of the various categories of native labour and the true Communist policy towards the native workers has been prepared by Comrade SP Bunting and accepted by the International Socialist League.

Before the war no trade union movement existed among the native workers, and such a thing as a strike was unknown. The first move in the direction of organised revolt was a strike of native workers on the dumping machinery of the Van Ryn Gold Mine in December, 1915. It was regarded as a novel affair by the white workers of the mine; but it appears that certain white men who engaged to keep the plant going were sneered at as blacklegs by their white fellow-workers. Prior to that, in the 1913 revolt of the white workers, appeals had been made to the native workers of the Kleinfontein mine to stop working, and it seems to have dawned then on the white workers' intelligence, or some of their most militant leaders like George Mason, that the native was really a kind of a workmate. In 1917, Comrade Bunting and other members of the ISL made an attempt to form a native workers' union.

A number of the more industrialised natives of Johannesburg were enrolled into the Union, which was named "The Industrial Workers of Africa" (an echo of the "Industrial Workers of the World"). It held meetings regularly, and the message of working class emancipation was eagerly imbibed for the first time by an ardent little band of native workers who carried the message far and wide to their more backward brethren. A manifesto to the workers of Africa was issued in collaboration with the ISL written in the Zulu and Basuto languages, calling upon the natives to unite against their capitalist oppressors. This leaflet reached a still wider mass of native workers, and was introduced and read to the illiterate labourers in the mine compounds. For the native of Africa, and the white too for that matter, the question is not yet "irrevocably put of bloody struggle or death." It is the era of awakening to the consciousness of class. The emphasis of the League on the new power of industrial solidarity, which their very oppressors had put in their hands, had as its aim to draw away the native's hopes from the old tribal exploits with the spear and the assegai as a means of deliverance. The power of the machine dawned upon him. In 1918 the propaganda of the IWA [Industrial Workers of Africa], and the pressure of the rising cost of living, produced a formidable strike movement among the native municipal workers, and a general movement for the tearing up of passports. Hundreds of natives who had burned their passes were jailed every day, and the prisons became full to bursting. Gatherings of native men and women were clubbed down by the mounted police. The International Socialist League was charged with inciting to native revolt. Comrades Bunting, Tinker and Hanscombe were arrested at the instance of the Botha Government; but the chief native witness for the Crown broke down. He admitted that the evidence of incitement to riot had been invented for him by the Native Affairs Department, and the case collapsed. The moving spirits of the IWA were driven out of Johannesburg by the police, some to find their way to Capetown, where a more permanent movement of native organisation has since been formed. It has also spread to Bloemfontein, where Msimang, a young native lawyer, is active in native organisation. In the Cape Province the natives are more advanced politically, and more permanently settled in the European areas. But the greater civil equality does not bring greater freedom to combine. Masabalala, the leader of the Port Elizabeth native workers, was imprisoned last August for his trade union activity. Trade unionism among the native workers makes the hair of the South African bourgeois stand on end. But the result of Masabalala's imprisonment was that his comrades rose en masse and tried to storm the prison. A massacre by the armed police ensued; and the "white agitators of the Rand" blamed as usual.

But the most portentous event so far in the awakening of the native workers was the great strike of native mine workers on the Rand in March, 1920. These mine natives are mostly raw recruits from the tribal territories from Zululand, Basutoland, far-away Blantyre and Portuguese Africa, all are here. For the time being all the old tribal feuds were forgotten, and Zulu and Shangaan came out on strike together irrespective of tribal distinction to the number of 80,000. Without leaders, without organisation, hemmed in their compounds by the armed police, the flame of revolt died down, not without one or two bloody incidents in which the armed thugs of the law distinguished themselves for their savagery. The ISL at the time was engaged in the general elections, printing literature on the Soviets and the Dictatorship of the Proletariat for its five candidates. The white workers were undecided as to their attitude towards the native strikers. The ISL came out with an appeal in *The International* and in thousands of leaflets entitled "Don't Scab," calling upon the white workers to play the game towards the native strikers. These were distributed in the mine shafts by Communist sympathisers among the miners. One or two were made the object of a prosecution by the police, but released later owing to the difficulty felt, no doubt, of getting at the ISL for propaganda in the heat of an election. The Capitalist Press, thinking to damage our election prospects, gave still further publicity to our appeal by reproducing it in full as a proof of our criminality! The Mineworkers' Union Executive called upon its members to side with the masters and endeavour to run the mines, and publicly condemned our propaganda. But such is the division of labour in South Africa that whereas either black labour or white labour can stop industry, neither can properly start the wheels going again without the other.

Native Political Leaders

There exists a body known as The Native Congress, with sections functioning in the various Provinces and for the whole Union. This is a loosely organised body composed of the chiefs, native lawyers, native clergymen, and others who eke out a living as agents among their compatriots. This body is patronised and lectured by the Government. It has weekly newspapers in the various provinces, *Abantu Batho* in Johannesburg, *Ilanga Lase Natal* in Natal, etc. These are subsidised by Government advertisements, which are often withdrawn when the Congress drops the role of respectable bourgeois which it normally tries to assume. It is satisfied with agitation for civil equality and political rights to which its members as a small coterie of educated natives feel they have a special claim. But to obtain these the mass cannot be moved without their moving in a revolutionary manner. Hence the Government is dubious about the Congress, and the Congress draws back timidly from the mass movements of its own people. The native workers of the IWA quickly grasped the difference between their trade union and the Congress, and waged a merciless war of invective at the joint meetings of their Union with the Congress against the black-coated respectables of the Congress. But the growing class organisations of the natives will soon dominate or displace the "Congress." The national and class interests of the natives cannot be distinguished the one from the other. Here is a revolutionary nationalist movement in the fullest meaning of Lenin's term.

Native Education, etc.

Apart from work done by Christian missions, the natives are thrown largely on their own resources for their education. Reading and writing are not necessary to their industrial function, so they have to acquire these at their own night schools, those who have the ambition. Here is a grand field for Communist activity given the necessary personnel and the money. In the Cape and Natal there are voices heard in favour of education for the natives. Far-seeing bourgeoisie like Sir William Beaumont in Natal are advocates of votes for the native, with education, in order, as he says, that the native may be taught to vote as a good citizen, that is, as a good bourgeois, The mining industry has been wobbling in its attitude towards the educational and civil advancement of the natives, being hindered by political organisations, and the franckensteins of race prejudices which it has itself conjured up, from reducing working costs by opening the higher industrial employments to natives and coloured men. In the last few years *The Star*, the Chamber of Mines daily, has incessantly declared in favour of the civil advancement of the natives, vigorously attacking the white unions for their denial of equality of opportunity to the native worker. These appeals, made in the interest of lower working costs, are nevertheless unanswerable in logic from the Labour point of view. The native does not care what the motive may be. He sees in his economic exploiters the champions of his civil rights. Now that the capitalist parties are safely seated in the Government saddle we may look forward to steps being taken to realise the programme. After the native strikes of 1920 the Chamber of Mines issued a newspaper for distribution gratis printed in the native languages. Its leading articles were chiefly devoted to discrediting the Socialists and white agitators generally. The ISL had under consideration the issuing of a Communist sheet in counterblast, but found itself unable to do this in addition to *The International*. This attempt to debauch the mind of the native workers while it is in the process of awakening is one which the Communist movement is too weak to frustrate; and we can only call the attention of the Third International to the fact.

The ISL and its Task

The International Socialist League, soon after it parted company with the Labour Party, declared for the solidarity of Labour irrespective of race, colour or creed. Imbued with the ideas of De Leon as popularised in the splendid series of Marxian pamphlets issued by the SLP of America and Great Britain, the League proclaimed the principle of Industrial Unionism, placing in the Parliamentary fight the fight to end parliaments, and to replace them by the class state of the workers functioning through their industrial unions. Therefore craft unions were declared odious as dividing the workers instead of uniting them on the larger basis of industry. And as part of this craft disunity the exclusion of the native workers from part or lot in the Labour Movement was denounced as a crime. To us, the rather mechanical formula of De Leon's Industrial Unionism (which was deemed capable of performing a bloodless revolution by "a lock out of the capitalist class") was made a living thing by its application to the native workers. Later on the word became flesh in the Soviets, and we no longer worry overmuch about the craft or professional form which the older unions have taken.

The League having thus been captured by the De Leonites, the reform pacifists gave us the cold shoulder, and several slunk back into the Labour Party. The League also formed branches which have had fluctuating success in the Reef towns of Krugersdorp, Benoni, Springs and Germiston, also at Durban and Kimberley. Durban has also had for years a small group calling itself the Social Democratic Party, followers of Hyndman in war and peace. This body refused to link up with the ISL on the excuse that we were only the Labour Party under another name. It was allowed to hold its meetings during the war by an arrangement with the police that it would leave the war out of its propaganda. At this time the ISL was being mobbed by the organised hooligans of the police and prosecuted for its class war propaganda. This SDP outfit still follows Hyndman in sneering at the Third International and the Russian Revolution, and may justly be put down as of no account. The Social Democratic Federation of Capetown was also unwilling to link up for other reasons. It was composed of pro-warites and anti-warites, and the Jingoes and Pacifists remained in peace together. The ISL was reformist because it fought elections, and the "men from the north," as they called us, were accused of trying to sow disunity in the Federation by its neophyte enthusiasm for Karl Marx as the only authority! Comrade Harrison, one of the members of the SDF, carried on a valiant open-air propaganda on anti-militarism and what he calls "philosophical anarchy," for which he was repeatedly prosecuted. Latterly a body of young class war enthusiasts broke away from the SDF and formed the Industrial Socialist League. Anti-political, they thought to emphasise the fact by the word "Industrial". It has now proclaimed itself the Communist Party of Africa. The ISL itself also suffered a breakaway of anti-political anarchists for its persistency in fighting elections. This group also formed itself into a "Communist Party", in unison with the Capetown group. The ISL has made attempts since the proclamation of the Moscow theses to unite these groups into the Third International. The reply of the Johannesburg group objected to the twenty-one conditions and "to the dictatorship of Moscow" (meaning the dictatorship of the Marxian principles). Comrade EJ Brown, a member of the ISL recently expelled from the Belgian Congo for trade union agitation there, has been more successful in Capetown in the matter of unifying the sound revolutionary elements, and forming a group anxious to fight under the banner of the Third International. The ISL waits on these elements to fall into line before definitely transferring itself into the South African Communist Party of the Third International.

The number of Leagues and Parties all claiming to be revolutionary must not be taken as indicating a large revolutionary following. The ISL's election results have been very meagre indeed. The best poll was that of Comrade Andrews in Benoni in 1917 with 335 votes as against 1,200 odd for the successful candidate. Since then the election results in Benoni have dwindled considerably. The mass of voteless native workers makes it impossible for us to win elections in South Africa. The necessity for propaganda, the need to keep the two streams of the proletariat theoretically one, the need to appeal on the political plane on class issues affecting the native, and above all the advisability of opening as far as possible the arena of civil right for the native struggle makes it imperative nevertheless that we fight elections. The League is by far the largest of the groups that I have mentioned, undoubtedly larger than all the rest combined, and the only one of any political significance. Any worker who puts up a fight for class solidarity in the Transvaal Unions is thereby deemed a supporter of the ISL. It has a large circle of passive sympathisers, as evidenced by the number that follow its banner in the May Day procession, in which the trade unions co-operate.

Nevertheless the League's membership has never exceeded four hundred at any time. And latterly the number of militants who have emigrated to Europe has weakened our organisation. It is denied the support and inspiration of the great mass of the propertyless proletariat on which the Europeans parties are able to draw. The revolutionary movement depends almost entirely on a few advanced spirits drawn from the thin upper crust of Labour aristocracy. Owing to the heavy social disabilities and political backwardness the natives are not able to supply any active militants to the Communist movement. The immediate needs of white trades unionism, in which a number of our members are actively engaged, tends to throw the more difficult task of native emancipation into the background. The white movement dominates our attention, because the native workers' movement moves only spasmodically, and is neglected. It requires a special department, with native linguists and newspapers. All of which require large funds, which are not available. The Jewish community, with its anti-war and pro-Russian sympathies, has given generous support to our funds. But as the revolution clarifies, this support is now confined to the Jewish revolutionaries proper.

It will thus be seen that the ISL has a particularly heavy task falling upon the shoulders of a few militants who have stuck doggedly to it for over five years. The present writer, having also left Africa for the time being, feels it his duty to appeal for some reinforcement to the South African movement, and to urge that it should come more directly under the purview of the Third International. A few missionaries, revolutionists who need a spell of

sunshine, would be very welcome. Primitive though they be, the African natives are ripe for the message of the Communist International. Speed the day when they too will march with "the iron battalions of the proletariat."
Nice, March 29 1921

Johannesburg Municipal Elections.

1915

THE INTERNATIONAL SOCIALIST

CANDIDATES FOR WARD 2.

D. IVON JONES, and **S. P. BUNTING, M.P.C.**

Late Gen. Sec: S.A. Labour Party.
Now Sec: Inter Soc. League.

Chairman, Johannesburg Central Branch, Inter. Soc. League.

WILL HOLD

PUBLIC MEETINGS

as follows, at 8 p.m. :—

Tues. Nov. 2, St. Augustine's Hall, Cr. Height & Beit Sts.

Wed. „ 3, Masonic Hall, Jeppe St. (All I.S.L. Candidates, supported by Colin Wade, M.P.C.)

Mon. „ 8, Jewish Synagogue, Kimberley Road.

Johannesburg municipal election leaflet for the International Socialist League (1915)

4

IN REVOLUTIONARY RUSSIA

(1921-1924)

Communism in Africa

Moscow [Journal of the Third Congress of the Communist International], June 9 1921

The South African delegates [Sam Barlin and DI Jones] were introduced to the bare footed, 12 year old delegate from the Novgorod Young Communists the other day. The first thing he asked us was "Why aren"t you black!'

Coming from South Africa, we feel quite apologetic about our colour. An African delegation should at least include Negroes. This will be remedied in time; but it would be a mistake to think that in future there should be no white South African delegates. The African revolution will be led by white workers. In Africa there are 150 million natives, it is true, and a few hundred thousand white workers. But the industrialised and semi-proletarianised native workers moving in and around modern industry do not number more than a couple of million. These are mainly found in the Union of South Africa, comprising the provinces of the Transvaal, Free State, Natal and the Cape. Here is the entry to the African Continent. The railway line 2,000 miles long, runs right up to Elizabethville to the Belgian Congo, in the heart of the dark continent.

Around Johannesburg in the Transvaal is found the world-renowned gold mining industry, the most modern and most concentrated of its kind in the world, extending over a 60 mile gold reef and producing half the gold output of the world. This is the economic university of Southern Africa and of territories to the north. Here natives and whites are exploited side by side under two sharply distinct standards of life. Here you have the proportions of native to white skilled very much the same as those obtaining on the world scale: namely, a European factory proletariat, viz-a-viz the mass of Asiatic and African cheap labour. South Africa is thus unique in presenting a replica of the world problem resolving a solution for it.

We are in the habit of calling these white skilled workers the aristocrats of labour. But they are not ordinary labour aristocrats. The white workers of South Africa had some very militant fights. In 1913, the white miners and other workers had a general strike, which led to a pitched battle between them and the troops in the streets of Johannesburg resulting in 21 killed and several hundred wounded. In 1914, a general strike on a large scale broke out and the government mobilised sixty thousand armed burghers from the veld and marched them into Johannesburg to crush the movement. South African capitalism then distinguished itself by deporting nine of the trade union leaders to England.

It was in the 1913 strike that it first occurred to some of the most militant white workers that the native workers are also a factor in the labour movement. And from that time there has been a growing minority of the white workers who realise that the emancipation of the white can only be achieved by solidarity with the native, and who laugh derisively at the superficial socialism which ignores the native working masses.

Since then the white workers of South Africa have participated in the general enthusiasm for trade union organization. But there has been a decline in general militancy although hardly a union, as such, escaped conflict with the masters during the last few years. The general tendency as expressed in the policy of the South African Industrial Federation [a trade union organisation] is one of collaboration with the masters on Joint Boards, etc. The master class has realised that the white workers have to be humoured as a protection against the native masses, and as a means of keeping white and black workers apart.

Meanwhile, the native worker is waking up. Progress is slow! but that is due no less to the lack of resources in the Communist movement than to the backwardness of the native himself. For it is the peculiar task of the Communist movement to shake the native from his age old sleep. The Communist movement is almost a purely white workers' movement so far, and has its work cut out to keep the revolution before the white workers. But it is just this question, solidarity with the native workers, that distinguishes the communist movement from all other sections of the labour movement in South Africa. The "left" anarchist joins with the Labour politicians in branding us a "kaffir" party. The native worker is the touchstone of revolution. He can only [Only he can] organise the revolution. The "kaffir stock market" [in gold mining shares] in London rests on his cheap labour. It depends on his remaining illiterate and backward, and content with his pig-level of existence. The very idea of native trade unions sends the master class into hysterics. Another shilling or two in their daily pay would create a panic on the market. But the native worker is not very worried about the problems of his boss. He is a typical proletariat. He is a lovable sort. We cannot listen to his loud uproarious laughter without being reminded of Marx's conception of a proletarian. He has already given some blind kicks to capital. Last year 80,000 unorganized mine workers spontaneously struck work for better pay. Before that, in 1918, the Johannesburg workers rose in protest against the passport system. Every South African worker is labelled and ticketed. [A list follows]. In the anti-passport movement referred to, hundreds were marched off to gaol. A strike of native workers in the Municipal services broke out at the same time. The movement so alarmed the authorities that several members of the communist movement were arrested, and a grand charge of incitement to revolt brought against them. To illustrate the loyalty of the natives to each other, it is worth mentioning an incident in connection with this trial. The chief witness for the government was a native named Luke Messina, a member of the Industrial Workers of Africa. This was a native union formed by the communists. Messina had been sent into the union as a spy by the Native Affairs department, and informed us of the fact. After reading to the court the elaborate affidavit placed in his hands by the authorities, he told the court the affidavit was false in every particular, and the whole case broke down amid great sensation.

Our concern in Africa is not to emphasise the native movement to the exclusion of the white, nor the white to the exclusion of the native. Our message to the white is "solidarity with the native workers". In the white political field we have a fine opportunity of forcing the issue on the attention of the white workers with immunity from the police. And the echo of this propaganda reaches the native workers as well. Touching on the political movement brings us to the South African Labour Party and the Communist movement which has grown out of it.

The Trade Union movement of white workers was naturally reflected by a fairly vigorous Labour Party, with a social democratic structure, to which the trade unions affiliated according to the votes of their members. It had a right wing led by Creswell, a mine manager; and a left or more class conscious element, led by Andrews, a mechanic, who today is the secretary of the Communist Party of South Africa. Before the war, the Labour Party had 8 MPs (South Africa, of course is a self governing dominion). In 1915 the issue of the war broke the Labour Party into two. The executive had a majority of anti-militarists of various shades. But the bulk of the trade unions followed Creswell. At the general election the Labour Party lost seats in spite of its beating the jingo drum. The International Socialist League, as the breakaway section called itself, also put up two candidates purely as a demonstration of its position and, as expected, got heavily defeated...

[Jones then states that when the ISL "declared for a revolutionary platform regarding the native workers", most members "slunk back" to the Labour Party].

What part will Africa play in the world revolution? Our Indian comrades are fond of that clause which says that European labour cannot emancipate itself without Africa and India; while the British comrades regard it as a moot point. This one thing is certain: the native workers of Africa feed by their labour a large battalion of White Guards in the West End of London...

[Jones describes the "fairly large Native Union" in the Cape (namely, the Industrial and Commercial Workers Union) and refers to a new group of black members in the Communist Party].

And it is evident that the black battalions of the proletariat of Africa and India must first be on the march before world capitalism can be brought to the ground.

Letter to Leon Trotsky

Russian State Archive of Socio-Political History
Retranslated from Russian
June 2 1921

Dear Comrade Trotsky,
I have answered some of your questions from the point of view of the general British situation. [*In response to Trotsky's questionnaire to Communist International congress delegates about the economic crisis in Europe and the USA*]. Now I shall discuss the situation in South Africa.

Your questions mainly deal, of course, with America and Europe. As far as South Africa is concerned I feel that they are not quite applicable to the conditions there and that you would have formulated them differently.

True enough, we in South Africa have a vast gold mining industry, concentrated in Johannesburg, based on completely new modern foundations and strongly centralised, with capitalised value of 500 million [pounds sterling].

Nevertheless all crises hit London and Paris first and only after that roll to South Africa. At the same time a national capital is coming into existence. But generally South Africa, as well as India. is only a fractional factor of the British capitalist hegemony, the field of cheap labour for England. Our proletariat fully depends on the fluctuations of the London stock exchange and it feeds the White Guards of West End, [a reference to City of London financiers] rather than the South African bourgeoisie.

We have in Africa a relatively small well paid white proletariat and a relatively big poorly paid native proletariat. They co-exist side by side in the same way as it can be seen on the world scale: a united European industrial proletariat and huge masses of African and Asian producers of raw materials.

Economic crises that you mention in your questionnaire do not exist in South Africa as an independent phenomenon of its capitalist economy because there is neither the capital nor the slaves subordinate to it.

In Britain the awakening up of the proletariat is the result of the economic Crisis.

In South Africa economic and political crisis will be the result of the awakening of the black proletariat.

In Britain workers will be awakened by the bankruptcy of capitalism.

In South Africa capitalism will go bankrupt because of the awakening of the proletariat.

South African natives are cheap labour. All the gold mining industry rests on this cheap labour. Their ludicrously small salaries of 2 shillings a day cannot be in any way substantially raised without a panic on the London gold shares market.

This mass of cheap workers owns no property whatsoever and has no desire to own any. The emancipation of white workers of South Africa depends upon the awakening of the native proletariat which will also be a significant factor in advancing the collapse of the world capitalism. These native workers are a perfect material for the Socialist revolution. But they are all illiterate and for this reason they are out of reach of the Communist propaganda. Their mental awakening demands educational institutions of either Capitalism, or Communism – whoever will be the first.

The white proletariat of South Africa is for the most part impenetrable for the revolutionary propaganda, while the native masses are still sleeping. The Chamber of Mines facilitates political, economic and mental development of the natives to increase their chances to compete with white qualified workers. But it is afraid of any radical reforms in this direction. It is afraid to balance living conditions of white and black proletariat the result of which could be the creation of a homogeneous toiling mass and giving white leaders to the dispossessed native masses.

But the Comintern should not have any doubts. Native workers are beginning to understand and master the idea of a Workers Organisation (see the report to the Congress) abandoning their hunting and military valour and their spears and javelins as weapons of emancipation. But a workers organisation in the midst of the dispossessed can only be revolutionary. All they need is Communist education and then their awakening will become a powerful factor in the World Revolution.

With greetings from South Africa
Yours D. Tom [sic] Jones.

Letter to MV Kobetsky

Russian State Archive of Socio-Political History
To The Secretary, Communist International
June 11 1921

Dear Comrade [Mikhail] Kobetsky,

In accordance with resolutions passed at yesterday's meeting of the Executive of the Comintern we wish to state that Comrade Ivon Jones will serve on the Executive Committee for South Africa with decisive or consultative vote according to the decision of the Bureau, (the strict meaning of the resolution provides a decisive vote for South Africa, but we do not press the point if the Comrades consider it disproportionate).

2. Comrade Ivon Jones will also serve for South Africa on the Oriental Committee.

3. Comrade Barlin will sit on the Theses Committee on the "World Crisis."

We remain

Fraternally yours,
Sam Barlin,
D. Ivon Jones
South African delegation [to the Third Comintern Congress] for the Communist Party of South Africa
Hotel Lux, Moscow

The Black Question

Russian State Archive of Socio-Political History
Speech to the Third Congress of the Communist International, Moscow
July 12 1921

"Comrades, I can see from your expressions that you are surprised to see a white comrade from South Africa, a country so generally associated with the Negro. And indeed I think the Comintern photographer was also dismayed to find the South African delegates white. I have seen a Negro brother in the corridor; I think he has been captured by main force for the photographer [*Laughter*]. I have been asked to deal with the Negro question in general. I hope that the fact that we are dealing with this vast question in the closing hours of this congress is no indication of our sense of responsibility.

It is now fifty years since Karl Marx told us that the open slavery of the colonies is the pedestal on which is built up the veiled slavery of European wage labour [*Capital* Vol.1 (1867)]. And he threw out the warning then, which is as serious a warning to us today, when he said that labour cannot emancipate itself in the white so long as in the black it is branded. I trust that in spite of the hurried notice given to the Oriental question at this congress, that warning of our master Marx will not be forgotten by the Communist International.

I agree that last year's theses left nothing to be said on the colonial question. We marvelled, in fact, at the comprehension of matters contained in it which we had only learnt by close association with the facts for years. We agree that these theses now need only local application on the part of the sections, and direct action on the part of the Comintern. This has been lacking so far. Comrade [Karl] Radek admitted in committee that they know very little of the state of the movement among vast working masses of India and China so far as definite Communist parties were concerned. We must not be misled into inactivity by the number of interesting and picturesque personalities from the East here who are of such interest to our photographers. We in Africa call for a more direct initiative in the Negro question particularly. The Negro has been the Ishmael of the human race. He must become the Benjamin [Jacob's righteous twelfth son in The Bible] of the Communist International.

In South Africa we have a replica of the world problem in miniature. Almost in the same proportions as on the world scale, you have there a mass of native workers side by side with a select white skilled class of workers. How is it that just here, where there is a mass of natives side by side with a labour aristocracy you have perhaps the largest Communist Party in the British colonies? The reasons for this form an interesting study. But we are only allowed five minutes and I cannot enter into details.

The Negro question manifests itself also in America, where it takes on a very acute form. There you have the proportion of the Negro in the ratio of one to ten of the whites, and it is just there that you have colony prejudices in its most frenzied form. It is only the other day that we read of the burning of 150 Negro worshippers in a Negro church by the mobs of lynch law [in Tulsa, Oklahoma]. As the disintegration of the bourgeoisie proceeds apace, we can expect more and more violent forms of this frenzy in America, which is today not only confined to Negro states like Georgia, but is spreading to the North as well, fanned as it is by the flames of economic competition between Negroes and whites.

In South Africa, on the other hand, you have the proportion of Negroes to whites in the reverse degree. The natives outnumber the whites by about ten to one. In America the problem will come more and more within the scope of the Communist Party there, as the party grows in strength, and as the workers become too oppressed by their economic oppression to be misled by colony prejudice any more. But in Africa we have a relatively small labour aristocracy, from which it is difficult to recruit militant workers for the Communist Party. So that as the natives outnumber the whites by ten to one, the task is beyond the small Communist Party to the same extent. We say nothing now of the vast native populations, working masses outside the Union [of South Africa] proper. Here is a strong case for the direct initiative of the Communist International.

While on this phase of the subject, I should like to mention India. India has nothing to do with the Negro question proper. But insofar as the subject is one of the relations between white and native workers, you have an interesting fact in the case of India, and it is this: There is also a thin upper crust of white skilled workers, much smaller than in Africa, but still it is there. One would have thought that this small labour aristocracy could easily be bought out by the capitalist class. But what do we see? We see white workers coming out on strike on the railways side by side with the Indian workers. Now, here is a good chance for Communist propaganda to get a purchase hold among the white workers. There must be fine opportunities there of bringing out white skilled leaders for the Indian working masses in the difficult early stages of the movement.

As for Africa, I would like to say in conclusion that although there are no brilliant examples of Negro Communists here in Moscow yet, I can assure you that the native working mass as a whole is going to be a brilliant example for communism. They are ripe for communism. They are absolutely propertyless. They are stripped of every vestige of property and caste prejudice. The African natives are a labouring race, still fresh from ancestral communal traditions. I will not say that the native workers are well organised, or have a general conception of communism or even of trade unionism, as yet. But they have made several attempts at liberation by way of industrial solidarity. They only need awakening. They know they are slaves, but lack the knowledge how to free themselves. I should like to say the same regarding colony prejudice. Although colony prejudice is there, I am glad to say that never has it taken on the form of mob lynching and the frenzy of the American outbreaks against the Negroes.

The solution of the problem, the whole world problem is being worked out in South Africa on the field of the working-class movement. In conclusion, I would like to admit this motion for the congress to endorse as a sentiment of solidarity with Africa:

> That this congress resolves to further the movement among the working masses of Africa as an integral part of the Oriental question, and desires the Executive to take a direct initiative in promoting the awakening of the African Negroes as a necessary step to the world revolution."

The Situation in Africa

Russian State Archive of Socio-Political History
To the Small Bureau of the Comintern
July 16 1921

The South African Delegation has already submitted a report on the state of the Communist movement in that country. Suffice it to say here that a United Communist Party [the Communist Party of South Africa] has now been formed by the linking of the various groups with the International Socialist League, which was the Left Wing of the South African Labour Party that broke away from the latter body in 1915.

In the reports and articles already submitted by us to the International comrades, we have tried to emphasize the peculiar conditions of the South African Communist movement, namely:

(1) The presence in South Africa of two streams of the proletariat, white and black, performing complementary industrial functions, with two widely different standards of life.
(2) The very primitive character of the Negro race, just emerging from the tribal system and the consequent exclusively white character of the Communist Movement.
(3) The Communist Party is forced by the logic of the class struggle to place the question of solidarity with the native workers in the forefront of its propaganda among the white workers. This principle is the touchstone of Communism for us. Nevertheless, owing to the slow development of the Native Labour Movement, the occasions on which this slogan can be made an issue are not so frequent as they otherwise might be with an accelerated native movement. A native strike gives the Communists ideal opportunities of placing the revolutionary test before the white workers, either to side with their masters or with their black fellow workers. But while the native workers remain unorganised, the white workers lag at the stage of Class Collaboration; and between the two, the Communist movement hangs fire.
(4) Normally, all the activity of the South African Communists is among the whites, although the subject matter of propaganda largely includes the native labour question. Our members and supporters find themselves in white Trade Unions, and are preoccupied with the fight against class collaboration there. There are hardly any native linguists among the white Communists. The common medium of expression between whites and natives is "Kitchen K*," a very inadequate kind of native esperanto. On the occasions when we have issued leaflets in the native languages we have had to depend on native translators. All Communist activity among the native Africans has to he mainly illegal. For this, the Communist Party organisation, besides being inadequate, is wholly unsuited.
(5) South Africa is the entrance to the great territories further north. We have to consider not only the negro population of the Government of South Africa. The railway line runs right up for two thousand miles to the Belgian Congo. Members of the South African Communist movement are to be found there also, although no Communist Group; and one member was recently expelled from the territory for Trade Union agitation. For this vast native population, however, the Communist movement can only draw on white sources for financial and other support. All natives are under the strictest passport control. The few educated natives are easily lured away by the enticements of social equality and an assured existence equivalent to their education. Thus, as the native population of South Africa, (to say nothing of territories outside the Union), outnumbers the whites by six to one. the task of the Communist Party is beyond its resources at least in

that proportion; in addition the presence of a slave cast side by side with white skilled labour makes the latter an unfavourable recruiting ground for obtaining the necessary minimum of Communist workers.

We would therefore suggest that, in a country like Africa, the small white working class should be regarded more as a purchase-hold for the direct action of the Comintern, than as wholly responsible for the Communist movement among the Africans. We white colonists are a shifting population. For some of us, the only tie with South Africa is the Communist Movement itself.

(In passing, we may point out that the presence of a small class of white skilled workers in India who have already given proofs of militancy by coming out on strike with their Indian fellow-workers, offers a good opening for the education of possible Communist elements, powerful and influential in proportion to their numbers, in India also.)

We consider that these conditions entitle us to urge upon the Comintern that the African Negroes, like the Indians, should come directly under its initiative. We have already shown in our Report that the South African natives, the most advanced in Africa, offer good material for the Communist movement. They have already given proofs of their willingness to fight against oppression.

We submit that the matter of the African Negroes is sufficiently important to send a Comintern representative to South Africa to survey the whole Negro question and its relation to the Communist Party. Comrade Rutgers, for instance, has taken a keen interest in the Indian and African movements. Incidentally, his Dutch nationality would make him a competent judge of the Dutch Nationalist movement in South Africa in its bearings on the negro question and its relation to the Communist movement.

In Comrade SP Bunting, of Johannesburg, the Comintern representative would find a member who has devoted his whole energy to the movement among the native Africans, so far as his work for daily bread allows, This comrade has been most active in forming education groups of young natives, and organising a native Union. But he is continually driven back by lack of funds and the pre-occupation of his fellow members in the work among the whites. He has tried to start a newspaper in the native languages. But the Party could not come to his aid without jeopardising the funds of its official organ, *The International*.

Owing to their miserable conditions, the natives are not able to give financial help for the necessary preliminary work. What is required is to assure economic sustenance to a few native workers as agitators and organisers, such as Cetiywe [Industrial Workers of Africa organiser Alfred Cetyiwe], Mashabala [Industrial and Commercial Workers Union and ANC official Samuel Masabalala] and others who have already made attempts, some successful, to organise their brothers. This primitive mass is waiting to be stirred. Given the necessary funds and a comrade like Bunting who is a capable administrator and journalist, we are convinced that great results could be achieved. A Communist newspaper in the native languages is a crying need; also schools for illiterate workers. The bourgeoisie are beginning to realise the need of satisfying the Negro's craving for education. It remains for us to decide whether that education shall be given to him in a capitalist or in a Communist medium.

We trust that the Comintern will take into consideration, and give us their instructions on the movement among the Africans. We hope that the Comintern will not content itself with Manifestoes from Moscow, which, owing to the lack of local machinery, will not reach the masses to whom they are directed. The pre-occupations of an early European revolution should not create an atmosphere of *laissez-aller* ['leave it be'] towards the Negroes. It should rather be an argument for forestalling the bourgeoisie against any attempt to use Africa as a base for the counter-revolution. Conversely, the idea of a prolonged lease of life for European Capitalism should also be an argument for action in the work of forming proletarian parties among the Indian and African populations to accelerate the world revolution. There is above all the supreme revolutionary duty of rallying all peoples to Communism irrespective of motives of strategy.

We hope that the Comintern will give us an opportunity for exchange of views On the matter before our return to South Africa.

With Communist Greetings,

D. Ivon Jones, Sam Barlin

South African Delegation to the Third Congress of the Communist International.

NB. The word "Negro" is never used in South Africa, except its corrupted form "N*" in an insulting sense. Technically, the Negro is the more northern native. The Southern race of Africa is known by their own term "Bantu" to ethnologists. But we have used the better known word "Negro" to cover the lot for the sake of clearness.

A Colonial Bureau of the Comintern

Russian State Archive of Socio-Political History
Letter to Matyas Rakosi July-August 1921

Dear Comrade Rakosi,

PROPOSED COLONIAL BUREAU OF THE COMINTERN

I have spoken to several Colonial delegates regarding the advisability of forming a Colonial Bureau of the Comintern; and I should be obliged if you would place the proposal before the Small Bureau or the Executive Committee [which elected the 'Small Bureau"].

In the present state of things the Colonial delegates feel that they have no plan of work, and no adequate scope for their activities. We feel that we could best contribute to the work of the Comintern by the formation of a Colonial Bureau, and thus feel of some use to the International movement.

We propose that such a Bureau should gather together all matter pertaining to the Colonies, Colonial exploitation, and the Colonial movements in India, Africa, Java, Palestine, Egypt, etc.

The collection of data and statistics, literature, etc., would be the task of this Bureau. It would also be its duty when called upon to advise the Secretariat regarding the various aspects of the Colonial movements. It would also keep watch over social and political developments especially affecting the Colonial working masses where there is no Communist movement or where it is too weak to make its voice heard.

For example, John Harris [organising secretary of the Anti-Slavery and Aborigines Protection Society] the Negrophile liberal, has succeeded in making an issue in the British liberal Press of the repressive measures of the British Administration in Kenya, where the natives have been subjected to compulsory labour and land expropriation. Such matters might also receive the attention of the Comintern, giving a lead directly or through the British Communist Party, and thus enhance its prestige as the defender of the unprotected working masses of the Colonies.

It is suggested that the Negro question as it surges up in its most frenzied form in America would also come within the purview of the Colonial Bureau to collect information for the Executive Committee and make proposals on developments from time to time. And the immense amount of matter arising out of the Indian movement, the necessity of collecting data on present political developments, non-cooperation, Swadeshi [supporting home produce against British imports], etc. and the part played by the young Indian proletariat in Gandhi's Boycott movement, as also the struggles of the proletariat in its own interests, where it clashes with the Nationalist movement and how far the two march together, – all offers a wide field for work which only the Comintern can do.

This work would of course require a Secretary and a Russian typist. An office fitted out for statistical work with a card system for the work of reference to all the collected data, and bookshelves with catalogue system for the collected literature. The Colonial Delegates, with any other comrades which the Executive might consider it advisable to add, would form an advisory Committee to control the Bureau and advise the Executive Committee on Colonial developments. The Colonial delegates would apportion out the work of reading up and collecting the material for current literature and journals etc., make a collection of same and advise the Archives Department what to order from abroad. Literature on the Colonial question now in the Library might form a separate section as part of the Colonial Bureau.

Trusting these suggestions will not be unwelcome to the comrades,

I remain,
fraternally yours,
D. Ivon Jones (South Africa)

Workers' Organisations in South Africa

Russian State Archive of Socio-Political History
Report to the Communist International
August 13 1921
Am awaiting latest particulars of the Party [CPSA] statistics etc.
Re leaders:
WH Andrews. Secretary, and Editor *The International*. Best known Labour figure in South Africa on the radical side. Before split of Labour Party in 1915 on war question, was its chairman, and its chief founder. Combines steady going characteristics of British Trade Unionist with a large grasp of the class struggle. Age 51. Mechanic (fitter or turner).

SP Bunting A lawyer in his leisure time! A graduate of Oxford. Son of Sir Percy Bunting, *Contemporary Review*. Comrade of great energy. Came into Labour Party in 1911, and was among the first to denounce labour participation in War of capitalists. Has suffered much Economic stress through boycott owing to International Socialist Activity. Man of great energy. Inclined to Leftism in question of Parliamentary elections, and advocates devoting Communist activity solely to the Negro workers. Age 46.

CB Tyler: A member and most prominent figure in the Building Workers Industrial Union. Came into Communist movement through SLP [Socialist Labour Party] group of Campbell (now left S.A.) Tyler works at his trade of shop fitter. Main activity consists in furthering Communist methods and propaganda in the Trade Union. Age 38.

Colin Wade: Dentist. Chief promoter of War on War League at outbreak of war, from which sprang the International Socialist League and now Communist Party. A lecturer on Russia and keen collector of all matter relating thereto. Best authority in Transvaal on Municipal Socialism and Town Planning Reform.

Charles Dines: Fitter, 30. Communist propagandist, with SLP training.

HW Haynes: 40. Miner, now office worker. Collaborator in *The International*. A Comrade of great experience in strike movement. Chairman of the Kleinfontein strike Committee which initiated the general strike movement in 1913. Keen student of Marxism, and leader of Marxian Club, Durban. Advocate of anti-parliamentary action, now he joins the Communist party under 21 Points [conditions of admission for parties to join the Communist International].

D. Ivon Jones: Office worker, 37. Was Secretary of the Labour Party at time of split. Was first Secretary and Editor of *The International* 1915-1920.

WH [Wilfred] Harrison: Capetown, Secretary of local Branch of Communist Party. Previously secretary of Social Democratic Federation, now merged in Communist Party. Was arrested several times for anti-militarist propaganda. Called himself "philosophical anarchist" before formation of CP Cabinet maker.

DL [David] Dryburgh: Capetown, previously SLP student, member of Industrial Socialist League. Arrested with his father (70) for "criminal slander" of Government in connection with recent massacre of natives at Bullhoek. Trial pending.

W. Green [LH Greene]: Cape Town. Propagandist, also arrested with above.

J. Chapman: Benoni. 40. Blacksmith. Communist worker & propagandist. Chairman of Executive Committee CP. Persistent advocate of revolutionary political action on lines now laid down by 21 Points.

Other propagandists & workers in the Communist Party. S.A.

H. Barendorgh: [Barendregt] fitter.

E.J. Brown: Experienced strike leader. Recently expelled from Belgian Congo for agitation there.

Sam Barlin. Party worker, and organiser of coloured tailors and other coloured workers. Member of E. Committee.

Ralph Rabb: Organiser of literature activity of the International Socialist & Communist movements. Great believer in printed word.

Ben Sigamoney: School teacher. Indian. Organiser of Indian workers in Natal.

Abe Goldman: Tailor. Propagandist and educator in Marxist theory. Prominent figure in Tailors Union.

W. Blake: Secretary of Building workers Industrial Union.

Gideon Botha: Tramwayman. Dutch propagandist of Communism.

[Thomas William] Thibedi: Negro school teacher. Propagandist of Communism among native (negro) workers.

Manuel Lopez: 25. Capetown. Tramwayman. Communist writer and agitator.

Tom Nortye: Dutch propagandist of Communism. Tramwayman. 33.

Jack Williams: Engine driver. Pretoria. Branch Secretary.

Tom Mathews: Fitter. Member of AEU [Amalagamted Engineering Union] Executive. Communist speaker.

South African Labour Party:

This Party has never recovered the shock it received in the 1915 split. In order to please the jingo press it expelled its left wing members who had formed themselves into the International League of the SALP. Its parliamentary representation was reduced from 8 to 4 members in the 1915 election. One by one the Trade unions disaffiliated from it. In the 1920 election however it increased its Parliamentary representation to 21 on the cost of living issue.

In 1921, its members in Parliament were again reduced to 10 members on the Industrial Issue. Its leader is FHP Creswell: One time mine manager. A most conservative type of Labour leader. Was defeated at the last election. Does not function as Party leader except through Parliament.

Thomas Boydell: member of Parliament since 1912 for Durban. Railway worker. Most painstaking worker in Labour Party, and adept at handling revolutionary phrases.

Kentridge, Waterston, Madeley.

The name Labour Party should not mislead one to associate this Party with the British Labour Party. No Trade Unions are affiliated to it. Even its open Branches are moribund, and only function for elections and at elections, – small groups gathered round the Parliamentary members as personal following. It survives on the prestige given it in the militant days before the ejection of the Socialists. Any proposal for affiliation of Communist Party should be viewed with these differences in mind. Moreover, the Labour Party has alienated the Dutch workers, hence in past de-affiliation of Unions. A broadening of the functions of the Communist Party would soon knock out the Labour Party in the industrial centres.

The South African Industrial Federation.

This Federation includes most of the Trade Unions of the Transvaal, and is aiming to bring in the other provinces. It functions in the Orange Free State, and is gaining over the Natal Unions. So far it has not been able to win over the Cape Federation owing to the radical difference of attitude towards the Coloured workers in the two Provinces.

The old Federation of Trades in the Transvaal which took up a militant revolutionary policy culminating in the uprising of 1913, was smashed up by the debacle of the 1914 movement, when Smuts brought 60,000 armed burghers into Johannesburg and deported nine Trade Union leaders to England. Crawford, was one of the deportees. He was then a noted exponent of Anarcho-Syndicalism. On his return to Africa at the outbreak of war he took up the honorary duties of the almost defunct Federation, and was in office when the resurgence of the Trade Union movement took place. He hitched on to the Chamber of Mines from the stand, and carried on the policy of class collaboration until today to an almost open champion of capitalist interests. There are spasmodic revolts against his policy, but since it is not yet bankrupt of results, the revolt has not yet taken definite shape.

Archibald Crawford has few other colleagues of importance. The opposition to his policy is reflected by the Communists, with Andrews, a metal worker, as its chief spokesman.

The Federation includes about 60,000 workers. The Railwaymen, loosely organised, & Coast Unions, not yet in the Federation, round number about 40,000. Statistical details to follow on receipt of same from South Africa.

"Epics of martyrdom"

Letter to George Eyre Evans

August 19 1921

Dear George,

So I hope to settle down for a few days stay at least, now that I have reached this objective and seen things. Russia as you see is suffering from famine, but is manfully coping with the menace. However, we shall tell all about Russia on my return.

Hope that Miss Jones is not vexed with me for running away so mysteriously. To me the world has become very small now, and a run over to Russia looks no more than a trip to Pontrhydfendigaid used to be in the old days!! Except that in the former case you have to watch the police! I did not know that I could get across until I got to Newcastle and from there; if I set forward the Norwegian Party were to tell me further. Hence I could not give much [information] of my goings and left JDS [friend JD Stephens] to tell you privately.

My health is fairly good, and yet not quite satisfactory. We are looked after here carefully and not allowed to share in the privations of the poor Russian people. But the food is not exactly constituted for a chest complaint. But my appetite is good, and I feel better even than I was in France, except that persistent mental work becomes difficult, and there is a lot to do here for South Africa in connection with the Communist International to which I am a delegate. The people of Moscow, although suffering from lack of food, look surprisingly well. You do not see the drawn and haggard faces of the British industrial centres. The reason is that the hours of work decrease as food decreases and becomes normal again as the food becomes normal. So that no undue strain is placed upon the people's health. Of course, we are not in the famine districts. There the conditions are serious indeed. The Moscow workers sacrifice a quantity of their daily ration, which is already small, to the relief of the famine areas. The result is that after the privations of seven years of war and civil war, and the Blockade, and now the Drought and the failure of crops, the people are beginning to show that lack of stamina and mental vigour which I feel after only two months with specially favoured food. What wonder that they have to appeal for outside aid. They have done wonderfully, performed epics of martyrdom, and will do so again.

The Russian people are like the sea, one never knows its depth,or what resources of vigour and sacrifice it may yet hold concealed to come forth when the occassion demands.

By the way, I wonder if the *Welsh Gazette* would publish a couple of articles, if they were not too communistic in flavour, on Russia. Shall I send one or two and see?

I still remember that afternoon tea with eggs and nice bread and butter!!

Au revoir old friend.

The Crisis in Colonial Nationalism

Russian State Archive of Socio-Political History
To the Executive Committee of the Communist International
September-October 1921

Comrades,

I wish to urge the formation of a COLONIAL BUREAU OF THE COMINTERN on the lines of my proposals placed with the Secretary, Comrade Rakosi.

A crisis is at present discernible in the Colonial National Movements which calls for the unremitting attention of the Comintern. Right and Left wings are emerging, and the dangers of compromise of Right Nationalists with the Imperial domination becoming more imminent.

Egypt: In Egypt, the Adly Pasha official delegation is gaining adherents and Zaghloul Pasha in the Nationalist Centre seems prone towards more pacific methods under pressure of the Capitulatory Powers. A left wing movement is appearing, calling itself Socialist, under Dr. Hussein, and the Communist Group has an important function to perform in keeping up the uncompromising struggle through the Left Wing Nationalist elements.

India: In India, Gandhi's boycott movement is gaining huge proportions, but is reactionary in its economic results as far as the movement back to hand spinning goes, although the native mill owners are meanwhile reaping the benefits. The recent rising of the *moplahs* [Muslim peasants in Madras province] reported last week indicate the lower mass struggle against both Indian and Imperialist exploiters, and Gandhi, with Mohammed Ali, the Moslem leader, have been requested by the Government to go and pacify the rebels. The need of a Communist Party right on the spot in India is very urgent.

Ireland: The Republicans in Ireland have concluded a truce which has produced a Left Wing movement among the fighting Brigades, which are composed almost wholly of working men. The Left Wing elements have turned towards the Communist Group for guidance and aid in renewing the struggle should any form of compromise take place. Unfortunately, the data at the command of the Comintern is meagre, and a joint delegate from the Communists and the Brigades who spent a week here on urgent business, had to return empty handed owing to the danger of provocateurs and the lack of the necessary information in our archives to confirm credentials, which information it would be the task of a Colonial Bureau to collect.

Africa: A Pan-African Congress of the Negroes of the world was recently held in London, Brussels and Paris promoted by Americans [August 28-September 6]. The negroes of Africa have no bourgeoisie. This Pan-African movement has therefore no progressive traits like the other Colonial National movements. The African Negroes are beginning to move along class lines. The Governments are using the Pan-African idea to divert them from it. The great COLONIAL AND SUBJECT NATIONALIST MOVEMENTS are unprovided for the technical apparatus of the Comintern, and it is my duty as a Colonial delegate to plead for the Comintern to place itself as the only co-ordinating head of these movements, not only in word, but by the formation of a COLONIAL BUREAU, at first to gather data and watch events, later to be extended to any function that may be deemed necessary.

D. Ivon Jones,
Communist Party of South Africa.

The Solidarity of Anarchism and the Fight against the Left

Communist Review Vol. 2 No. 1, November 1921

The "Anarchist" incident in the closing session of the Red Trade Union Congress is too significant to pass over without comment. It was not a mere misunderstanding which, through good fortune, was smoothed over. Given other conditions it could have developed into a grand combat with West European anarchism – the left menace to the Revolution. One felt we were back again in the old atmosphere of Marx versus Bakunin. Such a propitious ground of attack on Anarcho-Syndicalism philosophy may not appear again, as that arising from the request of the Anarcho-Syndicalist delegation for the Soviet Republic to release the Anarchists in prison, Anarchists caught with arms in their hands conspiring against the proletarian Republic. What will the workers of France, who in the mass do not care a fig for theory when they are faced with a fact, what will they think of such an astounding request? The only drawback to making an issue of the matter is that its proletarian exponents are the dupes of petty bourgeois ideology, and may themselves be quite sincere fighters for the revolution/ Although, in reading the reports of the Red Trade Union Congress, one cannot but notice the complete absence of all reference to the Soviet regime and the Dictatorship of the proletariat in the speeches of the anti-political Syndicalists at this congress. The vague word "revolution" is not enough to define working class intentions.

Are they Different?

Bucharin [Bukharin], in making his statement on the imprisoned Anarchists, said that Russian Anarchism is different from West European Anarchism. I think he said this more for the sake of good feeling than of good theory. In other circumstances he would probably have said that Anarchism is at a more advanced stage of expression in Russia than in Western Europe. Just as Communism is more advanced here, so its enemies to Right and to Left have their inherent propensities brought out more blatantly into the open day. What difference is there between the Machno [Nestor Makhno] bands which the say "Down with all governments," and the West European Anarchist who, with mellifluous libertarian phrases, denounces all interference, even proletarian interference, with individual liberty. The only difference is that Machno has passed to propaganda of the deed.

In Machno the economic basis for Anarchism is exposed. He hates all governments, because all governments rob the poor rich peasants of their hoards of bread. The White Government plunders him for profit. The Red Government takes his store of corn for the common good. The philosophic Anarchist does not confess even to himself the economic root of his libertarian phrases. He does not know their root.

(It is a mishandling of the Materialist conception to speak of the "Economic Roots of Ideas." Ideas are exploited but not produced by economic interests. Ideas clamour for admission. Ruling interests decide which ones shall enter the doors of publicity. In a larger sense, of course, the production of ideas is conditioned by the material surroundings as variously seen by thinking men. But the subject is too big to enter into here. It involves the "sincerity" of the propagandist, which is always a tough nut to crack for the counter-propagandist. See Marx in "Eighteenth Brumaire" on relation of petty bourgeois class to its representatives among the Intelligentsia).

As Plechanoff [Georgi Plekhanov] showed in his work on Anarchism, it is idle for the philosophic Anarchist to disavow the propaganda of the deed. Firstly, their writings, their phrases and their slogans, become the slogans of the Machno band and the bomb-thrower. Secondly, Plechanoff showed how the philosophic companions greeted the propaganda of the deed when any of the more ardent brethren bombed a Parliament or stabbed a king. While disavowing the act, they greeted the propagandist by deed as worthy of Anarchism. There is no halting place for Anarchism between the phrase and the deed. The very ethereal and refined Berkmans provide the watchword for the more practical Machnos. It is a true instinct, therefore, which makes the philosophic brethren of the West plead for the bomb-throwing brethren of Russia.

Anarchism and Anti-Parliamentarism

Anti-Parliamentarism in itself is no sign of Anarchism. Tom Mann was a doughty antagonist of parliamentary reformism in his old syndicalist days, before the conditions of revolutionary political action had yet fully evolved. Much that is healthy disgust with "parliamentary cretinism" goes under the name of Anarchism in Italy, France and Spain. The test of its sincerity is the willingness of such elements not only to acclaim the Soviet Republic (many bourgeois liberals do that), not only to acclaim the Communist International as the fighting head of the proletariat – both these institutions are far away in Moscow, and the petty bourgeois has a habit of acclaiming many things as good at a distance which be will bitterly oppose at home – no, the test of sincerity in such Anarchist or Syndicalist elements, so-called, is their readiness, to see in the Communist Party right at home the necessary weapon of emancipation, of the fight against the bourgeois state power.

At the Red Trade Union Congress the Anarchist-Syndicalist elements opposed any relation with either the Communist parties or the Communist International, and even evaded references to the Soviet Republic and the

Dictatorship of the proletariat. Without these weapons of revolution, the Anarcho-Syndicalists have failed to show, have not even attempted to show, how they will pull down and keep down the bourgeois State power, and how they will build up a proletarian State upon its ruins.

Anarchism and the Petty-Bourgeoisie

Without these conditions of struggle, the Anarcho-Syndicalists express only the aims of the petty-bourgeoisie, who wish to break up the big capitalist State, but not to build another in its place. Anarchism is the paradise of the petty bourgeoisie. Anarchism the the ideology of the disgruntled bourgeois, squeezed out in the furious race for profits. "Scratch an Anarchist and you will find a reformist, scratch a reformist and you will find an Anarchist," said Daniel De Leon. But while expressing the vague longings of the petty bourgeois tor a state of society, not where all shall be proletarians, but where all shall be petty bourgeois, Anarchism, especially in the form of Anarcho-Syndicalism, serves the purpose of the capitalist domination. The petty trader longs for some weapon against the big capitalist State which will not itself become an organised State power. It won't have the Communist Party for that reason. It has no weapon of its own except the futile one of non-resistance. He sees a weapon in Anarcho-Syndicalism, because it dissipates the power of the proletariat just at the point when it would become an organised State power. Thus both the big and small capitalists are pleased.

Anarcho-Syndicalism pretends that in opposing the Communist Party it only wants to keep the movement purely proletarian on the industrial field. It ignores the overwhelming power of the Capitalist Press, its power to give bourgeois minds to common proletarians. Thus, in the Syndicates without a party, instead of the clear-minded proletarians being able to move to a common watchword and close discipline unhampered by the amorphous mass, as they would be in the form of a Communist Party, they are assimilated to the general level of the mass. The mass can only see its immediate interests. The clear-headed proletarians, gathered together in the form of a Communist Party to direct the mass, see also the ultimate interests of the working class, and are able to guide the masses accordingly. Thus Anarcho-Syndicalism, in spite of its high-sounding phrases, by this very boycott of the organisation of the clear-headed sections of the proletarians into a common group – called a party – hinders most effectively the pursuit of the ultimate aims of the proletariat. It splits up the class movement into a false antagonism of political versus industrial. The amorphous mass of the trades unions, no matter how well organised, well led, are left wholly at the mercy of bourgeois press propaganda, and other bourgeois agencies at the crucial moments. The circumambient air is bourgeois. Even though the leaders be true, having no party following, their voices pitted against the tornado of the bourgeois press, are not heard even by their own membership. The mass moves to its immediate interests only. And Anarcho-Syndicalism in the hour of revolution would halt the proletariat at the stage of immediate demands, at the stage of disrupting the capitalist State power in the interests of the petty bourgeoisie, without going forward to the formation of a proletarian State power in the interest of the proletariat. We are here speaking class motives, class designs of an instinctive character imposed upon the workers by petty bourgeois Anarchism. In actual fact, of course, the conditions for the most effective struggle for the immediate needs of the proletariat are also, in the revolutionary crisis, the conditions for the attainment of the ultimate objective. The means and the end become one. The dualism of the peaceful era of capitalism vanishes.

Other Symptoms

It is this instinct of the petty bourgeois, this unavowed desire for a political instrument of destruction, which is behind such schemes as Guild Socialism. How it loves to harp on the "consumer." It longs for a state of consumers, based on Orage's [English author and *New Age* editor AR Orage] instruments of consumption. Meanwhile the trades unions are to control industry, including no doubt the State's Army and Navy! What abnegation! Here is the Anarcho-Syndicalist idea of the after-the-revolution period. Like the Anarchist pure and simple, it dotes on the saving power of the consumer. The proletarian forces, it will be seen, have been good enough to smash up the capitalist State, and then withdrawn to second place to make room for the " consumer," the universal customer. Anarcho-Syndicalism and Guild Socialism makes the proletariat pull the chestnuts out of the fire for the petty bourgeoisie. Because such schemes are Utopian, futile, childish in the extreme to any student of history, it does not follow that they are harmless. In the meantime the sabotaging of the workers' revolutionary party by the Anarcho-Syndicalists to the tune of seemingly ultra-revolutionary slogans does incalculable harm to the revolution.

The counter-revolutionary effect of the Anarcho-Syndicalist doctrine has been laid bare by the Kronstadt mutiny, where the slogan of the counter-revolution was "Soviets without the Communists." The Vienna Congress of the Two-and-a-Half International pledged itself to Soviets, but minus the 21 points. Thus Anarcho-Syndicalism, Guild Socialism and Reform Pacifism at last find their joint image in the slogan of the Kronstadt counter-revolution, in the camp of the White Guard. So long as classes have not disappeared, so long as the whole of the people have not been turned into producers, Soviets or trade unions without guiding hand of the Communist Party must inevitably deteriorate into amorphous bodies and become a prey to bourgeois influences. The petty bourgeoisie have no instrument of their own. They waver between the two big classes. They see an instrument in the trades unions, even in the Soviets, if properly misguided on the lines of Anarcho-Syndicalism. Hence why it is that in countries like France and Spain, with preponderant petty-proprietorship, the prevailing habits of thought tend to permeate the workers' organisations, disguised as anti-capitalist thought, but in reality not pro-proletarian. Thus we have the

Comite[s] Syndicaliste[s] Revolutionnaire[s] (CSR), appealing for a return to the Charter of Amiens, which is the identical appeal which Jouhaux, the henchman of Big Capital, makes. Forward to the Communist International, not back to the Charter of Amiens, is the test of true revolutionary policy to-day. As the pressure increases the rank and file must more and more look to a revolutionary political party of the working class to guide and direct the struggle, even though the Anarcho-Syndicalist leaders themselves may be too deeply rooted in old forms of thought, to say nothing of *amour propre*,[self-love, vanity] to change. Meanwhile, these leaders, who like the Bourbons, learn nothing and forget nothing, are doing a great dis-service to the proletarian cause by their separatism in regard to the Communist International and their solidarity in regard to the Russian Anarchists – two expressions of the one anti-proletarian idea.

The Crisis in the South African Labour Movement

International Press Correspondence February 28 1922

Johannesburg in the Transvaal is the centre of a coal and gold miners' strike. Apart from sympathetic movements which may or may not break out, not more than 20,000 white workers are directly involved. Yet the London Press is considerably perturbed. "K*", as gold mining stock is dubbed, are the mainstay of an important section of the bourgeoisie. And the Transvaal mines produced last year slightly more than half the total gold output of the world, produced moreover under the most modern forms of concentrated large industry. Hence its importance not only for the section of the bourgeoisie directly interested, but for the whole financial mechanism of world capitalism at a time when British bankers are striving to stabilize currency on the gold basis. But this big proportion of the world's gold output is not produced by the 15,000 or 20,000 workers directly involved in the present dispute. Apart from the coal mines, there are 200,000 native workers, many of them raw recruits from the tribes, employed in the Transvaal gold mines. These are the men who actually drill the rock, "lash" the blasted ore and do the hardest manual work. The white miners on strike are more or less go-betweens, gangers, possessing a legal monopoly as white men of the right to handle gelatinite and blasting fuses. No man of colour can by law hold a blasting certificate. This colour bar is the symbol of the white workers' privileged economic and social position in South Africa.

This double-barrelled character of the South African labour movement is only now dawning upon the white workers. Hitherto they have regarded themselves as all that was meant by "Labour". Under the illusion of being the whole of Labour (as the bourgeoisie have the illusion of being "the people") the white workers have waged several fierce struggles with gold mining capital. In the 1913 general strike things went so far that a pitched battle took place between them and the regular troops in the streets of

Johannesburg, in which 21 persons were killed and over 400 wounded. The capitalist class were panic-stricken, and the men's leaders, under the slogan of "The Martial Law of the Workers", scored a temporary victory. The following year, Smuts, after careful military preparation, avanged himself and deported nine of the trade union leaders.

When the war came, the supreme necessity of keeping the gold mines going forced the old politician type of magnate to withdraw from the scene, and Sir Evelyn Wallers, the arch-conciliator, was put in charge of the Chamber of Mines. Bain, Mason, Andrews and other old militant trade unionists were shoved into the background by their opposition to the war, and the Boards of Reference found Crawford, one time Anarcho-Syndicalist, a most suitable tool for carrying out the policy of class collaboration. After the war, the premium on the mint price of gold further helped the Chamber to concede much to the white workers, who gradually lost their fighting spirit.

Meanwhile, the native workers gave signs of awakening, and surprised the white worker out of his self-sufficiency. A strike of 80,000 native mine workers; a big anti-passport movement; strikes of native municipal workers; the formation of a native trade-union, an unheard of innovation; all these portents came after the outbreak of the Russian revolution. But the native still calls his white fellow worker "Boss" as an ordinary form of address. And so the white worker is assured his status.

But now the gold premium is vanishing under the better exchange position of the pound sterling. The mine owners declare that many low grade mines have been working solely on this premium as a source of profit. It has been for some years the dream of the gold magnates to abolish the colour bar, and introduce native labour into the more skilled operations. The *Star*, organ of the Chamber of Mines, is a champion of Negro advancement against the exclusiveness of the white labour unions, and sometimes its propaganda in this direction is a good handle for Communist Party propaganda. The white labour movement is placed in a false position against the undeniable justice of the capitalist plea for native advancement, although it is only a transparent cloak for more intense exploitation of the native. Comrade Andrews, writing in our Party organ, *The International*, holds out to the miners the only solution which they can employ and compromise their position in the labour movement: The following extract condenses the issue in a nutshell:

> As for the unions, they would do better for themselves if they urged and helped the natives to demand more pay for the jobs they do now, thus decreasing the competition of native with white and diminishing the danger of natives ousting whites. The white miners are perfectly justified in fighting to keep up the numbers and pay of holders of

> blasting certifications. They would get native support in this with the higher pay and better treatment of the blacks. However, owing to deficient class consciousness, we find them presenting the shameful spectacle of conspiring with their masters for the better exploitation of their fellow workers, which must inevitably, if gradually, lead to their own elimination. For a section whlch poses at the same time as both masters and workers must sooner or later collapse.

Let it not be supposed that a state of antagonism exists between the black and white worker at all comparable with that obtaining in the South of the United States. All our pogroms are governmental pogroms – the recent dastardly massacre of simple natives at Bullhoek, for instance, (passed over so lightly by the British Press). As a matter of fact, the white and black workers get on very happily together at the mines. The South African Bantu is a jovial fellow to work with. The white skilled mechanic functions as a teacher of the native labourer, though he may not be conscious of it. During working hours he jokes with him and even discusses the rudiments of social justice. The industrial functions of white and black are complementary. There is no industry where both do not labour together. The white workers can stop industry on their own account. So can the black workers if they have a mind to. But it takes both white and black to start the wheels going again. Under a Soviet system all the factors are present for mutual cooperation. Capitalist exploitation turns this industrial partnership into political antagonism. An abyss separates the standard of living of the blacks and the whites. It is this, and the fear of falling into the abyss, which generates the anti-colour prejudice of the white worker. It is also this which makes the white worker a strange combination of anti-colour conservative and anti-capitalist militant. He would honestly like a way out with justice to these "uncivilized children" as he naively regards the Bantu worker, but without "social contamination" with them.

The attack on the colour bar threatens to put an end to this, the best possible condition for cooperation of white with black. A competition in the same industrial function will introduce the more ugly forms of American race hatred. There are more compelling reasons for this challenge than the drop in the gold premium. The total world output of gold has dropped from 94 million pounds in 1913 to 66 millions in 1921. The drop in Transvaal output was only from 37.4 million 34.5 million. It will be seen that the proportion of the Transvaal output to the whole world output has risen from two-fifths to one-half. With the enormous inflation of the currency, this drop in gold production must be checked if the bankers' stabilization plans are to be realized. The-low grade mines must be kept going at all costs, and the low grade ore knocking about the higher grade mines must be made available, and new borings encouraged. These considerations are behind the undoubted determination of the mineowners to smash the colour bar. A reduction in wages is not enough. Some "larger perspective", equal to the discovery of the cyanide process of gold extraction in the nineties, is needed. And the cheap Bantu worker is the solution, the man for the job, fresh from the tribe and requiring only a loin cloth and the benevolent sunshine in addition to the needs of the inner man – for the time being. Just now the mineowners are only asking for a certain fixed proportion of coloured workers to white.

Since 1913, Dutch workers in large numbers have invaded town industry, forced from the land by modern methods of agriculture. The Dutch Afrikanders are in a majority in the mines today, as well as several other industries. The police force is largely Dutch Afrikander. Only in the skilled mechanical trades does the old type of British trade unionist still hold his own. Nevertheless, with one or two exceptions, the leadership of the labour movement is still in the hands of the more experienced British workers. The Dutch workers make splendid trade unionists, however, full of the fighting spirit, for the trade union movement gives them back a little of the lost glamour, the sense of combat, of the old voortrekking days. But they are as yet a drag on the wheel of labour progress. They are much more bitter towards the native than the British workers, owing to the slave-holding traditions of the Dutch farmers. They are an obstacle to the speedy rapprochement of the white with the black worker which is the burden of our propaganda as a Communist Party in South Africa. The Dutch workers form as a rule the left wing of the Dutch Nationalist movement, since the Labour Party by its chauvinism has forfeited their sympathy. Hence we have for the first time the participation of Nationalist leaders like Visser and Tielman Roos [Justice Minister 1924-29] in the present strike on the side of the men, and General Hertzog, the Republican leader, has had a conference with the Industrial Federation. The Nationalists seem to be utilizing the strike as a means of forcing Smuts out of office. The sympathetic elements in the police force and the absence of Imperial troops, are factors in their favour. In normal times the British workers would resent the interference of the Nationalists. But the attack on the colour bar is an attack on the very existence of the white section of the working-class, and it is therefore prepared to seek allies anywhere.

In the 1913 strike the more advanced white workers already encouraged appeals for native support. In the present strike in the coal section at Witbank, where the miners are more conservative than on the Rand (as the sixty-mile gold reef is called) the native workers are carrying on mining under the direction of officials. They approached their white fellow workers on strike and asked them what they were to do. These white strikers, still *solidaire* with bourgeois society, solemnly advised the natives to obey the big *mlungu* (master). But an increasing number of trade unionists stand for the solidarity of Labour irrespective of colour.

The Nationalist festival in South Africa is held on Dingaan's Day, the day when Dingaan's Zulu army was smashed by the Dutch invaders in 1838. This is now the holy day of Afrikander Nationalism. The honest Bantu has nothing to gain from Nationalist intervention in the present dispute. The Chamber of Mines is for him in the line of progress, if the white worker will only turn towards him as his natural ally and fellow worker. Should that come to pass, then gold, the "root of all evil", will have been for the Negro masses of South Africa the agent of proletarian development which has brought them in line with the great world movement.

Memorandum on the South African situation

Russian State Archive of Socio-Political History

To the Presidium of the Comintern March 15 1922

Comrades,

The news in today's *Pravda* indicates a state of bloody civil war in South Africa, arising from the strike in the gold mines [the "Rand Revolt" of white gold and coal miners]. I have submitted several notes on the Press reports of the situation. I shall only repeat here that the issue of the strike is the attempt of the Chamber of Mines, (which is all-powerful in the Government of South Africa) to break down the "colour bar", that is, introduce native (negro) labour at cheap rates into the skilled industrial operations. But this is only the form which the international attack of capital on labour has taken in South Africa. It has been the function of the Communist Party of South Africa and the International Socialist movement preceding it to preach this fact in and out of season for the last six years. It is a tribute to the persistent efforts of the Party in this regard that, in spite of the pernicious form in which the strike issue has been put, a form best calculated to arouse race hatred between the two sections of the working class, and in spite of the stage of armed conflict into which the struggle has passed, not a single instance has been cabled in the reports of attacks by white workers on the negro working masses, the unwitting occasion of the conflict. This splendid result is wholly due to the work of the Communist Party.

Our paper *The International*, which has been doing the work of the Third International in South Africa from the Zimmerwald days [beginning in September 1915 with the first international socialist conference against war], is the only working class paper in the country. The Labour Party in South Africa, though it has 11 members in Parliament, has no official press. The sacrifices made by our members to keep this paper going for over six years have been worthy of the cause, and have succeeded in keeping the paper alive against heavy odds without any outside help up to the present date. In our work on the negro question, and our efforts through the paper to achieve a rapprochement of the black and white working masses NO PARTY COULD

WITH GREATER JUSTIFICATION APPEAL FOR OUTSIDE AID, but, with the exception of five minutes discussion with the Budget Committee eight months ago, no consideration has been given to the matter by the Comintern in spite of repeated memorandums on the subject by myself. The negro masses have no votes to give us, no militants or funds to lend to the cause; they are new from the tribal state, and cannot do more at present than form rough and ready industrial organisations. Our work among these masses is therefore a missionary work, and our responsibility towards them is only slightly greater than the responsibility of the International in general. We came to Moscow with the idea of reporting to a General Staff of the world movement, but find that it requires "diplomatic" qualities to push one's case, and in these diplomatic arts the revolutionary movement in South Africa has equipped us very poorly!!

Our Secretary, Comrade Andrews, has been arrested in connection with the strike, on the charge of "inciting to violence". He is a mechanic by occupation. Before the world war he was the acknowledged leader of the South Africa Labour movement and chairman of the Labour Party. This position he sacrificed by his denunciation of the war from the class point of view. Nevertheless, although thrown into the background by the Jingo leaders during the war, and later by Communist propaganda on the question of Negro labour, he has never ceased to be the most respected Labour leader in South Africa, and his arrest is a sure sign of the progress made by the Communist solution of the present problems of South African Labour. If the present bloodshed results in a Republican-Labour block in the Government, Andrews is the one man who commands the unbounded respect of both the Dutch Republican farmers as well as Labour, and is the one man who by his record can restrain the pogrom proclivities of the Dutch farmer class against the negro masses, by any such coalition. In this matter I should be glad if the Presidium could find time to tender advice to the Party.

Owing to the return of a number of our most militant comrades to England, the Party was not so strong numerically of late. The unemployment crisis also brought the funds for carrying on our paper into low water, so that latterly *The International* has been kept alive by the profits of our printing press. Now, however, owing to large printing credits to the Trades Unions during the strike, and the impoverishment of the Unions, our printing shop is also in financial difficulties, and the paper must collapse without outside aid.

I feel it my duty to proceed without delay to South Africa, (although I had definitely returned to England when I was instructed to proceed to Moscow). I should therefore be glad of an early consideration of these matters by the Presidium.

With Communist greetings,
D. Ivon Jones

Further Statement on the South African Situation

Russian State Archive of Socio-Political History
Moscow March 25 1922

To Comrade Kuusingen, Secretary, Comintern
The latest news by mail from Africa tend to modify my previous statement that there had been no outbreaks of violence between black and white workers. It appears that several tragic conflicts of minor character occurred between Black and white workers side by side with the main struggle with the Government forces.

These incidents are all the more tragic in that they make the task of the Communist Party far more difficult in the future, unless a great change of attitude takes place in the minds of the white workers as a result of the present events.

It is precisely because of the new political alignments that will result from the conflict that it may be wise for me to await some report from the Party before returning to South Africa, especially if in the meanwhile the proposed Anglo-American-Colonial Bureau will be formed.

The strike and insurrection was not officially led by the Communist Party, although participated in by Communist speakers. Comrade Andrews, our Secretary, was arrested with five other members of the Left Wing Movement, on a charge of "inciting to violence". Meanwhile, the actual leaders of the Commandoes, especially a member of Parliament named [Bob] Waterston) who has no fixed principles and disclaims any revolutionary intent, were left unmolested by the police right up to the open conflict. The Government seemed to have welcomed an armed clash, as long as it was led by volatile, non-Communist elements, in order to settle once for all with the white workers, and gain a free field for the exploitation of cheap native labour.

The Communist Party office, in common with that of the Trade Unions in the same building, is occupied by the police; and there is no doubt that our printing press and Party newspaper *The International* are suppressed. The charge against Comrade Andrews and the others will no doubt be now changed into one of High Treason, making it a question of life and death. The best of our membership will have suffered terribly in the conflict, and the whole organisation shattered.

It remains to ascertain whether the conflict is the last revolt of a non-revolutionary white working class driven to arms by the very insecurity of their economic position over against the native masses. In that case the conditions for a Communist Party based on white militants have disappeared, and the Comintern will henceforth have to take over the direct responsibility for the native masses.

On the other hand it is possible that along with the discouragement of the workers on the economic front, a political revulsion may ensue which will result in a Labour-Republican block. In such a block, Comrade Andrews, by the universal respect which he commands with the rank and file, would play an important role for the Communist Party; and the anti-Imperialist forces, hitherto divided by chauvinist cries, would be for the first time united. This implies an extension of the principle of the United Front to include the Anti-Imperialist farmers Party [viz. the anti-British National Party]. But in Colonial questions the Comintern has already recognised this tactic in principle.

It is for the Comintern to decide whether these Colonial movements play any part in the general revolutionary process, whether the world revolution is not all one piece and not a European or Central European affair, whether these outbreaks at the periphery of capitalism are not as essential to its general collapse as those at the centre. It is to be regretted that by working on the opposite theory the Comintern takes an interest in these movements after the crisis, and when it is already too late. Moreover, the absence of clear knowledge as to the place of the Colonial movements in the Comintern strategy leaves Colonial delegates and revolutionaries undecided. For example, I have no personal ties with South Africa apart from the Comintern, and my home is England equally with the Colonies.

The whole of English speaking society, especially American and Colonial, is afflicted with a festering sore in the question of the negro race. Whether Colonial movements play a part or not in the revolutionary movement, the Revolution will later on be confronted to its peril with this terrible incubus of colour hatred implanted in the breast of the English speaking peoples by generations of slave dealers. Apart from the immediate strategy of the Revolution, the Comintern has a universal human appeal to make also (in other words, grand strategy), especially in regard of the Negro Race. In South Africa we have tried hard for the last seven years to concentrate on the issue, for in our complex Society it is immediately bound up with the issue of the Revolution. We were too weak however to bring about the desired rapprochement of the Black and White workers in time to influence the present crisis. After this and the aftermath of animosity aroused between black and white I am afraid we shall be weaker. The Gold Mining Capital or the Rand, which Walton Newbold [Communist MP for Motherwell, Scotland, 1922-23] declares to be the fulcrum of world finance capital, enters upon a new era of further expansion in Africa as a result of the crushing of the White workers' revolt.

There remains the need for agitating and informing the Labour movement in London in order to check the ferocity of White Guard Justice.

1. The Presidium should decide whether this should be done. either by myself or someone else.

2. To decide if the Smuts Government maintains its political as well as military position, and the milieu for Communist Party still further narrowed as a white workers party, whether it will take on direct work through a South African Bureau among the Native masses.

3. To decide, in the event of a political revolution, the role of the C.P. in an Anti-Imperialist block.

4. To decide the question of financial support.

5. The formation of an Anglo-American-Colonial Bureau.

D. Ivon Jones

(South African delegate.)

Application to Proceed Home

Russian State Archive of Socio-Political History

April 1922

Dear Comrade Kuusingen,

With reference to our conversation today regarding the situation in South Africa, and my desire to return home without delay, I have the following points on which I desire the advice of the Presidium.

1. The critical situation in the South African movement, the armed uprising and its suppression by the Government. The arrest of Comrade Andrews, our Secretary, who is also one of the most respected Labour leaders there. The probable smash up of the Communist Party, the police having occupied the premises, and the armed conflict scattered the membership, and made open activity impossible. Also the need from the International point of view to stiffen the white workers to resistance in order to prevent Imperialist Capital from breaking through into wider spheres of Negro exploitation which is necessary for its existence, – ALL THIS BACKS UP OUR APPEAL FOR FINANCIAL AID FROM THE INTERNATIONAL TO CARRY ON THE FIGHT.

2. The necessity for me to immediately proceed to London on my way to South Africa in order to acquaint the Labour Movement in England of the true merits of the colour issue which started the conflict, and which is liable in English circles to be construed to the disadvantage of the white workers of the Rand now in the struggle. White Guard justice will follow the conflict, and ruthless suppressions and executions are most probable. It is necessary for me to move Press and Trade Unions in England to come to the aid of our comrades.

3. I am now engaged with Comrade Borodin and Andrews in drafting an appeal to the International movement on the question for submission to the Presidium.

4. I also wish to have the advice of the [Executive] Committee on the application of the United Front in Africa after the present events. Comrade Andrews, who was up to the war Chairman of the Labour Party and member of Parliament, by his denunciation of the war forfeited these positions and his leading place in the Labour movement. The present. struggle is calculated to restore him to leadership, at least of a very considerable section of the left wing and militant elements. He is also much respected by the Boer Farmers

or Nationalists for his stand in the war and his defence of the Boer rebels in Parliament. He is a champion of the negro labouring masses, and this has still further kept him out of official position. But he is the one man who combines the sympathies of all these three sections of the anti-imperialist forces to any degree. It seems impossible that the Smuts Government can retain power after these events, even in the case of a Labour defeat in the field. A Labour-Republican block [an alliance between the SA Labour Party and the National Party] is probable. HOW FAR SHOULD ANDREWS AS A REPRESENTATIVE COMMUNIST TAKE OFFICIAL POSITION IN SUCH A BLOCK FOR THE COMBINED ANTI-IMPERIALIST CONFLICT? This question carries us forward to the idea of participation in a left bourgeois Government with Labour in the centre, which is more than anything contemplated in the United Front under European conditions.

5. The status of Colonial or consultative delegates also might be considered by the Committee for report, as I consider that under present conditions our position is not sufficiently well defined.

Letter to V.I. Lenin

Russian State Archive of Socio-Political History

April 5 1922

Dear Comrade Lenin,

I am sending you herewith copies of memorandums on the South African situation, thinking you may be interested to know the state of affairs disclosed therein. Also copy of an article on the recent conflict of the Johannesburg miners, as well as the draft of an appeal that was ordered by the Executive Committee. This appeal was not sent for some reason; but as it gives an idea of the operation of the colour issue, I enclose it also.

I am leaving Russia in a few days. Comrade Wilkinson, the Australian delegate, and myself, would feel very grateful for a short interview with you before our return home, if your health and the great pressure of your public duties would permit. The revolutionary movements of Australia and South Africa have problems in common on which we should be glad of your advice, and we know how keen is your interest in the Colonial movements.

We earnestly hope that your health will be completely restored.

With Communist greetings,

D. Ivon Jones.

(Delegate for the South African Communist Party)

Room 7, Lux Hotel, Moscow

Collecting Material on the South African Revolt

To the Secretariat, Comintern

May 9 1922

Dear Comrades,

Comrade Rakosi has conveyed to me the difficulty which has arisen regarding the budget submitted by me in connection with my journey to South Africa to collect information on the South African workers revolt.

I am asked to report regarding the possibility of (1) organising the collection of this material from Moscow through London: or (2) in the alternative to state the minimum expense on which the journey could made.

ORGANISING FROM MOSCOW. The drawback to organising the collection of the information from Moscow is that the comrades on the scene of the revolt who could efficiently do the work are in prison. But there are two or three comrades available at Durban and Capetown who could be engaged to go to Johannesburg to collect and forward the material. The London comrades are out of touch with the movement and its personalities in South Africa, but the Labour Research Department might be engaged to direct the work from London, and we would supply the names and addresses from here. In the alternative I might be sent to London to direct the work. It would require about 50 pounds sterling to enable Comrade Haynes to leave his work in Durban and make a thorough collection of material in Johannesburg, under the direction of the Labour Research Department. If the Presidium decides to send me to London to direct the work, it would involve a total expenditure of 125 pounds.

If the Presidium thinks that either of the above methods are likely to prove unsatisfactory, and that the best results would be obtained by sending me to South Africa, the MINIMUM cost would be the cost of the travelling expenses to South Africa and back, leaving the local comrades to bear the expense of my work there.

RESUME. In the order of efficiency the respective methods would cost as follows.

(1) Organising the work from Moscow through Labour Research Department, London... 50 pounds.

(2) Sending Jones to London to direct work (50 + 75) 125 pounds.

(3) Sending Jones to South Africa, travelling expenses there and back... 200 pounds.

With communist greetings,

D. Ivon Jones

Letter to Grigory Zinoviev

Russian State Archive of Socio-Political History

May 11 1922

Dear Comrade Zinoviev,

Owing to the very serious character of the matter claiming your attention at the last Executive meeting, I did not care to worry you about the South African question. Especially as I knew that the Presidium ['Small Bureau"] had dealt with the matter, but the result had not been conveyed to me.

I would not worry you further did I not know that Comrade Lenin and yourself are still as anxious as ever to gather the full details about the revolt. But the whole of the arrangements for carrying the idea into effect seem in a state of confusion, and the latest communications from South Africa show that the matter is urgent.

It is now a month since it was decided to send me to Africa, and today my departure is held up. According to Comrade Rakosi there are no funds for the project. Comrade [Heinrich] Brandler gives other reasons.

I have therefore given a report on other methods for gathering the material, copy of which I enclose. I have also suggested that, if Presidium decides that only by sending me to Africa can the work be done efficiently, the expenses for this might be reduced by getting the South African comrades to bear part of the expense.

But I now see from the latest issue of the London *Communist* [April 29] an appeal from the Capetown Branch of our Party to the British movement for financial aid in the present crisis. Although the organisation has been smashed up, the comrades killed and imprisoned, almost the whole membership in Johannesburg, they are determined to keep the flag flying.

Smuts has ordered a Commission of Inquiry which will sit concurrently with the trial of comrades. It is urgent that our enquiry should proceed at the same time, in order to avail ourselves of all material, and while the matter is fresh. Two months have already passed since the events.

I feel that now or never the Comintern should give some token of solidarity with comrades, no matter how distant, in the tragic position revealed in the letter to *The Communist*. The Comintern lost a great opportunity, for some reason not yet explained, when it suppressed our draft appeal ordered by the Executive.

I urge that we do something in connection with the appeal in *The Communist*. In any event, I feel it my duty to return to encourage the remaining comrades.

With kind regards, and communist greetings,

D. Ivon Jones

Hotel Lux, Moscow

The South African Question

Russian State Archive of Socio-Political History

Letter to M. Rakosi, May 23 1922

Dear Comrade Rakosi,

Regarding your suggestion over the telephone to draft another appeal for South Africa, I have thought it over and consider the time inopportune until we know definitely the state of affairs there.

I moreover confess to a lack of enthusiasm for drafting another after the suppression of the one drafted by Comrades [Mikhail] Borodin, [Tom] Bell and myself immediately after the revolt, addressed not exclusively to South Africa but to British Labour as well and attempting to embrace the vital issue of colour prejudice in general. You will remember that the reasons given for suppressing that draft was that it was unsuitable and not understandable to working men. I could only repeat the general tenour of that draft.

I would urge that the new appeal can wait until we make enquiries through Comrade Borodin as to the state of things in South Africa. It is to be regretted that, though a Party Branch [Cape Town] has appealed to the English Party [ie. the Communist Party of Great Britain] for support in the present crisis, no responsible comrade has written to me or the Comintern since the revolt. There has been no lack of communications on my part, with continual articles to our Party organ. But the feeling of a real bond with the Comintern has dwindled perceptibly among the South African comrades since Comrade Barlin"s return, and I can only attribute it to a general discouragement that our Party, the most active of British Colonial parties as events have proved, has been so far ignored in the allocation of material and moral support. By the suppression of the original appeal and the change of plan regarding my journey I am in the position of having failed to do anything for my Party in the most serious crisis of its existence. That is why I wish the Comintern to do something as an expression of solidarity with the South African section.

1. I propose that the application for a subsidy of 250 pounds to our Party organ *The International* already made to the Finance Commission be considered by the Presidium. The comrades in Johannesburg are endeavouring to revive the paper in spite of the reaction.

2. A Party message from Comrade Zinoviev as head of The International (or if possible, Comrade Lenin, whose interest in the Colonial movements is so great), would give the South African comrades a valuable sense of a bond with the International, and would be the best expression of the Comintern"s solidarity now that the opportunity for a general appeal is past. [An appeal from the Executive Committee of the Comintern to 'Save the Workers of South Africa!' was soon to be published in *International Press Correspondence* on June 7].

3. That Comrade Borodin be asked to get information as to the course of the trials, especially as to the fate of Comrade Andrews.

4. Owing to the repercussions of the South African conflict in Australia and Egypt, I urge that these questions be also hurried up for report in order to cope in time with the situation.

An article in the current *New Statesman* attributes the inspiration of the revolt to "The Marxian Socialists".

A letter from a Johannesburg Mine Manager in *The Daily Telegraph* forecasts a recrudescence of unrest at an early date.

The Minister of Defence, speaking in the Capetown Parliament, attributes the leadership of the last stages of the strike conflict to Andrews (our Party Secretary), and [Percy] Fisher (Left Trade Unionist and Red military leader). After eight years exclusion from leadership of the mass movement through his devotion to the International during the war and after, Andrews was called upon to resume it in the middle of a disorganised conflict at the greatest possible personal risk, from which he did not flinch. For this reason I feel that the Comintern should take a special interest in Comrade Andrews' case.

With kind regards and Communist Greetings,

D. Ivon Jones (South African delegate.)

American Imperialism and the Negro

Communist Review September 1922

IN March of last year *The Philippines Review* reported the farewell address of Governor-General Francis Burton Harisson, after eight years of office in the Philippine Islands, "carrying out the policy of the best President of the present generation,"as he himself described it. It had evidently been President Wilson's objective to grant complete independence to the Philippines, relying solely on the silvery threads of finance. But the sorrowful Harrison had to confess his great disappointment that he was not the last Governor-General. He had on a previous occasion gallantly offered to resign in favour of a Philipine Governor-General. "I am convinced that you are ready to take your place among the independent nations of the world," he said. But he hoped to return again to pay his first official visit to the first President of the Philippine Republic at Malaccnaby Palace.

However, that was not to be. The "best President" made way for Harding. And instead of the Jeffersonian Harrison came Major-General Wood, and a large contingent of American Jesuits to take the place of the Spanish Catholic missionaries hitherto established in the Islands. And so the Philippinos were taught the elementary lesson that financial bonds are not the last, but only the first, stage of imperialist occupation.

And Wilson himself knew that; for even while he was drawing up the notorious Fourteen Points, were not his troops and marines in actual occupation of the Negro Republic of Haiti? Six times the Wilson Government made overtures to this island republic for the control of its customs during the imperialist war.

The need was urgent. The Island of Haiti, with its 2,000,000 negroes, is in a strategic position in the Carribean Sea commanding the Panama Canal. (To understand the menace of American imperialism in the Carribean Sea the reader is referred to an illuminating article on this point by J.F. Horrabin in the *Plebs* magazine for July). Finally, the disturbances of July 27th, 1915, afforded the pretext for securing control. We know very well that the United States is never at a loss for "disturbances," whenever it finds it necessary to intervene in any country covered by the Monroe Doctrine.

Since then the American occupation of Haiti (sketched in the May number of the *Labour Monthly*) makes a long and gruesome story, in which the browbeating of the negro islanders, putting them to forced labour, torturings and persecution by negro-hating Southerner officials (see *Negro World*, May 6th), in the approved style of King Lynch, are the dominant features. The description given in the *Negro World* of the "free" elections to the legislature is a typical example of the extent to which imperialist violation is prepared to go in keeping up the outward farce of democratic forms for purposes of home consumption. The anti-American votes were indicated by pink papers, and the pro-American by yellow papers. American marines, fully armed, stood on guard to see that fair play was observed, and to do some observing of their own. There were piles of pink papers nicely tied up in bundles for anyone who might have the temerity to trouble the registration officer to untie them, while the yellow papers lay ready to hand for all who came to vote. The result, of course, was an overwhelming majority in favour of the nominees of the glorious Democracy of the West.

It is now announced that the United States Government is trying to force a loan of 14,000,000 dollars on the island, in order to liquidate certain European creditors. The loan is issued under such ruinous terms that even the puppet President himself is kicking against it. It will involve the Haitian budget in an annual deficit of 1,000,000 dollars. The scandal of the occupation is arousing the liberal elements of the States into vigorous protests. But the Government sits unmoved.

Dr. Burghardt Du Bois, the leader of the Negro intellectuals, announces in his paper, *The Crisis*, that the Republican and Democratic Parties have come to a pact not to compete for the Negro vote. And Du Bois exclaims: "May God write us down as asses if we ever support these parties again." The reason for this conspiracy of silence is obvious. Harding, in his election addresses, denounced the employment of American marines to subjugate a free and independent people, and proclaimed that he would never, no, never, be a party to such an outrage. Since his coming to office the American Government is digging itself in upon the island with a vengeance. The Senate Commission on Haiti has reported that things are very much better there now, thank you! And there the matter of America's little Ireland now rests.

Meanwhile, the distressed Negroes have been buoyed up with hope by the passage of the Dyer Anti-Lynching Bill through the Lower House of Legislature. But great difficulties are being experienced in its further progress through the Senate, in spite of the fact that the lynching horrors and burning of negroes have again broken out at the rate of eight in two weeks in the Southern States.

But the American Senators are not altogether blind to the positive advantages to be derived from the Negro Movement, especially from the "Back to Africa" cry of these poor, hunted and harassed people who are looking for any way of escape. Senator [Torrey] McCullum, of Mississippi, and Senator [Joseph] France, of Maryland, have both expressed their sympathy with the "Back to Africa" movement of the Negroes. The former has introduced a resolution in the State Legislature to petition the President to use his good influence in securing from the Allies sufficient territory in Africa in liquidation of the war debt, "which territory should be used for the establishing of an independent nation for American Negroes."

Senator France, on his part, put the matter in the following noble terms: –

> We owe a big duty to Africa, and one which we have too long ignored. I need not enlarge upon our peculiar interest in the obligation to the people of Africa. Thousands of Americans have for years been contributing to the missionary work which has been carried on by the noble men and women who have been sent out to that field by the churches of America.

This was spoken in the Senate. Translated into plain English, Senator France wished to say it was about time that American business followed up the labours of its own missionary agents-in-advance in Africa.

This proposal was immediately followed by a timely interview with Dr. Heinrich Schnee, a former governor of German East Africa, in which it was suggested that America should take over the mandatories of Great Britain and France in Africa for the colonisation of American Negroes. Marcus Garvey's paper, *The Negro World*, was jubilant, and headed the announcement with big block letters, "Africa's Redemption Draws Near."

Secretary Hughes, no doubt, will keep that pot simmering for a suitable occasion. Meanwhile, he is taking practical steps. The United States Government has in one stride stepped across the Atlantic and planted its foot in the little African republic of Liberia. Liberia was founded about a century ago as a refuge for American slaves in West Africa. Within the last few years its narrow confines have very much been encroached upon by French and English expansion in the neighbouring colonies. Liberia has a foreign debt of 1,650,000 dollars owing to J. Pierpoint Morgan & Co. and his financial confreres in New York, acting for themselves and for European banks. The United States has drawn up an elaborate agreement with the

Negro president for the granting of a loan of 5,000,000 dollars to the Negro republic. Detailed stpulations are made regarding the spending of the money. One clause provides for the immediate repayment of the money owing to J. Pierpoint Morgan & Co., with the result that the market price of that loan has already jumped up from 75 to 98, putting over 300,000 dollars in the pockets of Morgan & Co. at one stroke of the pen.

But that is only a little side-pocket money. The most significant clauses in the loan agreement refer to the appointment of a Financial Commissioner, with 21 other American officials under him. This official will control the finances and customs of Liberia. Certain provisions are also made for the control of the Legislature. The financial commissioner will determine the size of the Liberian police and frontier control force, which will be commanded by American army officers. He will have the power of veto over the Liberian budget, and the right to order the passing of any financial legislation which he may desire. He is empowered to limit the annual expenditure of Liberia to a total of 650,00 dollars, of which 109,700 dollars will go to pay the salaries of the American officials. In short, he will be the well-paid dictator of Liberia, with an armed force of American trained police to do his bidding.

This control is to last for the lifetime of the new loan; and a special clause prohibits the contracting of other loans without the sanction of the financial commissioner, so that there is no chance of Liberia trying to buy itself out of Uncle Sam's clutches. The loan therefore promises to have a long life, long enough, in fact, to enable American Imperialism to get a foothold on the African continent, and to follow its religious agents further afield into the interior as opportunities arise.

In 1900, says the New York *Nation* (which gives the text of agreement in its issue of May 31st), we sent a mission to Liberia, which was much impressed by the high-handed methods of the British in assuming control of the Liberian customs and frontier force. This commission reported that "It is difficult to find among the Liberians anyone who has entire confidence in the disinterestedness of Great Britain"; that "French interest in Liberia is apparently that of an heir-expectant"; that "Germany has lent her at least a sympathetic understanding," but that since Germany had "ambitious designs in Africa," Liberia naturally turned to the United States for disinterested help.

Nevertheless, it took thirteen long years for that wave of disinterested emotion to flow eastward in the shape of a financial dictator and an American police force.

The American bourgeoisie finds itself obliged more and more to renounce the angelic role of "pure democracy," and to take up the openly Mephistophelian one of Imperial expansion. The Negro question bids fair to become the moral lever for it. And soon we may have the whole history of England's criminality in starting the slave trade and the plantation system raked up as a preliminary to the reconsideration of the African mandates.

The Negroes themselves are being encouraged to look forward to a change of slave drivers for Africa. Marcus Garvey, the religio-racial charlatan who claims to voice the needs of the Negro masses, carries on a persistent campaign in his paper, which has a large circulation among the Negroes, for the liberation of Africa from the European Imperialists, and welcomes with joy the new loan to Liberia as a start in this direction. He is assiduous in the sale of excursion tickets for Liberia to his Negro dupes, on "The Black Star Line," the steamships of which are not yet built! A short while ago he was arrested for obtaining money on false pretences in this manner. But nothing further has been heard of the matter, and he now seems to be as busy as ever denouncing the Bolshevik members of his race. But even the *Negro World* is compelled to expose the crimes of American Imperialism in Haiti. So that Garvey and his organisation, "The Universal Negro Improvement Association," typify the immature consciousness of the Negroes in the first stage of awakening.

But the growing band of young Negro radicals, who look to Soviet Russia for guidance and inspiration in the struggle – they are not deceived. Under the banner of the African Blood Brotherhood, and in close touch with the class-conscious white workers of America, they are pointing the way to proletarian emancipation as the only hope for their oppressed Negro brothers in Africa and America.

The Workers' Revolt in South Africa

[Retranslated in part from German]

Communist International, October 1922

The armed uprising of the gold miners of Johannesburg was very little understood, not only in Russia but also in England. While the American labour press portrayed the outrage as an event of world importance and the Australian trade unions, in keeping with their traditional contempt for bourgeois public opinion, passed many resolutions of solidarity, the British labour press, the trade unions and the Labour Party remained silent throughout. And when the Daily Herald finally broke the silence, as if the causes of the strike had hitherto been a secret, it described the insurrection in a manner biased against the cause of the insurgent workers.

It would appear that General Smuts is now a kind of [US President] Wilson and infallible in the eyes of European liberalism. When he slaughtered a thousand innocent Negroes at Bullhock the previous year, the British press acknowledged the affair with a dark paragraph. International finance looks after its own. And in the face of imperialist capital's latest assault on the standard of living of white workers in South Africa (where more than half the world's gold is produced), Smuts has managed with diabolical cunning, in the role of protector of the native masses, to fulfil the bloody task.

The poor tortured workers, worn down by a seven-week strike, by hunger, exhaustion and despair, and seeing their labour increasingly performed by low-paid Negroes under the direction of white strike-breakers, finally succumbed to an outbreak of racial hatred, no doubt provoked by Smuts, which the warnings and pleas of the leaders could not prevent. This lasted only a day or two. The Negro-baiting took place mainly in the most disreputable neighbourhoods of Johannesburg. There were unmistakable signs of police provocation, but that was enough to allow Smuts to stand as the unshakeable hope of the Manchester Guardian with his hands stained with the blood of a thousand white labourers. International finance guards this nerve centre of its organism as it would guard no other. With the exception of that section of the British press which is endeavouring to use the uprising as an argument against Soviet Russia, the murdered workers of South Africa have been the victims of a conspiracy of silence unknown even to the history of Indian and other colonial oppression. The world witnessed the events of Amritsar; but during the last twelve months, large-scale violence has twice escaped public attention.

Nonetheless, this uprising holds lessons of the greatest significance for the working class movement.

1. It presents us with the problem of colour prejudice within the ranks of the workers in its acutest form, there, where the conditions for its solution are already maturing.

2. It is the first great armed revolt of the workers on any scale in the British Empire.

3. It presents one of the most striking examples of the use of the aeroplane as the supreme capitalist weapon against the workers, and suggests serious problems for the military mechanics of revolution.

4. It is a victory for imperialist capital, on the one hand extending its tenure of life by expansion, on the other performing a revolutionary role by drawing in still wider masses of the backward peoples into the world movement.

Causes of the conflict

The Johannesburg gold mines produce more than half of the world's gold. They are concentrated in a single management, with the ultimate control in London. The workers employed are 200,000 natives, mostly still primitive, and 25,000 whites. Herein lies the root of the conflict. The white miners are a block to native progress. Their legal privileges are an anachronism. Yet no Communist can withhold support from their resistance to the capitalist offensive. The unconsciously revolutionary effect of capital on the backward races can be moulded by the working class into a conscious force. The class struggle, the struggle for power, has given the white workers their proper place in the historical movement. This struggle for power, blind and improvised as it was, suffered a fiasco this time. The white workers were bloodily crushed.They will rise again, but then hand in hand with the native masses.

The figures for the mining industry do not give a true picture of the usual relationship between white and black workers. In the mechanical engineering industry, which was also drawn into the strike, the number of white workers predominates. The ratio does not give a correct picture of the relative significance of the two types of workers. The native masses are the lowest possible form of cheap, unskilled labour drawn from one of the most primitive peoples in the world, politically passive and industrially unorganized, recruited on indenture from the tribal reserves, and housed around the mines in closed compounds under strict police supervision, with hardly a vestige of civil rights. This relates to the native gold miners. As for the rest, the native workers are more advanced, live far better, and a certain steadily increasing percentage in industry is gradually becoming permanent.

The white workers therefore yield a power quite out of proportion to their numbers. They can stop industry. But this passive native mass is a constant menace to them, and is used against them by the capitalists, whereas the white workers fail to take the surest means of securing their position by common organization with the natives, as advocated by the Communist Party.

The state of affairs explains the circumstances of armed conflict from which the general strike emerged. In the end it was a conflict for the control of the industry, for the abolition of the Chamber of Mines, and for ousting Smuts from power.

This was not the first time that Johannesburg gold miners had resorted to armed rebellion. As early as 1913, a street battle took place between the strikers and the troops in Johannesburg in which 21 workers were killed and many hundreds wounded. At that time, English workers were in the majority in the mines. Today, Dutch-speaking Afrikaners make up the majority.

Dutch nationalism

Dutch nationalist sentiments had nothing to do with the armed uprising, as some newspapers portray. The Nationalist leaders initially supported the movement, but then rejected it. In the end, the armed uprising was suppressed by the mobilisation of armed farmers and British white guards. The recent influx of a fresh and vigorous element of Dutch workers from the surrounding districts had made an armed conflict likely, before the workers had recognised their defeat. [Tom] Matthews, the president of the Engineers' Association, a true English trade unionist, who was certainly not prone to fiery speeches, was the first to warn the Chamber of Mines and the Government that their behaviour must inevitably lead to bloodshed before the miners would submit.

Incidentally, there are signs that the Nationalist party was badly shaken by the desire of the poorer farmers to support their kinsmen in the strike.

The outcome of the colour question

Similarly with the Coloured cause. It was not a conflict of whites against blacks, but a pure class struggle between the politically conscious workers, who happened to be white, and the capitalist class. The international offensive of capitalism spreads to the colonies including Australia and South Africa. In South Africa it takes the form of a demand on the part of the Chamber of Mines that the mining regulations be altered to allow cheap native labour into more skilled positions. This means larger gangs of natives working under fewer skilled whites This was accompanied by a demand for a general reduction of wages and a reduction of one fifth in the number of white workers. Hence it was for the white workers a question of their very existence. The Chamber of Mines knew how to take up the slogan of promoting the blacks and to strike the pose before whole British world as the champion of the natives. But the bloodbath among the natives caused by Smuts showed the true character of these friends of the Negro. In order to preserve its profits, gold-mining capital must deny the colonial masses any application of European bourgeois democracy, and it has no time to apply "free" education and the benefits of a bourgeois press. It rules directly by the bayonet and the policeman's baton. It brutalises whole masses of the backward peoples. But white democracy itself has become an obstacle to the further expansion of gold mining capital in South Africa. Not only the nationalist farmers, but also the local bourgeoisie were more or less sympathetic to the strikers in the first days of the strike. Throughout the strike and the ensuing bloodshed, the London financial papers could report only a slight decrease in the output of the gold mines and looked forward with hope, after a successful settlement of the strike, to a great development of the industy in the undeveloped eastern and southern areas.

The gold mining industry of the Rand has been described as the fulcrum of world capital. Twenty years ago the old Boer republics became an obstacle to the Chamber of Mines, and the whole British army was requisitioned to blow them out of existence. In the old Boer republics the English labourers were foreigners without the right to vote. That was the complaint that brought about the intervention of the English army. After the job was done the Rand magnates got leave to import fifty thousand Chinese workers under indenture. Their working conditions were no more economical than those of the natives. But they served the English Liberals well as an election slogan for a long time after the mining magnates had realised, to their dismay, that the Chinaman was too much of a revolutionary to be profitable. Since the repatriation of the Chinese repeated attempts have been made to open up the skilled positions to the natives, and to break down the legal monopoly [on such jobs] of the white miners. From then on, the [South African] Labour Party had two leaders before the war:

Creswell, a Liberal, a former mine owner, who posed as a supporter of the Labour Party, but who in fact represented the interests of the local bourgeoisie in maintaining a white working class population and increased demands, and [Bill] Andrews, a metalworker, president of the party, who represented the needs of labour as a class and later led a section of advanced workers into the Communist Party through his opposition to the war.

The question became acute at the end of 1921. The low exchange value, of the pound sterling had for two or three years enabled the mining industry to sell gold at a premium. With the improved position of the pound sterling as against the dollar, the premium is disappearing, and the mining industry is compelled to work on the bare mint price of four pounds five shillings. A mere drop of wages could no longer satisfy the ambitions of the employers. A further perspective became necessary to entice capital to open up the undeveloped areas of the reef. A thorough reduction in the number of skilled white workers and more extensive exploitation of the cheap indigenous labour became necessary in order to remedy the weakness of gold capital.

The strike and the Worker-"Commandos"

This was the situation when the strike broke out on January 9, a strike in which both the whole white workforce, as well as gold mining capital, jeopardised its entire existence.

The strike lasted eight weeks. Almost immediately after the strike was declared, the local strike committees began to form "commandos" (the old military unit of the Boer civil army) and to organise Red Cross detachments etc., i.e. to make open preparations for an armed conflict. The Central Strike Committee, although it did not officially support these preparations, gave local initiative a free hand. In fact, a struggle between the different factions of the movement seems to have taken place in the central executive, and the executive of the association was expanded to include the active elements leading the strike. The strike committee at Germiston (nine miles from Johannesburg) was at one stage of the struggle prevented from negotiating a compromise with Smuts only by the violent intervention of the leading strikers who held their executive prisoner during the election. The authorities allowed weeks of unrestrained drilling and marching by unarmed or poorly armed "commandos", a sure sign that a bloody conflict was considered the most welcome, clearest and most appropriate outcome of the strike which could open a new era in the gold mining industry.

The workers' "commandos" made tours of the mines, intimidating and arresting the strikebreakers, taking them to workers' homes for interrogation, etc. In the first week of March, such a commando arrested an electrician in Boksburg (12 miles from Johannesburg) without carrying any visible weapons. On the way, they stopped in front of a prison, raised three cheers in honour of one of their captured comrades and sang the "Red Flag." A squadron of mounted police, believing them to be planning an attack on the prison, killed three strikers and wounded several others. This incident threw the entire working class of the Rand states in turmoil. It was clear that the employer class was determined to fight a decisive struggle.

Although masses of natives under the supervision of white strikebreakers guarded the pits, no violence had been made against them on the part of the white workers – only against the skilled workers who blacklegged. Natives were not regarded as scabs, their whole outlook and mode of life being too primitive (sic) for the conscious workers to attribute any responsibility to them. But a few days after the Boksburg incident, tragic outbreaks of violence against the natives occurred in one of the dirty parts of Johannesburg. Despite the passionate appeals of the strike leaders, the innocent natives, who were not strikebreakers at all, became the target of the fury of the white workers. Nineteen workers were killed in this clash. The cry of native rebellion, with its mythical horrors of rape and massacre, always conjured up to confuse the class issue, was again set going; and it diverted many of the strikers for two or three days from the real issue. Police provocation was undoubtedly behind it. The case probably served as a moral justification for the carnage that followed. During this whole time negotiations with the Chamber of Mines were held and broken off, in the course of which the tone of the speeches and counter speeches became more and more threatening.

On March 7, an incident occurred that outraged the entire mass of strikers. A large number of strikers were gathered around the telephone exchange. The British police cleared the square. The women's "commando" was next to the telephone exchange and tried to call out the women telephonists. According to the sworn statements published in our party paper *The International*, the police attacked the women:

> Then, unexpectedly, another pack fell upon a white man and struck him a blow to the neck from behind. The man strolled on calmly. Then another policeman fell upon him and plunged his bayonet into his body. After pulling out the bayonet, he left him on the pavement and attacked the women.

Another sworn statement gives a more detailed account of this incident:

> Then, unexpectedly, another pack of policemen approached me. One of them, seeing me cross his path, lowered his bayonet towards me as if he wanted to stab me. A man from the crowd, who had behaved quite harmlessly, came up and said: "Don't do that to a woman, she's the mother of several children! Do it to me instead!" Then the policeman thrust the bayonet into his body, I jumped over the fence and saw nothing more.

The renowned Fordsburg "Commando" heard of the incident and launched a furious attack on the entire mounted and foot police, who, either from shame or cowardice, turned and fled. That was the mood on the eve of the general conflict.
Three days later, martial law was proclaimed. In such a situation, this meant nothing less than a declaration of civil war. The outlying mining towns of Benoni and Brakpan were already dominated by the armed strikers. In a few hours aeroplanes were hovering over the scenes where commandos were mobilizing. Boer commandos were soon on their way to fight for the government against the insurgents, against their own flesh and blood. Vigilantes were put on standby, and artillery was deployed. Boer General [Jacob] van Deventer, with the help of aeroplanes, carried out a raid against the outlying towns. An aeroplane dropped a bomb on the Benoni Workers' Hall, and blew the whole building full of executives and strikers to atoms. The fact that the pilot who performed this deed was found pierced by nine bullets from the strikers when the aeroplane landed may give an idea of the low altitude at which the aircraft were able to operate.

Around the centre of Johannesburg, the worker commandos took possession of the working class suburbs of Fordsburg and Jeppe, about a mile from the centre. They also entrenched on the neighbouring low hills overlooking the military camping ground. Here half a dozen aeroplanes operated on these positions with deadly effect. A bourgeois journalist of the kind we remember from the Paris Commune indulges in tirades when describing the sinister grace with which these machines of class warfare hovered low above the entrenchments of the workers, leaving torn human bodies behind with every advance, only then to float back to their former position. Artillery bombardment proceeded at the same time, but the position was stubbornly defended, and only given up after terrible losses. Here where no bourgeois property was endangered, the aeroplanes could operate with impunity.

For these reasons Fordsburg, the last bastion of the worker commandos, had so far been spared destruction by the planes. The streets that separated it from the centre had been provided with fencing and sand walls on both sides. This was the only section of the workers' armed forces that threatened the centre, but otherwise the reports of a concentrated attack on Johannesburg, which have been partly circulated, seem to be exaggerated. The commandos stood and fought where the troops found them. After the bases of Bononi and Brakpan in the east, and those of Maraisburs in the west, had been completely destroyed and the Jeppe side had also been cleared, the White forces gathered against Fordsburg under the direct command of Smuts. Smuts sent an ultimatum in which the refusal to surrender was threatened with bombardment. Fordsburg is situated on a gentle slope, just opposite the inner city, and therefore offered an excellent target for the Whites' artillery. The Boer commandos who, just like the regular troops, had rushed to maintain law and order, gathered for the final attack. Here, in those few tragic hours, the brave victim of capitalist ferocity atoned many times over in blood and tears, and deeds of heroism that move the proletarian heart, for the anti-native outrages committed in their name a week before. Here the red forces were directed by [Percy] Fisher and [Harry] Spendiff, two miners' leaders followers of the Communists, and while ardent strike militants, most fervent partisans of the negro workers at the same time. Fischer ordered the decisive battle. "No surrender!" And hastily scribbled down his will for his wife. A bourgeois journalist derisively mentions the singing of the "Red Flag", the English anthem of the revolutionary workers, by the Red defenders. But the entire South African uprising, with all its errors of racial prejudice, with its immaturity and its complicated proletarian character, can only be adequately appreciated when the full fervour of the workers' internationalism breaks through everything. This final singing of the "Red Flag" raises the Reds of Fordsburg to the level of revolutionary martyrs:

The people's flag is deepest red,
It shrouded oft our martyred dead,
And ere their limbs grew stiff and cold,
Their hearts' blood dyed its ev'ry fold.

Look 'round, the Frenchman loves its blaze,
The sturdy German chants its praise,
In Moscow's vaults its hymns are sung
Chicago swells the surging throng.

It well recalls the triumphs past,
It gives the hope of peace at last;
The banner bright, the symbol plain,
Of human right and human gain.

With heads uncovered swear we all
To bear it onward till we fall;
Come dungeons dark or gallows grim,
This song shall be our parting hymn.

The bombardment was expected to last ten minutes. It went on for seventy minutes. Covered by the defence, the government troops surrounded the workers' stronghold. The streets of a colonial town are unsuitable for barricade fighting because they are wide and scattered. It was only a question of time, and the issue was never in doubt, for Smuts only directs final assaults for political acclaim when the issue is absolutely safe. Fischer and Spendiff, English leaders of the Dutch and English Reds, were found dead here, in their own beloved labour halls, having fought to their last breath. They are true martyrs of the proletarian revolution. On Spendiff was found his membership card of the Communist Party. Thousands of prisoners were taken, and the militants weeded out for the court martials. All the important Communist leaders had already been imprisoned in the course of the conflict. Nevertheless, through its leader, Comrade Andrews, the Communist Party won a place in the hearts of the workers.

The London press cabal got into the habit of exaggerating the size of the force threatening the mining industry, and the same seems to have been the case when man attributed well thought-out plans and good weaponry to the insurgent workers. So far we have only the capitalist press as the source of our information. A hastily written letter from a party member in the midst of the struggle mentions the expansion of the reaction, the ban on wearing red badges and the many arrests that took place as a result of these "crimes" alone. This comrade writes the following: "Comrades in Russia! A crowd of workers, who only had a few pistols and a little ammunition, rose up against the Chamber of Mines, against its infantry, cavalry, machine guns and aeroplanes; and died defiantly..." The frail little woman whose short letter I quoted above is not only the sole survivor of the office staff, but of all the inhabitants of the Trades Hall who were thrown into prison. She still tries every day to penetrate beyond the confines of this building and defies the police ban, which has outlawed and banished everything Red, by holding on to her "Soviet badge" to the last. In two words, she describes the grandeur and magnificence of a working class defeat.

> As I approached some well-dressed members, they said: "Oh, it's over with the party now, it's absolutely over in this country." But communism is already approaching again in the form of a dusty, unshaven labourer, whom you hardly ever seen before, and he grabs you by the hand with a "By God, comrade, we've got some organisational work to do now!"

"The government is talking about friendship and protection of the black workers against the slogan of the strikers who are in favour of a white South Africa," the letter continues. "But that is the hard nut to crack in this strike." The gold mining industry believes that now that this bloodbath is over, it can move on to the full exploitation of indigenous labour. But the strikers' slogan of "White South Africa" does not at all mean that the blacks will be eradicated from the minds of the strikers, but merely that the white standard of living should be maintained. The skilled white workers need the unskilled black workers as much as the capitalists, but united in a harmonious industrial partnership they can very well do without the capitalists. Imperialist capital exploits the backward races by denying them the same democratic rights which form the basis of the exploitation of European labour. But while in India it can logically adhere to one system and in Australia to the other, in South Africa it cannot harness both to the same yoke without constant convulsions, which can only end in the bourgeois idea of democracy giving way to the proletarian soviet one. Then the goal dreamed of by the workers will no longer be a "White Africa", nor a "Black South Africa", but "A South Africa of the united working class." A surprising photograph was published in a capitalist newspaper: a procession of strikers carrying a banner with the inscription: "Workers of the world, unite and fight for a White South Africa!" In the crowd, several black workers were to be seen. Till the fifth week of the strike this slogan did not betoken any race enmity. That dastardly evil was left for Smuts to do.

The South African uprising must be taken to heart, especially by Australian workers, and lessons learnt. The sophisticated Australian trade union movement was very generous in its expressions of solidarity with the brave fighters for the workers' cause in Johannesburg. We have here a working-class community that is even freer from the illusions of the British movement than the South Africa one which, with a firmly organised workers' party, is constantly moving to the left and becoming more and more communist in its ideology, a community of 800,000 trade unionists out of a population of 5½ million heads, threatened by a capitalist offensive equipped with the experience of the South African butchery. Melbourne's labour halls lowered the red flag to half-mast in honour of the South African martyrs. Today for solidarity. But tomorrow, Australian labour will stand as the avenger of their cause. There has always been a close bond between these two movements. After the March events, their community will become a real one as equal members of the international workers' movement, hitherto recognised only academically in Europe. Capitalism has no frontiers so distant that we cannot bridge the space between Australia and South Africa. Their hearts are ever-present. The colonial movement can play a role in the world revolution that canot be imagined today.

Be that as it may, the deed of indictment against capitalism filling up from every land and every clime; and the roll of honour of proletarian heroism from Africa, Australia and India to the outermost ends of the earth, grow to enrich the new communist world order that is being born everywhere.

The United Front and Labour Parties

The International January 19 1923

It is over two years since Lenin formulated the special tactic to be applied to Communist Parties functioning side by side with Labour Parties, with special reference to the British Labour Party. This form of political working class organisation is uniquely British. Its Australian counterpart is a still more perfect example of a trade union party. Before the war the South African Labour Party was also of the same type. Up to the special Conference in August, 1915, most of the important trade unions were affiliated to the Labour Party. After the adoption of the See-It-Through policy and the expulsion of the Internationalists, the trade unions, for various reasons, one by one dropped away from the Party, until it finally became a mere election apparatus. There was a period when it revived as a machine, sported a club—indeed, a sporting club – for was it not endowed by a well-known racecourse sport for favours received or yet to come, I know not which, in regard to Betting Legislation in the Provincial Council. Why, I remember very well on the never-to-be-forgotten evening of the debate in the Special Conference on the See-It-Through Policy in the Selborne Hall, how Creswell used the racing element newly arrived in the Party to move the closure – there was the *Evening Chronicle* racing scribe and the bucket shop delegate of Auckland Park, and the white-waistcoated straight-from-the-horse's-mouth man, all jumping up to make the longest speech they were ever capable of: "Move the question be now put"; and how they voiced their glee at the motion which put Andrews, the old trade union warrior, out of the chair, while Creswell played the Tin Napoleon over a party of the workers in the interests of the war-mongering capitalist class. Since the exodus of the trade unions, Creswell and a few electioneering agents are still exploiting the prestige of Labour for election purposes, quite uncontrolled by any real Labour organisation.

When Lenin wrote his treatise we thought that the absence of the trade union element from the Party made a difference in our case. We thought that we could break the remnant of the Labour Party and substitute a revolutionary party in its place. But one thing we overlooked; the people, the working masses, did not know that the Labour Party was no longer the labour movement. They gave long credit to the Party for its work in the past. They also attributed the prestige of the British Labour Party to its South African counterpart. The very name made it impossible for the ordinary worker to conceive working class political action except in the Labour Party. And so a few men in possession of the electioneering machine filled in just what they liked into the blank cheque given them by the working people; while the trade unions, the rightful owners of the cheque, the rightful controllers and promoters of the mactiine, allowed it and still allow it to be used by uncontrolled politicians. Here is the situation in South Africa to-day.

We cannot liquidate the Labour Party because the people think it is the trade union party. The first step, then, is to insist that the trade unioms shall control it. A Labour Party seams to be part of the flesh and blood of the Anglo-Saxons. The Americans are just beginning to talk about forming one, and it is part of the task of the Communist Party there to throw itself into the movement and be in the swim at the start. So long as the Labour Party stands in the mind of the people as the only form of political action, and that party is in the hands of a private junta, our slogan should be "Trade unions back into the Labour Party." Then we should have a chance, while retaining our distinctive revolutionary character, to co-operate in the daily political struggle of the masses.

We have somewhat neutralised our sound position on the native question in the past by our horror of partial demands. We should have no difficulty in finding planks of common interest for both black and white workers, provided only the workers are sure of our loyalty to their tangible interests as distinct from what. appears to them a revolutionary theory of their interests. And here it seems to me the old Labour Party platform: "Abolition of indentured native labour," is an excellent plank upon which the whote gamut of the United Front Movement from Jim Sixpence to Creswell can find a common aim. Even the white miners will now be not averse to it. For what is this but the old bourgeois democratic principle of equal rights thrown away by the bourgeois themselves and now picked up by Labour in the interests of the revolution. This sort of thing is happening everywhere as an incident of the revolutionary class war. The German workers are the only real defenders of the German bourgeois republic, etc. And in the fight for it they will set up a Soviet Republic. However, that is another story.

Now, I have dictated at far greater length than the limits of an article. My chief desire was to modify the aittitude of good revolutionists like Comrade Lopes, rather too prone to find reasons for not taking action. All political action is action among shoals. If we point out dangers it should be in order to navigate better, not to keep our ship rotting in harbour. We do not admire the goodness of the monk who never moves in the crowd, nor the superlative revolutionary who stays at home to read Karl Marx in the middle of a strike.

Another point about the United Front it is necessary to make, because Daniel Renoult and others of the French Opposition (now liquidated) persisted in regarding the break up of the Council of Nine as the failure of the United Front. Nothing of the kind! Whether we make or break with the leaders, the United Front tactic contemplates some gain, some forward march, for our Party, because thousands of German workers were disillusioned by the action of their leaders, especially the refusal to put the cancellation of the Versailles Treaty on the programme of action. As Trotsky said in his great speech on the French question in the Enlarged Executive: "It is not the repetition of the same ideas, marking time on the same spot of ground, but the tactic of struggle that will swell our forces." Don't let us wait for an apocryphal revolution. This is the revolution now here. And those who are with the masses in their daily struggles will guide the revolution.

Aloopka, Crimea, 31st October, 1922

Some Remarks on the United Front

The International, January 5 1923

Comrade Lopes wrote an able article in *The International* for August 18th. By the time it got to the Crimea, and these remarks return to South Africa, the matter may have lost its political significance, such is the speed of the crisis of Capitalism. Be that as it may, the article in question has inspired a few observations even in this distant part of the world.

Comrade Lopes pleaded that the United Front was not applicable to our Party in South Africa for various reasons. Now I wish to refer to a common misapprehension regarding the United Front. It does not consist of making "bedfellows" of the opportunist leaders. It is not proposed to unite with Colonel Creswell or Sampson, OBE, as Comrade Lopes suggests. In this respect the United Front idea is liable to be misinterpreted. The problem is how to unite the workers, and then how to keep the Communist Party in touch with the workers, and ready at any moment to take the lead, and constantly offering a lead, a common slogan of immediate demands.

The Third Congress of the Comintern raised the slogan, "To the masses and with the masses into the revolutionary struggle." At the Conference on the United Front the Italian Opposition said: "Let us go to the masses, not to the chiefs." Zinoviev, with that sledge-hammer logic of his, replied: "How are you going to get at the masses? Do you think you can go out one fine morning into the streets, looking for the masses, and say, 'Good-morning, masses, come with us!'" No! The problem is how to get at the masses, and the United Front solves that problem.

To-day every struggle for the daily needs of the workers is a revolutionary struggle, because capitalism is becoming too bankrupt to throw sops of reform to alleviate the position. The reformist leaders in all parts of the world are sabotaging this struggle for partial demands, where once they used to make political capital out of it. Because they cannot identify themselves with the daily struggle without furthering the revolution. This was seen in the engineering lock-out in England, and is very clear to-day in Germany.

It remains for the Communists to lead this struggle. But the masses are still behind the reformist chiefs. How, then, to get the masses to move? How io get them to realise the true character of their chiefs? By openly declaring our willingness to combine for certain definite action under definite slogans for certain definite working class demands, and forcing the chiefs either to reject our proposals, and thus betray their true character to their following, or make them line up in the active struggle for the partial demands. From that struggle the Communists are bound to return with an increased following, for only the Communists struggle to the uttermost with the workers.

That is the United Front, and it does not necessarily imply that we should ever exchange a single word personally with the chiefs. It is a public parley between chiefs in the presence of the workers on the fate of the working class. Certainly it does not preclude personal contact with opportunist leaders as to technical arrangements. But Communists who are sure of their principles should be the last to fear such contact. We do not believe in the monastic virtues.

The position in the Colonial movements somewhat differs: from that in Europe. In the Colonial revolts we see reformist labour men in the active struggle. Colonial exploitation is an absentee exploitation, and local bourgeoisie fight under Labour slogans. Although these bourgeoisie are represented by the Creswell type and others, like Waterston who – after marching his men up the hill and down the hill again in the good old Duke of York style – runs away to Capetown when he finds that the workers are not in a playing mood. So that this coquetting with revolt only means that. Crawford has played out the old game of spoof by collaboration. The pitifully apologetic speeches of the Labour members in the Capetown Parliament showed that the Labour Party in South Africa is just as afraid of going the whole hog for the present needs of the workers as its confreres in Europe. Hence the need for the Communist Party.

Comrade Lopes suggests that our Party in South Africa is not yet sufficiently large nor sufficiently clear in principle for the United Front; at least he quotes [August] T[h]alheimer as saying that such parties should refrain from attempting it.

But what of that? If the party is negligible, the other parties can ignore us, and there will. be no united front. If in the United Front we get submerged and the workers fail to see the difference between us, then certainly the party is not characterised by clear-cut thinking. But the problem remains, how to make the workers learn the difference between us and the reformist parties? By the United Front! The United Front is not a suspension of the struggle, but the pursuit of the struggle on a wider field. It is only formally an agreement between chiefs. In substance it is a challenge to the opportunist leaders to fight for the workers or quit the arena.

It seems that the United Front is developing more in the direction of an agreement with the Nationalist Party (to the exclusion of the CP) than of purely working-class action. This is our weakness in action. It proves one of two things: either that there is no need for a Communist Party in South Africa, or that the Communist Party is not correctly applying the tactic of the United Front. The former is by far the least likely reason. A United Front in which the Communists do the donkey work but in which the Communist Party is ignored is a travesty of the whole idea.

Creswell and Hertzog have identical aims: the protection of the interests of the small local bourgeoisie – one of the towns, the other of the country. The local bourgeoisie, the shopkeepers, etc, sympathise with the strike up to a certain point, because the Chamber of Mines threatened to reduce the number of their best customers. Creswell's white labour policy was a policy, and is a policy, of the local bourgeoisie in search of more customers. There is an identity of interest between the local bourgeoisie represented by Creswell, which desires more white customers, and less black labour, and the Nationalist farmers, who desire more of the black labour now grabbed by the Chamber of Mines. This union is not a working class union. It is an anti-Imperialist union, quite desirable after true working class unity has been achieved. But such unity can only be accomplished on the Left by the Communist Party. The Party must, in its turn, become the link on the left between the white and black workers. It can most effectively do this by first gaining the confidence of the white workers.

That is the whole problem, comrades, how to gain the confidence of the white workers, and having gained their confidence, how to make it operate effectively to our Party advantage, and to the mutual advantage of both black and white workers. Herein lies the problem of how to apply the tactic of the United Front in South Africa.

The Proposal to Call a World Negro Congress

Russian State Archive of Socio-Political History
Letter to the Executive Committee, Comintern
January 8 1923

I wish to support the proposal to hold a Negro Congress at Moscow. I directed the attention of the Presidium to the two Bourgeois Congresses of Negroes held last summer under [Marcus] Garvey [an International Convention of the Negro People of the World in New York in August 1920] and [WEB] Du Bois [the Second Pan-African Congress in London, Brussels and Paris in August-September 1921] respectively, and the confusionist effect of their propaganda.

1. There are certain difficulties to overcome. It will not be sufficient to send out a call to a Congress, but COMINTERN representatives would have to work on the spot to assure a representative gathering of proletarian and radical Negroes.

2. In South Africa, for example, where the native African Negroes are the most advanced industrially, the passport supervision of the negroes is very strict and underground work of shipping delegates would therefore be very difficult. I am inclined to think that a special All-Black route through Persia via Zanzibar would have to be organised for all or most African Negro delegates from the Congo Southwards. A Negro in Europe making for any Baltic port would be immediately marked.

3. Failing such a plan however, the delegates could work their way on ship as seamen. In any case it is necessary to bear in mind that if the Congress is to bear a proletarian complexion the problem of bringing the delegates here is a serious one, requires many months of preparation.

4. Regarding the objection that we should be exaggerating the race consciousness of the Negroes by calling such a world Congress, instead of their class-consciousness, it is only necessary to point out that the Negroes more than any other race are a labouring race, with only a slight crust of Bourgeoisie in America. The Negro problem exists, and has to be tackled. It only remains to influence the content to be given to the common action of the Negroes as a race. The capitalist class are quite glad to encourage militant, anti-white racialism among the Negroes *a la* Garveyism in order to divert them from the class issue, which is ever present owing to vast preponderance of workers in any Negro gathering. It remains for the COMINTERN to give this common feeling of the Negro race a proletarian content. The Moscow Congress of Negroes would have a resounding echo throughout the world. Not the liberal bourgeoisie but the Communist International, not Manchester but Moscow, would then become the known protector of the oppressed Negro masses.

5. The South African delegates and negro masses generally would derive enormous benefit from intercourse at Moscow with the best proletarian Negroes of America, such as the leaders of the African Blood Brotherhood.

6. Should the proposal be adopted I suggest that a committee be immediately appointed to consider the draft Manifesto sent from America. It requires some of its too literary turns of expression to be simplified for the average Negro reader, and also the avoidance of references to the "Negro farmer" and "peasant". We should appeal to the industrial and agricultural working masses. The word "peasant" is also not used for any American section. It is a slavish copying of Russian conditions to bring in the word for all countries.

7. The term "Negro" is not used in South Africa. The word "Bantu" is the inclusive term for negro races South of the Equator. This word "Negro" has also the stigma of slavery and association with the word "N*" attached to it, although it is the widest understood. But if the COMINTERN should popularise the far more inclusive and more dignified term "ETHIOPIAN" as a sign of the race's emergence to proletarian consciousness, it would be an achievement. But perhaps this had better be left to the Congress.

8. A special Manifesto would be necessary for Africa, if the present one is adopted for America. And a short all-embracing Manifesto to the whole Negro race suitable for Radio transmission, issued as well.

9. Here arises the question of publicity, the advisability or otherwise of making world wide public appeals to the Negroes, and thus increasing the difficulties of organising the appointment and despatch of delegates. But probably such difficulties would be greatly overweighed by the political "reclame" [*reklama:* publicity, advertising] among the Negro races of such a world-wide call to Moscow.

10. For America and South Africa the work can be undertaken by the respective Communist Parties on the spot. if the suggestion as to the admission of the Egyptians and Moors [non-Egyptian North Africans] be adopted, the Egyptian Communist Party will also be able to help. Comrade Avigdor of the Egyptian section has already discussed the sending of Egyptian native delegates to Moscow.

11. There remain the other parts of Africa, such as Kenya, Uganda, and Portuguese Africa. In the last named region there exists a pro-negro Social Revolutionary Party which would undoubtedly help to organise the

Congress, and line itself up with Moscow in the process. In the British East Africa colonies aforementioned we have no connections. The CP of South Africa has correspondents in the Belgian Congo with its fifteen million natives. But we have no connections with British Nigeria and the Gold Coast, nor with the French Congo, unless this can be worked through the French Communist Party.

12. Our experience in South Africa is that as soon as a Negro attains any measure of education he becomes spoilt as a proletarian and loses touch with the negro working masses, because he is immediately snatched up to be a lawyer's or agent's tout, or to be a parson. Hence great care will have to be exercised to select working-class delegates in touch with the labouring masses. The point here is that all this requires many months of preparation for the congress, which should be decided upon quickly if it is intended to hold it at the same time as the Comintern Congress. In that the short RADIO Call should be deferred till later, and the special manifestoes sent out now more privately for translation and circulation among Negro Masses.

A Further Note on the Proposed Negro Congress

Russian State Archive of Socio-Political History
Letter to the Executive Committee, Comintern
23 March 1923

I wish to supplement my note of the 8th January on the above with further considerations which suggest themselves against the idea. The former note contains information regarding problems of organising said Congress which may be yet useful.

I believe that some kind of a Congress of radical negroes for America and the neighbouring islands might he of value. But we have to regard the negro race as a permanent section of the American population, and the encouraging of ideas of repatriation, "back to Africa", has a confusing effect upon the classes, just as the "back to Palestine" cry has had that effect upon the Jewish proletariat in the past. Garveyism depends on this diverting of the attention of the negro masses from the immediate class struggle to the distant hope of free Africa.

This danger is still more apparent in the case of South African natives. These natives have no highly developed intellegenzia like the American negroes, and practically no bourgeois class. It is a race of labourers newly emerging from tribal communism, individually uncultured but possessing a high sense of communist solidarity. Their emergence into industrial life breaks down their tribal animosities. But this break down of tribal animosity takes place in the actual necessities of the class struggle. For example, a few years ago, faction fights between tribes, in which fatal casualties occurred, were frequent among the natives working on the Rand mines. In 1920 all these natives in one mass upheaval forgot all their tribal distinctions and struck work to the number of 80,000 as fellow workers. The Communists were blamed for this as for all other manifestations of awakening among the natives. There are two native newspapers subsidised by the Government which carry on a bitter warfare against the Communist propaganda of solidarity of labour irrespective of race, colour or creed. And the one antidote which they purvey to this class propaganda, and encouraged by the Government, is precisely this one of Garvey, solidarity with negro races against the white men. Garveyism is invading Africa. And the Africans are made to look to America, just as the Americans are made to look to Africa.

Before this lesson is properly learnt, that not the white man, but the capitalist, is the enemy of the negro, and before some measure of alliance has been achieved between the white and black on the international field, it would be a source of confusion to have a racial congress.

Therefore I think that we should limit ourselves to urging the Communist Parties to send negroes in the delegations whenever possible. In Africa, owing to the lack of Communist funds, the newly formed native Unions are in danger of being pocketed by bourgeois agents. If the Communist Party could retain control of these Unions and also have the means of a Native newspaper to fight the Government subsidised ones, it would have far more effect in the fight against Imperialism than any Congress. It seems absurd to speak about Congresses when we are not prepared or notable to [or worthy to do] this preparatory spade work. If Mahomed cannot go to the mountain, the mountain will surely not go to Mahomed. In Africa we witness a struggle where it is touch and go whether Imperialist Capital is going to win field for expansion. A little attention to these native masses in the past on the part of the International might have proved [provided] a different result. It is still time to stiffen up the negro masses in Africa by work on the spot.

Africa's Awakening for a World Negro Congress

International Press Correspondence June 14 1923
The International, July 13 1923

The Negro is the greatest living accuser of capitalist civilization. The wealth of England and America is built upon his bones. The slave ships of Bristol and New York, with good Quaker prayers to speed them, founded the fortunes of many a Christian home. Every capitalist government is drenched with the blood of the Negro. British capitalism in South Africa, the French in the Cameroons, Belgium in the Congo, and the German Empire in Damaraland – they all constitute the blackest record in human history of mass slaughters and human violation of every primitive human right continued up to the present day. Even the liberation of the American slave was only an incident of a civil war between two factions of property holders engaged in a quarrel over the forms of exploitation, and was not the aim of the war as is commonly supposed. And as an aftermath of that war there was created a social attitude towards the Negro race which leaves the one time chattel slaves still degraded outcasts among the peoples of the earth.

This artificially generated race animosity towards the Negro pervading the whole of Anglo-Saxon society infects also the large working masses. The African Negro is the hewer of wood and the drawer of water even for the white workers of Europe. The workers of England are trained from childhood to regard the Zulu and Matabele wars as heroic exploits, rather than foul pages in English history. Hence the apathy and social prejudice towards the Negro race, for we hate most what we have injured most. But this period is passing, just as the days of the Second International are passing. The workers of Europe are no longer sharing the profits of their masters. The Communist International has appeared, and calls into the one great proletarian family the Negroes of Africa, as well as the peoples of the East, along with the revolutionary proletariat of the capitalist countries.

This is the first ray of hope for the Negroes throughout the centuries of their oppression. For the first time, the Negro Communists appeared at the Fourth Congress of the Communist International, and a resolution was passed declaring in favour of a World Congress of Negroes. There have been World Congresses of Negroes before. But they have been composed of members of the very thin layer of Negro intelligentsia, who have placed vain hopes in professions of loyalty to their oppressors. The London Congress of 1921 greeted the recruitment of Negroes into the French army as a mark of citizenship. Among the huge toiling masses of Negroes such a Congress passes by without notice.

There are also the Congresses held by the association headed by Marcus Garvey, a Jamaican Negro who has captured the imagination of the Negro masses in America, and whose slogan "Back to Africa" and "Africa for the Africans", are even spreading into Africa itself. This organization is strongly flavoured with religious and racial charlatanism. The proletarian character of the Negro mass is not so distinct in America as for instance, in South Africa. In the latter country the Negroes form a race of labourers, without any shopkeeping or small tenant element. Probably the small property psychology of the tenant farmers and the small trader element in America reflecting on the purely labouring Negro masses, has a lot to do with what is now notoriously known as "Garveyism", a charlatan exploitation of awakening race consciousness which, in so far as it takes anti-white forms, is secretly encouraged by the capitalist class both in America and in South Africa. The number of Negro farmers, mostly with very small holdings, according to the last American census was 949,889, which with their families represents a big proportion of the Negro population in America.

But awakening race consciousness in Africa tends to have a positive side among the large industrial masses, namely, the outliving of old tribal sectionalism. What the South African bourgeoisie calls a native hooligan is one who having worked some time in the towns, no longer recognises the authority of his tribal chief. Race consciousness, in the case of the Negro in Africa is a step towards class consciousness, because his race is a race of labourers. The coming World Congress will have to decide the question, how far the movement towards race consciousness can be directed into proletarian forms. The foremost leader of the Negro intelligentsia in America, Burghardt du Bois, a graduate of Harvard, stands apart from the Marcus Garvey organization. He is an author of several books of high literary merit, in which appears a glimmering apprehension of the truth that Negro emancipation can only come through proletarian emancipation. But the organization of Negro Communists, known as the African Blood Brotherhood, has achieved considerable progress. Undoubtedly, America will supply the leaders of Negro emancipation.

But Negro emancipation is not an American question; it is a question of Africa, as our American comrades themselves have declared. Who is to get this great Africa, the capitalist class or the Comintern? And when is the European proletariat going to stretch out the hand of brotherhood to the masses of Africa, and wipe out centuries of capitalist wrong? The status of the American Negro cannot be raised without the awakening of Africa. But it is no less true that the European proletariat cannot obtain a real link with Africa except through the more advanced Negroes of America.

To the South African Negro, every white man is an oppressor, a master, a "boss" Even the oppressed among the whites appears to the black the most violent curser of the Negro. And therefore it is no wonder that news of class emancipation in Europe must appear to him a purely domestic affair of the whites. A few young industrial workers are beginning to hear news of the Communist Party and of its actions on behalf of the blacks, and these are beginning to spread the idea. They see Communists gaoled for declaring the solidarity of black and white workers. But a more imposing gesture is needed to convince the Negro masses that a new dawn is breaking, that "white man" and "oppressor" are not one and the same thing, that there is an army of liberation coming to aid him, the revolutionary proletariat. Time is pressing, the Negro armies of Imperialism are already on the Rhine. Only the Communist International can reconcile the Negro and the white races, and only through proletarian solidarity can this reconciliation be achieved.

The Fourth Congress [of the Communist International] appointed a committee to draw up the plans for a World Negro Congress. It is to be hoped that this committee will report to the forthcoming Enlarged Executive, and that the delegates will be equipped with definite ideas on the subject. The Congress will undoubtedly be a proletarian Congress, but the extent to which non-proletarian representatives will be invited will also be a matter for the Enlarged Executive [of the Comintern] to decide.

The foregoing notes are written as part of the Committee's publicity campaign; the Committee hopes that the Party organs in Britain, America, Belgium, etc., will devote special attention to the Negro question and to the preliminary work necessary for the calling of a World Negro Congress under the banner of the Comintern.

Last Letter to George Eyre Evans

January 25 1924

Dear George Eyre,

Either the post has miscarried, or my sins have cried out to heaven, for some reason or another there has been a complete stoppage of news from you.

It is now two and a half years since I made that unseemly flying visit (thinking that I would be back in a couple of weeks), have written you several times but with no result. I wrote to to JDS [friend JD Stephens who had supported the Great War] a week or two ago for the first time, thinking the conditions now better for communications.

So far I have felt it somewhat of an imposition to compel a friend to receive a letter with a Russian stamp, which under Curzonian circumstances may bring unpleasant visits!! [Lord Curzon, British Foreign Secretary 1919-24]. And I am assuming that by now these conditions no longer exist.

As you can see I am now at Yalta. I wrote you from here last year. I went back to Moscow and got a bad relapse, so bad that I spend the most part of my days in doors, the weather just now being severe, and sunny days an exception. I have succeeded in getting the upper hand once more over my enemy, but these continual relapses due to premature return to work compel me to resign myself to a a quiet existence for the next few years (and not too many of them left in any case!). Just now and for the next few weeks the weather here is very much like an English winter, with snow on the ground, and temperature just round freezing, but still so severe as to prevent the admission of fresh air.

In Moscow just now with 20 degrees of frost centigrade, double doors, and double windows all puttied up to the joists, you can imagine that houses are perfectly badly ventilated and most unhealthy, especially for us Westerners. Russians are somewhat acclimatized to the lack of oxygen.

I often sit here and muse over Ty Tringad – how nice it would be to sit by the fire in that library – and wonder how things are with you there. But I feel that there is an estrangement – since my experiences of Nice. (Now I wonder why I had stayed there so long.) I had not realised that "Communism" had made a vast difference – the spectre of it had made friendly relations, not to speak of friendship, between those who seriously take opposite views of the Russian revolution a matter of impossibility. One could wish that a person's personal belongings might not mar the serenity of his or her views as to the ultimate good in society nor distort his judgements as to what is best for the majority, nor blind his vision as to the substance of slavery all round him – but so it is, personal property does have these effects in all but the idealist spirits; hence how I am now prepared for rebuff without too much lamentation. Life after all is a stern affair, unless we look to turn our backs on it. I remember how you once sent me a card. I was then at Lampeter – "Follow the gleam lad, come what may" and I did not think, nor do I now, that you made any reservations, even if the gleam led one to paths which then would have shocked us both at the very mention thereof!

As I write these lines news is still fresh of the death of Lenin. There has passed away the greatest figure of the present century, and for the wideness of his influence, the greatest figure of centuries, this may appear to you absurdly overdrawn but think that in no country on this wide earth is there a worker that does not know the name of Lenin, and in no country is there not a party formed to carry on his ideas. Such a man, whether seen from near or from afar appears rarely. Such a sense of world responsibility, such monolithic sincerity, in word and action, such a love of the oppressed in all lands – combined with a science of action for their deliverance.

But I must not bore you, although I am at present under the immediate sense of a great loss.

As for me, I don't know my plans. They depend upon my health. I am occassionally doubtful about prospects. But I think that it is inevitable that I leave Russia, when the snow thaws up north either to settle in England or go back to sunny SA. Everything depends on how I get on. I should have left Russia last year but was stopped by my relapse in August. In any case I shall come to Aber and finish my visit if you have an invitation for me. Otherwise barring staunch old JD. Aber has only painful memories.

Lampeter, has far more attractions, it is free from the associations of snob pauperdom of one's early life, which meet one in ghost form at every corner in Aber. Ah, the beautiful Teify, the trout, the trees, the jovial people there, the touch of pagan humanism which respectable Aber has not.

Perhaps I may yet taste it. What say you? (That is a GEE query.) Well old fellow, my friend of long ago! I hail thee once more.

David

Tuberculosis Institute, Yalta, Crimea

Last Letter to Bill Andrews

April 1924

Dear Comrade Bill.

I was pleased to receive your long (at any rate long for you!) letter. I didn't know whether you had alreday left England or not. But now you are home, and your account does not make me feel particularly glad. In reality, there is no sign of success as yet that might cause us to feel glad. I have started a letter to [SP] Bunting on that very theme – that the stream of workers in the party is small in number, and because of this we are cut off from the masses.

From references to it in *The International* I realized that they had received one of my letters. But I've written several of them, including two articles – I allowed myself this since you had already left. However, your letter is the first I have received from South Africa. Perhaps I have adopted the wrong tone in my writings, have been too bombastic or shown some other errors?

Raithaus wrote to me from Sevast where he has a niece or someone. He apologised for not having called in at Yalta, blaming it on the timetable of boats departing for Odessa and Constantinople. He is hoping to come here again, as a party delegate to the Fifth Congress [of the Communist International]. I think it would be a mistake to elect him as a delegate, only because he can afford such a trip. He is a typical representative of those elements in the party which are its financial support, and at the same time, the cause of its weakness. He is a sympathizing petty-bourgeois. If we can't send an active party worker, it's better not to send anyone at all. A short advance notice of the congress clearly indicates that now that the foundation of the Comintern has been laid, representatives from the parties of distant colonial countries should not necessarily be expected to attend every time. And since we now have to admit our lack of success (excluding young people) there is no reason for us to send a delegate. We need to concentrate on the future, when we will be able to send Edward Roux from the YCL and together with him a genuinely class conscious Negro worker. We must set ourselves this goal and within two years create the conditions for sending such a delegation.

Up till now the party has spent a lot of time campaigning for assistance so any saving from the delegates and other funds will be timely. *Young Worker* has devoted itself to the question of pupils in a businesslike way. What a long chalk this is from the old Socialist Labour Party's hatred of all "reform", although, of course, if the situation ceases to be revolutionary, our struggle for "reforms" must inevitably become reformist, yet we are learning how to combine the struggle for reforms with the revolutionary struggle, or rather how to make the struggle for reforms revolutionary. I have just been reading one of Lenin's early brochures of 1902, where he declares that the political struggle of the working class is not exclusively a struggle for the economic betterment of the workers, but also a struggle in which the party of the workers enters in defence of every oppressed section, even non-worker sections, of society. For example, he cited the call to the workers to demonstrate against the Czar drafting students into the army. A positive attitude on every issue!

It is a pity you did not include just a few cuttings in your letter – interviews and other material. I receive individual copies of *The International*, probably even most of them. I see the lay out has changed again. I like the new title drawing, it's just a pity that the hammer and sickle are missing. But overall it is a definite improvement. Now a big question: what will Bunting live on – will he have to return to his old job? I am sure that the perspectives outlined, if not his own, then in any case your perspective, as well as those of the party as a whole, are not to his liking. I expressed the opinion to Bunting that even if we had to return to the idea of a Johannesburg committee with an unpaid secretary, it would be worth doing in order to guarantee ourselves a point of support in the working class. We have lost the trade unionists, but I doubt if that is anything peculiar to us; it is a general South African, if not a British trait, the difficulty of forming a real mass organization. How many active branches has the Labour Party got? Apart from the special excitement of electioneering, which the name "Labour" gives it, it has no more organizational cohesion than the CP.

Our trouble is isolation. (We allowed them to keep the name in 1915). The point is how to get a foot in again. Now it will be very hard. There may be a chance during the elections to put you up as United Front candidate with the LP somewhere. The CP would be justified in a little manoeuvring to get this. The CP as an affiliated section, with members in SALP branches, would be the thing of course.

As a cold matter of fact, there is no room for a CP in white South Africa except as the watchdog of the native, as the promoters of rapprochement, watching, within the broader organizations, for every opportunity to switch the movement on right lines on this question and scotching every conspiracy to rouse race hatred and strike breaking of race against race. We have done something on this question since 1914, even if the damage is great. But history does not count damages, organizational damages, in order to shift forward a peg. And this peg could not have been shifted forward as it has been without the tremendous sacrifices, the wanderings in the wilderness of the last nine years. We must be humble and satisfied, satisfied that we did our best. And I hope that Bunting, with all his wonderful devotion and self-sacrifice of the last nine years, will not feel that his labours have been in vain. We have made our protest. We have insisted on certain questions. We stand for Bolshevism, which since 1917 has come to our vindication, and in all minds Bolshevism stands for the native worker. Now we can safely review tactics, if necessary even dissolve temporarily except for a nucleus for the paper, in order to give comrades like Bunting a breathing space, and use this in order to get in through the proposed Trades Councils, Trade Unions, etc, into the Labour Party machine. It would be a great asset to have the govt. pay our organizing and travelling expenses.

April 14 1924

Excuse the poor paper and ink. As always, I am writing this lying in bed. Spring came late and the cold, damp winter had a bad effect on my health. Up till 1 December I was well on the way to recovery and began to walk, but during the winter months I again took to my bed. Just when the weather began to improve and I could count on continuing the treatment, I started getting terrible neurological pains in my lower back and legs, especially in the knees. These lasted until last week. I've become totally helpless; I can't move around or even cross the room without assistance. I feel especially weak in the knees. The doctors evidently don't fully understand what is happening to me, let alone the general exhaustion of the organism and the deterioration of my condition during the winter. The disease of my lungs is no worse than in December, but other ailments have now started tormenting me. The pain has been so acute that I couldn't get to sleep without morphine. Hence I am pretty well resigning from my claim to "futures", and preparing to close my accounts as they stand, with all the mistakes and "damn foolishness" thrown in! The next few weeks will show what my prospects are, and if it appears that the trouble is chronic, I shall put in my checks. I don't know but that I have been a burden too long. After all, it is an egoism not compatible with Communism to lie bedridden indefinitely, waited upon by people who might do useful work. The time will come when it will be considered a piece of obsolete individualism, or even superstition, to wait and wait until the last breath heaves out. Just as a midwife's function is to help people in, so a doctor's should be to help people out once it is clear they are no longer any use. But it is hard to get the truth from doctors. That's the situation I am in. I don't know what will become of me, but I feel I have little chance of recovering and leaving Russia. Still, we'll see. But meanwhile let's talk about something more cheerful.

You may be interested to learn that your letter, written on the 9th March and bearing the Johannesburg postmark of the 10th reached me in my room on the 11th April, bearing the Moscow postmark April 6th. I think this is very quick travelling! Consider the number of re-sortings it has to go through – Cape Town, presumably England, Moscow, Sebastapol. In 1921 a letter from Odessa to Moscow took more than the present letter from South Africa. So we are getting on!

Today I read about [Britain's Labour Prime Minster] MacDonald's defeat on the housing question. But he is still holding on to his post. He is the most unprincipled and despicable time-server of all those who have been in the post. Baldwin and Lloyd George occasionally showed they knew how to put up a good fight, but MacDonald's only wish is, apparently, to show the capitalists what a good boy he is. The position he has adopted on India is disgusting. It's interesting that Menshevism has the same features everywhere and is repeating itself in England, despite your "reading of history." Equally, the same basic features of revolution must reveal themselves everywhere – if not in form, then in substance. Your "reading of history", dear William, smacks of the petty-bourgeoisie, and always has done. But your understanding of the present is quite correct. For you haven't learnt to read history from a class point of view. And if England didn't follow the example of France in 1792, then a reading of history from a class point of view reveals the reason for this: (1) By the time the bourgeoisie had already, to a significant extent, gained hold of power, the feudal system had largely gone into decline and the industrial revolution was maturing. (2) Cromwell had already accomplished everything that was necessary in the previous century and the French, basically, just followed the example of the English. The revolution led by Cromwell did not go beyond the bounds of legality and logic. It introduced sufficient revolutionary changes. like the French revolution, it moved from a petty bourgeois platform (yeomen) to a strictly bourgeois platform (the class of entrepreneurs). You are accustomed for several years now to consider England as a country doomed to compromises. But the Chartists had no respect for law and order. Only recently the British workers acquired such respect. I am convinced that once the masses realise that government and capitalists are one and the same thing, whatever ministers are in power, there will be unrest in the country and the workers will not stop at the abolition of the constitution. It is quite possible that an explosion will occur as a result of the people defending the constitution, which will have to be thrown overboard in the very process of its defence. In America the CP now has a flourishing daily paper. The movement for the creation of a workers' party, in which the CP is taking the lead, is spreading despite the opposition of [US trade union leader Samuel] Gompers. Once such a party has been created, it will adopt positions further to the left than Gompers' supporters. The USA is somewhat exceptional, but Britain will soon find itself drawn into the flow of current events. Even in complete calm one must always be prepared for a sudden squall.

April 15 1924

I have had to break off. Much writing tires, and the pains interrupt. The spring is late, but we have not yet got regular sunshine; although for most people it is already nice enough weather if somewhat cloudy, owing to the tendency of the mountain range to gather mists, so long as snow lies in Russia. Since you have left we have had a currency reform, so far successful, silver coinage, but this place has not yet received any, as an enormous quantity is required, but what remains of the Soviet rouble is stabilized, because the government has announced a firm price, 500 (000,000) to 1 kopek. So now everybody counts in kopeks and roubles as pre-war. I have seen specimens of the new silver coins, very beautiful, and in full go in the large centres. Meanwhile the government has to observe most stringent economies to avoid revenue escape.

How is [C.B.]Tyler? I had plans to write to half a dozen comrades, but in present state I must postpone. And [Ralph] Rabb and Ada Rabb? I started writing to Haynes, thinking he was fully active in the party, his "Para" being then in the paper. I hope that my suggestions for improving [the paper] were not used as a pretext for a diversion. There are now some very epxensive books in your catalogue, with a marked tendency to make book-selling take priority over the propagation of communist principles, with the aid of spiritual fare. There are some really unlikely books in the catalogue, while some propagandistic publications which have long established themselves are missing. Why for example do we no longer find John Reed's *Ten Days That Shook the World* – the best communistic reporting in all literature? I propose that Ralph think of opening a bookshop with a neutral sign, such as "Books for Workers", which would be under the control of the CP and act in co-operation with the party. The shop should, of course, have a stationary section. The most suitable person for organizing such a venture is RB as he loves books, loves propaganda through books, loves seeing books on shelves and stroking them lovingly. He could combine his new duties with other types of his economic activity if he were given a girl as an assistant who was trustworthy and capable of running the shop while he was out. This would be extremely valuable for the whole labour movement. At the same time the existing press could be turned into the press of the "Books for Workers" society, its activities should be expanded to those of a fully-fledged publishing house. Gradually Ralph would concentrate entirely on working in such a publishing-house. It should be opened in the centre and not in some side street. Everyone agreed? Resolution passed! Next business!! Of course my regards to Ralph, I often think of him and the other comrades, and wish I could grasp them by the hand once more. I see from papers that Sam Barlin has left Johannesburg. Any news of John Campbell? Whenever you happen to be in Natal give my regards to Lawrie Green. I suppose SMC is clean out of it now. His creditors will demand it of him, and the clearing up of the point re Free Masons in the Communist International puts him before an irksome dilemma. Well, we exploited SM ruthlessly, some of us must allow. I have not written to him for a long time. I gather that Kathleen and Willie are well and hearty. Have you seen Mr and Mrs Newbury yet? Give them my regards and also to Isabel Schikling. And of course the Chapmans, although I do not agree with Jessie Chapman as a candidate, but one can object to a friend's nomination! Chapman is very faithful to the cause. Where has Dan Bekker gone to? By the way you should ask Alper to give you the letter from the Association of assistance to Jews in Russia, which I sent to him in 1922 from the Jewish Relief Association. From this letter it is clear that not a single penny from the thousands of pounds which were collected by Jews in South Africa has arrived in Russia. But Russia has the burden of 300,000 orphans who were victims of the Jewish pogroms.

Now dear Andrews, I must finish this letter. When I can I'll write again. Give my warmest love to everyone. No doubt I shall think of others as well. Where is Parky? And Mrs Hockley, etc.

Your old friend and Comrade
Ivon

(Tell Bunting to write)
[In a PS Jones compared the words of *The Internationale* as sung in South

Africa with the version used in Britain and Russia and urged that a new version be used.]

INDEX

C

S

T

U

V

W

Y

Z

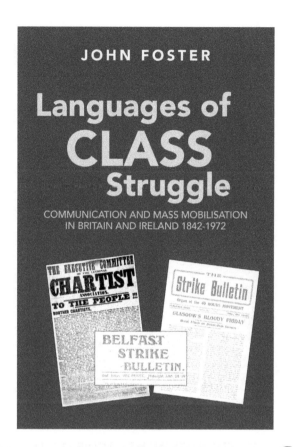

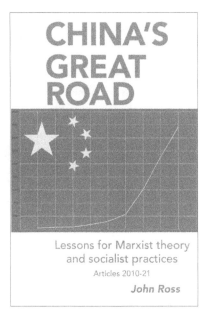

OTHER PRAXIS PRESS TITLES

MAKING OUR OWN HISTORY by Jonathan White
A brilliant introduction to the Marxist approach to understanding and participating in social change.

MARX200
Leading scholars and activists from different countries – including Cuba, India and the UK – show that Marx's ideas continue to provide us with the analysis we need to understand our world today.

A PROMETHEAN VISION by Eric Rahim
"This small book is a very useful account of how Marx came to develop his materialist conception of history." Michael Löwy, *New Politics*

LINE OF MARCH by Max Adereth
A new edition of Max Adereth's historical analysis of British communism, focusing on the development of the party's various programmes. First published 1994.

1000 DAYS OF REVOLUTION
A fascinating account of the Allende Presidency, the dilemmas of peaceful and armed struggles for socialism, the role of US imperialism and domestic right-wing forces, and a self critical evaluation of the role of Chilean communists.

HARDBOILED ACTIVIST by Ken Fuller
A critical review of the work and politics of writer Dashiell Hammett, crime fiction legend, communist and staunch opponent of McCarthyism.

For more details, contact praxispress@me.com

ORDER online at www.redletterspp.com

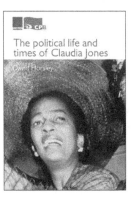

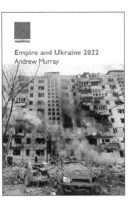

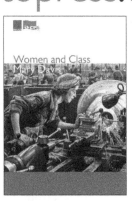

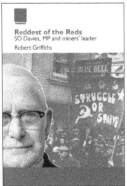

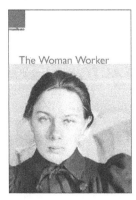